BRIERLEY

BRIERLEY

The Man Behind the Corporate Legend

Yvonne van Dongen

VIKING

VIKING

Penguin Books (NZ) Ltd, 182–190 Wairau Road, Auckland 10, New Zealand
Penguin Books Ltd, 27 Wrights Lane, London W8 5TZ, England
Penguin USA, 375 Hudson Street, New York, NY 10014, United States
Penguin Books Australia Ltd, 487 Maroondah Highway, Ringwood, Australia 3134
Penguin Books Canada Ltd, 10 Alcorn Avenue, Toronto, Ontario, Canada M4V 1E4

Penguin Books Ltd, Registered Offices: Harmondsworth, Middlesex, England

First published 1990
1 2 3 4 5 6 7 8 9 10

Designed by Richard King
Typeset by Typocrafters Ltd, Auckland
Printed in Singapore

ISBN 0 670 83124 7

CONTENTS

PREFACE

The idea of a book on Sir Ron Brierley was suggested to me following the publication of a series of four articles I wrote about him in early 1987 for *National Business Review.* It was at the height of bull market fever and Brierley had become something of a cult figure. Shareholders seemed to believe they had bought shares in the man as much as the company. But despite Brierley's overwhelming popularity little was known about him personally.

Friends and colleagues were not forthcoming with information, and the only reason I was able to write a lengthy profile was thanks to the frank disclosures of his mother, May Brierley, and the then deputy chairman of BIL, Bruce Hancox. I must admit their outspoken bluntness took me aback at first and I wondered if somehow I had caught them both off-guard.

I have since learned that this is, in fact, a characteristic of Brierley's associates and certainly a feature of the corporate environment of BIL. Most of his friends and colleagues are outgoing, down-to-earth people who are not afraid to criticise and not threatened by criticism themselves. This is a tribute to Brierley and a godsend to any writer, for Brierley is not an easy subject for scrutiny. He had already defeated the best efforts of two earlier would-be biographers and I was advised by a number of his colleagues that I should expect the worst.

I found that he was by turns unco-operative and silent or loquacious and agreeable. However, even when he was being interviewed, I discovered he still wanted to retain the air of mystery which over the years had shrouded so much of who he was and what he had done. In all I spent some thirty hours talking to Brierley, and while his stories were entertaining and generally informative, he was often reluctant to provide details or to be questioned further. Nevertheless he was always courteous, witty and charming company.

In the two years I spent working on the biography I interviewed at least 185 people. I interviewed some of these people many times, often for several hours. Only a few spoke 'off the record'. I tried wherever possible to verify all details of an incident or conversation with all the main participants rather than relying on a single source. However, no writer can recreate historical events with complete accuracy. Documentation is often scarce or inadequate and memories can be unreliable. It is always worth remembering this journalistic limitation.

There are too many people who helped me to thank individually but a few deserve special mention. I am especially grateful to Don McDonald for adding this project to his list of concerns. No one has done more to assist me with the book, and for no reason other than a loyalty to his friend Ron Brierley and the company he worked for.

I would also like to thank BIL and IEL for allowing me unrestricted access to their libraries and unquestioning use of their facilities. The goodwill and assistance of their staff was much appreciated.

My research also brought home to me the truth of one of Brierley's earliest discoveries: that libraries and librarians are underestimated resources of immense value. Librarians Hetty van Hale at BIL and Julia Stewart at IEL deserve a special vote of thanks for their help, especially Hetty for her unshakeable confidence in me and my project when I needed it most.

I am also grateful to Bill Loewenthal for enduring numerous interviews, even while he was on holiday in New Zealand; Bruce Hancox for his outspoken honesty and good humour; Bob Blackburn for his hospitality and assistance; Prof. Don Trow for his superior teaching skills and patience in dealing with the novice accountant; May Brierley for her entertaining tales; and my editor, Graham Adams, for putting in more time that he had bargained for.

Bryan James of the *Otago Daily Times* kindly let me use his manuscript 'The Gumboot Takeover', and all the directors of the BNZ I spoke to freely gave hours of their time. Also I found former employees of BIL and IEL such as Chris Castle, Jill Hatchwell and Geoff Pickles to be immensely helpful. I am thankful too to the publishing director of Penguin, Geoff Walker, for his sympathetic sense of timing. He knew just when to put pressure on but understood when it needed to be relaxed.

No vote of thanks would be complete without mentioning my long-suffering friends Bronwen Reid, Laurie Hilsgen, Wixi McDonald and Sandra Coney, all of whom had the job at one time or other of boosting my flagging spirits. Also my heartfelt thanks go to James Holland. Without his loving support the book would not have been possible.

Finally I must also thank Sir Ron Brierley. Whatever misunderstandings and difficulties Sir Ron and I might have had, his benign acceptance of my seemingly endless research into his life was greatly appreciated. At all times he has allowed me to pursue my research without any interference.

I know that as the manuscript came closer to completion he felt increasingly uncomfortable with the prospect of its publication. I had been told to expect this. Even before I began working on the book, his executives had warned me that Brierley would not like anything he had not written himself. This is understandable. Having a biography written during your lifetime would be a daunting experience for most people. None of us would emerge as we would ideally like and it is helpful for any biographer and reader to be humbled by this knowledge.

Yvonne van Dongen
Auckland, 1990

Note: As far as currency is concerned, the reader should know that, unless specified, Australian transactions are referred to in Australian dollars and New Zealand transactions in New Zealand dollars.

PROLOGUE

Forty-eight hours before the end of 1987, two men pull up outside the Motueka Cricket Ground in a green 1961 Bel Air Chevrolet. It is one of those hot, languid days one expects after Christmas in the South Island, with just a soft pilgrim cloud drifting across a flawless sky. On these days everything seems to move with a voluptuous lassitude and even the cricket looks slower than usual.

The two get out of the car and, although they are the same height, you can see at once how different they are. The one in the short-sleeved T-shirt looks tanned, self-contained and decisive, as if he has weathered a few storms. But his friend is pallid and walks with the gait of an old man. He is only now taking off his tie, a grudging concession to the heat and informality of the occasion.

They walk onto the grounds and join the crowd. There's the usual summertime debris of beer cans, picnic baskets and that sweet smell of suntan lotion reminding you of summers past. At the wicket Central Districts is playing Otago.

They could have been any two men watching the game and this could have been any day, except of course it isn't. Just about everybody there knows that the chairman of the country's premier bank and the nation's third-largest company, Ron Brierley, and his deputy, Bruce Hancox, have just walked onto the park. It is likely that some of the people there are shareholders in Brierley Investments Ltd. Almost one in fifteen adults in New Zealand owns shares in BIL at the time, and the company itself is worth a staggering $2 billion.

But they weren't to know that the following day Ron Brierley would be elevated to the position of Knight Bachelor in the New Year's Honours List. Only Brierley knew this as he sat watching the cricket. He had just flown into Motueka from Australia and was looking forward to the public announcement in a little over twelve hours' time.

The local reporter may have had an inkling of this when he photographed the pair at the cricket. In any event, a picture of the two of them appeared the next day with the usual how-do-you-feel and what-do-we-call-you-now questions.

Brierley replies coyly. He 'hadn't the faintest idea who nominated him', and as to whether he should be called Sir Ron, he said, 'Well, if you think so, I suppose I should.' He didn't even have to say, 'Just call me Ron' or 'It'll take some getting used to', for the press, like a good host always eager to give an event its proper tone, described him as down-to-earth and unassuming.

They weren't to know this was the best news he had heard since he discovered tax havens. Brierley shows his emotion by implication rather than expression, so it is hard for those not close to him to tell what he is feeling. The press, in particular, could never have guessed how much he wanted that knighthood. It didn't fit the Brierley they knew.

The Brierley they knew had shown himself to be no respecter of convention. During his career he had criticised complacent directors, Establishment boards and stultifying regulation. Laws had been passed to curb his activities, but he had found other loopholes to slip through. He had poked, prodded and provoked more regulatory authorities and politicians than any other businessman, and thrived on the drama. By all accounts he was a happy renegade and most willing outcast.

Personally, too, he had shunned all the trappings of respectability. He had never married and never wanted to. He had few possessions, few needs and had at one stage been content simply living in a hotel.

Brierley saw business as a game and liked to think he played it with an intellectual purity. Unimpressed by wealth, unmoved by convention, he seemed to be playing it for its own sake. In his commitment and detachment he was probably the most unusual businessman in Australasia.

But now people learned that the stakes had been much higher than they had ever realised, that all along the ultimate prize had been old-fashioned respectability. Only his friends and colleagues knew how much he wanted the knighthood and how much effort had gone into getting it.

Brierley had known about the impending announcement for over six weeks, and as soon as the appointed day arrived, he felt duty-bound to inform a few select people.

Back at Hancox's Stephens Bay house, Brierley rang his as-yet-untitled friend and rival, property developer Bob Jones, at eight that Saturday morning. Jones was on holiday with his family, and his wife, Ann, answered the telephone. She heard Ron pointedly referring to them over and over again as Mr and Mrs Jones.

A telegram from former IEL investment manager Geoff Pickles, which arrived later that day, read: 'Congratulations. You only did this to annoy me and Bob Jones.' Brierley telexed back the next day: 'You are absolutely correct.'

Ron Brierley then rang another friend, lawyer and cricket enthusiast John Oakley, who had also made the Honours List that day.

'I see you've just been awarded a CBE,' said Brierley.

'Yes, and I see you've just got a knighthood,' replied Oakley obligingly.

IEL's general manager Bill Loewenthal also got a call from Brierley, which began, 'About that knighthood, Bill . . .'

People rang him, of course. One call came from the Internal Affairs Department informing him there had been a terrible mistake. They were very sorry but he was not a knight after all.

Brierley was silent and then began to consider which one of his friends would play such a cruel and clever trick. It was so good, he might have thought of it himself.

'Is that you, Rob?' he asked and the former trade unionist and then deputy chairman of the BNZ, Rob Campbell, laughed out loud.

So nine months after he became chairman of New Zealand's largest bank, and on the last day of the year, Ron Brierley finally received the ultimate recognition of his achievements, something he thought even money couldn't buy.

The apotheosis of Ronald Alfred Brierley appeared complete. In 1961 he had started his investment company with the minimum of capital and the maximum of confidence in his conviction that New Zealand and Australia were ripe for a Brierley picking over. That judgment had proved to be correct and, despite the recent sharemarket crash, he was still seen as practically the patron saint of capitalism in both countries.

To his shareholders he was the incarnation of the trickle-down theory. In making himself rich, he had made many of them rich too, and they would have weighed him in gold as the Ismailis do the Agha Khan. For a moment he could have been forgiven for feeling invincible, respected by all around him and as buoyant as newly opened champagne.

But curiously, at the very time his star was in the ascendant in the wider world, it had already started to wane within his own ranks. Those who worked side by side with Brierley knew he had a special talent, and some called him a genius, but lately they had begun to question some of his judgments.

When the biggest sharemarket crash to ever hit New Zealand had struck two months earlier, the company's executives had looked to Brierley for leadership. They knew he had endured many crises in his twenty-six-year career and they hoped to benefit from his lengthy experience and wisdom. But so far Brierley had kept his own counsel and the executives were becoming restive. They were willing to wait as he lapped up his moment of glory, but their patience was fast coming to an end.

ONE

Little Old Tom

THOMAS BRIERLEY, Ron Brierley's grandfather, was a Christian in the austere mould. He looks out of photographs with the wintry, impenetrable stare of a man whose authority was rarely in question, as if some icy black cloud of original sin was passing before his very eyes. In his lifetime he embraced two churches, the Plymouth Brethren and later the Christadelphians. Every Sunday he obliged the church by taking his wife and nine children to hear the Word of God. Some, like his son John, hated going — there were two sets of steps to the church door and he always took the steps furthest away in a mute and childish statement of his rebellion. In any case it made little difference. They were there every Sunday, head in their hands, spirits in their feet, listening as the minister's voice droned on. It worked for some; one son later became a missionary.

But Thomas Brierley was best known for his business activities, which he pursued with the same uncompromising rigour as his religion. It is said that at the age of twenty-seven he came to New Zealand from Nottingham with £26 in his pocket, worked hard, and by 1930 owned the second-largest bakery in Wellington. He hated parting with money and said of his two wives that the first one used to rob him for the church and the second thought he was a millionaire.

Despite his gruff manner, he was well known and well liked enough to have a nickname, 'Old Tom'. There was always someone around to bundle Old Tom into a tram when he was too drunk to find his way home.

Old Tom's first wife died leaving him with nine motherless children, so he married again to solve that problem. The only time he liked having his children in close proximity was when they worked for him. He made most of them do a lengthy stint in the bakery whether they liked it or not, and most of them didn't. But by the time they felt bold enough to leave they were too old to do much else. On the whole the Brierley kids were a bright, unambitious bunch. None of them could ever muster as much enthusiasm for money and business as their old man.

After Tom died the family didn't see a lot of one another. They were never close, although Ron's uncle Harry tried. He even visited his brother John, but John told him he never wanted anything to do with his family.

Harry has a story about why they turned out such a distant, touchy lot. He remembers a typical evening in the two-storey house in Vivian Street Tom Brierley built for his family. Old Tom's second wife and the children's step-mother, Lily, is with him and they are counting the day's takings. The children have been told to stay downstairs and amuse themselves, but they are fighting. There is no one to stop the bullies of the family intimidating the quieter children, and for them the evening is hell. They can either give in or withdraw into themselves, smouldering with resentment.

Upstairs Lily and Tom count their money and some of the children fancy they can hear the chink, chink, chink of the coins falling neatly into place. In the end, says Harry, they reckoned money was all Tom cared about, because every evening he sat upstairs, counted his pennies and rarely came downstairs to see his children. He was like Old King Cole. Harry still calls him Old King Cole Brierley.

People tell stories in order to live. They want to know why the man jumped off the bridge or what motivated the woman to steal from her employer after thirty years' loyal service. They want to make sense of it all, to see a shape in the moving clouds or a face in the water.

May Brierley is often asked what makes her son Ronald Alfred Brierley tick. What makes a man pursue money to the exclusion of all else, what spurs him on after the first million, what kind of person is Ron Brierley? He's always been a 'funny' child, she says. His focus in life has always been quite different from any other child she has ever known, and to explain she tells a story about Ron at six years of age.

She and her husband, John Brierley, lived with their two sons in Island Bay. It is one of the colder suburbs in Wellington and in winter they always had a fire. At the age of six, Ron had already developed a fascination with coins and on many evenings he would sit in front of the fire polishing his pennies. In those days May's father was living with the family and occasionally he would bring friends home. The visitors were enchanted by the sight of Ron rubbing his coins. Licked by the firelight, boy and pennies must have looked like something out of a Norman Rockwell painting.

'What are you doing, Ron?' they would ask, and Ron would oblige by stating the obvious: 'Just polishing my coin collection.'

'Well, let's see,' someone would say, delving into his trouser pocket. 'I might just have some coins you would be interested in.'

Every time his grandfather's friends came to visit, Ron would quietly materialise with his coins and sit unobtrusively by the fire. 'And my, my, how those coins grew,' observed his mother.

The story about Ron and his coins is uncannily similar to the Old King Cole tale of his grandfather, told and retold until it has become a family myth. As a child Ron may have heard that story many times, and it is possible he might unconsciously have been acting out that myth. Or it might simply be that in spite of his father's rejection of his family, Ron Brierley's genetic inheritance harks back to his grandfather. It is impossible to know for certain, but Thomas Brierley was Ron Brierley's only close relative to show any interest in running his own business.

Old Tom did in fact leave a more visible genetic stamp on his grandson — young Ron turned out so like his grandfather that as a child his family called him 'Little Old Tom'. He had the same sleepy, hooded eyes, the same drawn-down lines around his mouth, and he would make his mother and her friends laugh at the way he tottered about as if his bones were brittle with age. He could be bad-tempered, too, and insist on doing things his way like a crotchety pensioner. 'I'm glad he's not mine,' said May's friends, eyeing Ron's scowling face.

From the outset May realised he was 'funny' and learned to accommodate her unusual offspring as other people eventually would. In fact, all his life people have treated Ron Brierley with the special tolerance reserved for old people and children, probably because he has always resembled both. As a child he was like a little old man, and as an adult he is closer to his childhood self than most people ever remain. He has the same interests, obsessions and mannerisms he had as a boy. His world still largely revolves around cricket, stamps and, most of all, money.

'Ron has only ever been interested in one thing really and that's money,' said his mother. 'If he had a shilling it was a prisoner straight away.'

His father was mystified and disappointed by his son's interest in money. The two never really developed a rapport, although they were both quiet and aloof — 'real Brierleys', according to May Brierley. Like many New Zealanders who survived the lean years of the Depression, what John Brierley wanted for his children was a good education and a secure job in a large shock-proof organisation. With the memory of the Depression riots, child malnutrition and a hundred thousand unemployed still fresh in his mind, John Brierley valued security above all else.

His first son, Ronald Alfred, was born at the tail-end of the Depression, on 2 August 1937, and three years later Ken arrived to complete the family. They lived in a plain, working-class neighbourhood in Wellington's Island Bay. When Ron Brierley recently visited the suburb where he grew up, he remarked on how little the place had changed. He said he didn't know whether to find it quaint or depressing.

That comment is probably a reflection of the fact that his childhood spanned some of the most suffocating, bland years New Zealand has ever known. The Depression and the war that followed had a numbing effect on the nation, and instead of greeting the end of this era with cheer and optimism, New Zealanders opted for thrift, security and caution.

Ron's father was no exception. He had been one of the bullied children in his own family, and he retaliated by rejecting everything his father stood for. He wanted no part of business and had no particular desire to advance himself. All he wanted was an easy, peaceful life.

An insular, unadventurous man, John Brierley began his working life as a taxi driver and during the Second World War worked in the telephone section of the Air Force. By the time he died in 1963 he was happily employed as a clerk in the Audit Department. His wife encouraged him to study accountancy in the evening, but he said he preferred to relax. Later, she says, they discovered he had developed heart trouble as a result of a childhood bout of rheumatic fever, and she wonders now if that was why he was so inactive.

Nevertheless, they got on wonderfully well. She found him frustrating at times, but she was bold enough for both of them. Though she was an only child, she had learned from an early age that if you want something you have to fight for it. May Brierley can't remember a time when she didn't fight with her headstrong Swedish mother to get what she wanted. She said they 'loved each other like poison'.

May's family came out to New Zealand from London in 1921, and her father, Alfred Reader, worked in accounts in Kirkcaldie and Stains, Wellington's most prestigious store. May is proud of the fact that her father once worked in Hockleys in Bond Street, London. Hockleys was an exclusive courtier whose clients included the royal family. One of Alfred Reader's tasks was to travel to Paris, pick up the latest designs, have them made up at Hockleys and, on completion, present them to the palace.

Later, when Alfred Reader grew old and infirm, his wife refused to look after him and he went to live with May and John.

John was relieved to unburden many tasks on to his spirited wife. When it came to most issues, including child-rearing, John would turn to May and say, 'You do all the talking, Maisie. You're better at these things than I am.' So she did. One of the tasks she enjoyed most was to go to Old Tom's bakery and help herself to his bread, a sight, she said, which used to make him 'nearly cry'.

It was May Brierley, then, who nurtured and disciplined her two sons, and by her own admission she was tough as tungsten steel. She remembers relatives criticising her for being too hard on the boys, but she took no notice, believing the discipline would stand them in good stead.

Yet if anyone filled the boys with a sense of possibility it was their mother. She looked out beyond the hemmed-in horizons of her husband and preached the ethic of self-propulsion through maxims such as, 'Work hard and it shall be yours,' and the one Ron obviously took to heart, 'Put your money in your money box and watch it grow.'

This was simple orthodox Calvinism, but May mixed it with a strong unorthodox anti-authoritarianism. She would dispute anything that offended her sense of fair play, and anyone from the local car dealer to Ron's headmaster was a potential target. Long before consumer rights were fashionable she was demanding them.

Not surprisingly, Ron was closer to his mother than his father. Ron and his father never argued openly, but there was obviously hostility between them. When Ron Brierley eventually started R. A. Brierley Investments Ltd, his mother and brother took shares in the company. His father refused. This was not the future he wanted for his son.

Today, psychoanalysts recognise this as the typical family dynamic of a budding entrepreneur. Though the success of the entrepreneur cannot be attributed solely to background, it is a major motivating factor.

A classic study of the psyche of entrepreneurs was made in 1964 by Orvis F. Collins, a professor of management at Michigan State University, and David G. Moore, then dean of the New York State School of Industrial and Labor Relations at Cornell University. Interviews with 150 entrepreneurs revealed that the typical childhood was one of a young boy who felt close to his mother and disappointed in his father. The mother lets the son know at an early age that she feels let down by her husband in some way, and that he can win in the rivalry with his father. The message may be overt or subtle, but the son accepts the need to outdo his father.

All this lies buried in the unconscious, but it may be the reason why the son usually resents being told what to do. He is unlikely to connect the fact that his resentment of authority is linked to his rivalry with his father, but he simply feels that he does not want anyone telling him what to do.

The son's desire to continue his close relationship with his mother is manifest in other ways as he grows older. In Brierley's case, it is probably most obvious in his unwillingness to look after himself. Ever since he was a child he has handed over the responsibility for the mundane practicalities of life to someone else.

If his parents were away on holiday, it was not Ron, the elder brother, who was expected to run the household. It was his younger brother, Ken, who had to make his bed and feed him. No one would have dreamed of asking Ron, for no one expected him to be able to cope. A similar reputation for incompetence had him exempted from duties such as marching in cadets at school. He was so inept he was given another, much better, job of delivering messages.

Today he is as cheerfully ignorant of the basics in life as he was as a child. He doesn't know how to make tea and he burns toast, declare his friends. He has avoided the need to learn how to look after himself by living with his mother for many years, then wisely choosing a hotel when he could afford it. He did flat with his friend Colin Beyer for a while, though Beyer said it was like flatting with no one. Brierley was never there.

Somehow Ron Brierley has always found someone to take care of the practical details of life such as paying parking tickets, buying shirts or arranging a morning suit for his investiture. Colleagues often joke that Ron doesn't need a wife, he needs a mother, and they are closer to the truth than they realise. By handing over such responsibilities to others, he is simply trying to recreate the relationship he has enjoyed most — the relationship with his mother.

As a child, Ron's appearance helped him to avoid responsibility. Although he was judged to be the most beautiful baby at a Wellington Harbour Board picnic, he grew up to be an unprepossessing youngster. With his wire-frame glasses, spindly legs and ears like wind sails, he looked sickly and sorrowful most of the time. He also has the mannerisms of the timid — a slight hesitation of speech, awkward gestures and a faltering walk. All the same, it was his healthy-looking brother who caught most of the childhood illnesses. Ron remained stubbornly well.

His feeble appearance invited bullying and he was often beaten up by school thugs. His mother had taught him not to respond to this intimidation, but it happened so frequently that the headmaster called her in to see him. He told her that Ron would have to start sticking up for himself. So the next time Ron was about to be pummelled again, he retaliated and showed such surprising strength and tenacity he finally had to be pulled away from his tormentor for fear of doing damage to the boy. Not surprisingly, the need to fight never arose again.

Though enjoying his own company more than most, he always had plenty of friends and he was a member of a group known among themselves as the Island Bay Five. Four out of five of the group, including Brierley himself, played an important role in Brierley's company in later years. The others were Neil Breingan, Trevor Beyer, who became a BIL director in 1971 and still is today, his brother Colin Beyer, a director in 1961 and lawyer for the company, and Denis Kelly, who was also company secretary of BIL from 1978 to 1982. Ron retains these friends today out of loyalty or sheer familiarity, a point on which there are many views.

At school boys generally grouped together according to suburbs, which were a rough indicator of class. However, social differences were not as distinct and isolating as they are today. The working-class boys of Island Bay and Northland all went to Wellington College, but so did the sons of Kelburn and Karori professionals. When the waterside workers were locked out during the 1951 waterfront dispute, there was tremendous sympathy for the affected families and their boys at the school.

Although Brierley displayed a remarkable memory as a child, easily memorising any fact he was told even before he could read, he resented learning at school. The regimentation offended him and he couldn't see the point of continued study. His views on education these days can be summed up as never letting your schooling get in the way of an education. Brierley believes in testing your mettle in the marketplace, and his progress reflected his dwindling interest as he slipped from 3A to 6D. He only just scraped through School Certificate and had to sit University Entrance.

Brierley did, however, receive the book-keeping prize although, being an unfashionable subject, this was rated a dubious distinction. In fact, he was so good at book-keeping his teacher, George Halliday, regarded him as a stand-by. If he couldn't find the answer to a problem, he was sure Ron could.

Despite his unremarkable academic career and inoffensive nature, Ron Brierley was remembered by many teachers at Wellington College. It was known that young Ron Brierley knew a thing or two about business, but one day he took his interest a step further than the school was happy with: he acquired a dealer's certificate from the New Zealand Stamp Dealers Federation, hung out his shingle and sold his first set of stamps to the teacher who ran the stamp club. He then put out notices around the school which declared: 'Buy, sell and exchange stamps at Room 4 during interval.' Brierley also cast his net wider by advertising in newspapers and magazines. During class he was often seen furtively counting his takings under his desk lid. The Kiwi Stamp Company, as he called it, was in business.

The headmaster, Alec Heron, was furious when he discovered what Brierley was doing. Apparently he marched into the staffroom, slammed his diary on the table and roared: 'That boy Brierley is using this institution for his commercial gain. This has got to stop.'

Perhaps it was the way Ron conducted his business that particularly infuriated the headmaster. Ron had acquired a typewriter, on which he solemnly tapped out reminder notices to those owing money. The parents of these offenders received letters from the Kiwi Stamp Company informing them their son had an outstanding debt with the company and asking them to pay the debt forthwith. It was a remarkably confident move by a young boy, and all the more surprising given that paying one's bills has always been low on Ron's list of priorities.

In any event, this was the beginning of a lifelong interest in stamps for Ron Brierley and a hint of what was to come. He was, in fact, learning about the very principles that would guide him in business, for in many ways collecting stamps is not too dissimilar to buying shares. Both are pieces of paper denoting value, and the trick is in picking that value.

Many of his peers, such as Bob Jones and Bruce Judge, share a love of stamps, but Brierley is one of the rare enthusiasts who does not desire ownership. Right from the Kiwi Stamp Company days, Brierley showed himself to be more of a stamp trader than collector. Not for him the pleasures of building up a collection or paying a high price for a rare stamp. He preferred to buy a grab-bag of stamps and sort through them in the hope of spying a rare stamp. For him there is a deep, private joy in discovering a hidden treasure and knowing that that single stamp is worth ten times the price he paid for the whole bag. He may sell the stamp immediately or hold on to it and sell at a time he thinks is more advantageous. Sometimes he buys as many of a special type of stamp as possible, thus cornering the market and forcing up the price.

It is the same process he applies to business. He begins by investigating companies, followed by identification of value, then acquisition and maximisation of value either by selling, adding to it or holding on. These days the monetary value of this hobby is minuscule compared with the sums he deals with in his business, but he has continued trading stamps for relaxation.

Brierley also finds stamp collecting satisfying because it confirms his judgment, albeit on a small scale, and it provides an important touchstone of common sense and value for him. If asked about his current wealth, he sighs and says, as if burdened, that money becomes meaningless when it reaches the upper limits. What do they really mean, all those figures, those millions and billions, he asks. Stamp collecting, on the other hand, provides a restraining influence or, as he puts it, keeps him in touch with 'real value and real people'.

For his successor at BIL, Bruce Hancox, it simply shows how hard Brierley is prepared to work to make a dollar. He remembers going to see Brierley one day and informing him that since the company's share price had gone up by so much that day he was now worth an extra $5 million. Ron looked up at him from his desk where he sat sorting through stamps and said, 'Fancy that. Here I've been trying all day to make sure that I've put together a stamp collection of only $49 to sell for $50.'

His interest in stamps waxes and wanes, but at one time he co-opted a staff member to help him. For years one of the IEL librarian's tasks was to bid at auction for stamps she and Ron Brierley had selected. He collects only British Commonwealth stamps dating from the mid-nineteenth century to the Second World War. After big spending sprees in 1978 to 1980, they had built up quite a sizable collection, which was deposited in an IEL safe and valued in the 1983 accounts at $500,000. That was the last year they appeared as a company investment, but the stamps stayed there until IEL was sold.

At about the same time he started the Kiwi Stamp Company, Ron Brierley was also spending a lot of time following his other passion — cricket. He was first given a cricket bat by his father when he was four years old and his love affair was immediate. He read cricketing annuals whenever he could and when he played he was the one who always kept a careful record of the scores. From the outset it was a serious pastime and he would come home spitting with fury if his friends had decided they wanted to relax the rules and have a friendly game.

He is a keen sportsman and what he lacks in ability he makes up for in tenacity. At school he is remembered for coming last in a school running race, but with a bravado few could forget. He had a slow, hobbling gait and it was not long before everyone left him far behind. In the end he was several laps behind the pack, but he persevered and the crowd began to take an interest in this determined, limping fellow as he made his way around the track. By the time he crossed the line, they were on his side and they roared their approval. Ron, smiling all the while, waved his arms in mock triumph.

When he grew older he took an interest in other sports. A friend who remembers playing squash with Ron when he was a beginner said it was 'dead boring'. He was hopeless. But Ron plugged valiantly away at the sport and eventually won every game against this friend.

Later he played A-grade table tennis for university and was credited with being one of the first people to introduce the sponge-rubber bat. This game suited him better than most, since it required technique rather than athletic ability. With his nifty sponge-rubber bat and a few crafty moves, he made a devastating table tennis player.

Brierley also developed a special technique for ball games which earned him the epithet 'Ron the Lob' in tennis. The technique relied on aiming the ball high in the air to confound the opponent. He used this skill to good effect in cricket as well as tennis, and in the end his determination to succeed paid off. He was promoted from Saturday morning cricket for boys who couldn't make the school teams to playing inter-school competition.

His best memory of cricket at school was his weekend job on the scoreboard for the Wellington Cricket Association. A Wellington College teacher recommended him for the position and he held the job for four years. In winter he did the scoreboard for the Soccer Association, but it was the cricket season he adored. He says he made only one mistake and that was in the first game. Instead of recording ten runs for no wickets, Ron put up ten wickets for no runs. The local paper photographed the error and Ron was embarrassed by the mistake, but delighted to be noticed.

He loved being part of the cricketing milieu. The beautiful muted order, strategy and class of the game enchanted him, and he silently worshipped the players. He even devised a cunning way of getting closer to them. Entry to the club lunch room was gained by means of a ticket. Ron quickly noticed that all club lunch tickets were the same, so he and the other boy who kept score were able to slip into the lunches by using discarded tickets. Eventually someone discovered their trick and stopped them, but by then he had at least had the glorious opportunity of mingling with his idols.

Ron Brierley's grandfather, Thomas Brierley, in 1940 when he was sixty-six years old

May and John Brierley at Karori, Wellington, 1935

Ron Brierley (centre) aged three years with two friends

John Brierley with Ken (centre) and Ron (left) at Akatarawa, 1950

May Brierley with Ron standing in the back yard at Island Bay, 1954

Ron Brierley, now with contact lenses, enjoying a drink with friend Rae Ezzie (centre) and Don McDonald in Sydney

Don McDonald

The determined face of Ron Brierley in the early 1960s

Given his joy at being a part of this fraternity, it seemed unlikely that he would resign from the scoreboard role, and even less likely that it would be over a point of principle. But that is exactly what he did. Sports day at school coincided with a four-day cricket test for which Ron was keen to keep score. When his request for permission to have school sports day off was refused he was furious. He knew full well his absence would not have been a great loss to the sporting world. His mother was also incensed on his behalf and together they told the headmaster that he would have to get someone else to do the scoreboard. Ron wouldn't be coming back.

In the end the school had to eat humble pie. They were unable to find an immediate replacement for Ron and so he was asked to reconsider his resignation. Mother and son were emphatic: Ron would not be coming back.

TWO

Think and Grow Rich

NEW ZEALAND IN THE 1950s was as fresh and heavy as new milk. After the cheerless 1930s and '40s, the '50s promised jobs for all, economic comfort and relative peace. The news media emphasised this complacent innocence with photographs of girls parading their own hand-sewn garments, young folk gathering at the new, fashionable milk bars, and endless pictures of the Queen in different outfits when she visited in 1953. It was the first visit to New Zealand by a reigning monarch and they said she added gaiety to our lives. Of course, there were darker moments, like the 1951 waterfront dispute and the Tangiwai disaster in 1953, but on the whole the mood of the country was like the weather — sunny and easy.

It was in this climate that Ron Brierley pondered his future. He knew he would have no trouble getting a job, for in early 1955, the year he started work, there were only sixty-eight people unemployed in New Zealand. He took a position at the Sun Insurance Co. Ltd (now Sun Alliance Insurance) and studied accountancy part-time at university with the aim of acquiring a Bachelor of Commerce degree.

So far he was meeting his father's requirements of gaining an education and a secure job, but after two years he gave up university study with the confident assertion that they had nothing to teach him. He was probably right — accountancy was little more than book-keeping in those days and Ron had excelled in that at school.

But if accountancy bored him, at Sun Insurance, where he worked for a year, he discovered what was to quickly become his life-long passion: the sharemarket. In those days the New Zealand share-market was small indeed. When the Barclays index started in 1957, market capitalisation was something in the order of £300 million and the market was dominated by historic heavyweights such as New Zealand Breweries, South British Insurance and Wright Stephenson. There was only a limited interest in matters financial, and the business section of the newspaper in the late 1950s consisted of half a page in between the racing and golf results.

Nevertheless, when Brierley read the quotations in the paper something clicked into place. He says he knew deep down this was for him, even though he did not know what the quotations really meant. This was it, the map to Treasure Island, and £ marked the spot.

He found out more in a chance meeting on the street with a friend who knew something about the market. They talked and Brierley says he could feel anticipation mounting inside him. He wanted more. He wanted to know everything; he craved involvement. All the numbers and values, all the gossip and competitive nature of it. This was the way to make a fortune and to enjoy doing it, he thought.

The stock-broking firm of Hamilton Buckleton & Nathan was in the same building as Sun Insurance, so once Brierley had done a little research on a company he was interested in he went to see Andrew Hamilton. Hamilton was something of a legend in Wellington financial circles, known for his autocratic nature and short temper as much as for his ability. Hesitantly Ron asked him about a speculative stock called Ampol Exploration and waited for the dazzling torrent of information he expected. Instead the great man frowned and said, 'I don't know much about that one. Let's look up the book to see what it says.' He didn't even know what the share price was and Ron then realised that he knew more about the stock than the expert.

Brierley might have been disappointed in Hamilton, but the broker took a liking to the young man and allowed him to practise margin trading through his firm. (Margin trading is where you buy shares with a good deal of the money borrowed through brokers or a bank.) Ampol Exploration shares, however, were not Brierley's first purchase. He first bought shares in the Auckland Gas Company. Shortly afterwards the city council began talking about nationalising the company and Brierley watched as his shares rose from 7s 6d to 10 shillings. He was hooked, and so were his friends.

It was around this time that a tentative social life, extending beyond six o'clock closing in pubs and drinking flagons in the kitchen, started to develop in New Zealand. The first coffee lounges and licensed restaurants opened and these were eagerly frequented by Brierley and his friends. Their favourite was the Café du Boulevard in Victoria Street, which had a sign showing a Frenchwoman with her poodle dallying at a street corner. It was run by Bart Cox, an Englishman who would later become a director of BIL.

Cox was interested in the market and he had a bit of money to spare thanks to a £10,000 win on Tatts, an Australian lottery. His coffee bar attracted a large number of businessmen, since Cox made a point of going to the Wellington Stock Exchange each day to pick up the daily callsheet, which he pinned to the wall of the café.

Brierley and his friends met there frequently to discuss the market, and the group, which included regulars like Alan Perry, Bill Hallam-Eames and Trevor Beyer, was dubbed the Brierley Boys. Later, when Cox sold his coffee lounge, they regrouped at Suzy's, a coffee house in Willis Street. Eventually the group expanded and started having regular Sunday night dinners at Cox's place, a ritual that would continue for twenty years.

It was amiable enough meeting at these coffee bars or at the Midland Hotel, taking flagons to parties afterwards, playing cards late at night and with women as yet on the rim of their world, 'out there', and not spoiling their fun. All the young men came from similar hardworking, modest backgrounds and all of them nursed aspirations for a better future. While the choice of wine, salami and shoes might have been limited in the 1950s, the future unrolled before them like the night sky, limitless and beckoning with promise.

Jobs were plentiful, the country had an impeccable record in social welfare, and education, like the school milk, was free. Although the Beyers' father was a waterside worker and Brierley's father was a clerk, the young men all knew they would not be repeating the past. Ron's friends dreamed of becoming millionaires and joined investment clubs in hope.

Investment clubs were new in New Zealand, although they had been popular in Britain for some time. Perhaps since several of Brierley's friends were British immigrants, they were not slow to start their own group. He and Trevor Beyer belonged to a club started by Bill Hallam-Eames which was noted more for its sociability than success.

In 1959 Brierley and Beyer formed a company called Investment Funds New Zealand Ltd. Its purpose was to make investments in other companies, although it also engaged in factoring of debt. (Factoring involves the discount purchase of debt, which the purchasers then attempt to redeem at face value.) The only significant investment it had was 10 per cent of General Finance Ltd, an unlisted public company that invested most of its funds in second mortgages.

Beyer remembers that at first he and Brierley lost money with Investment Funds but later these losses were recovered.

Brierley was clearly casting around for the best way to make money. His dreams of becoming a millionaire were as recurring and fervent as any of his friends' fantasies, and he knew that the first step on the road to riches was to develop the right attitude. In search of that attitude he joined the Napoleon Hill Club.

Today Napoleon Hill's name has disappeared from view, but in his day he had a large following and the book of his teachings sold millions of copies. During the Depression, Napoleon Hill was engaged by the American steel king Andrew Carnegie to discover why some people continued to do well throughout this period. Napoleon Hill contacted these people and asked what motivated them.

The result was a book, *Think and Grow Rich*, which was based on thirteen principles of success. These were a collection of homilies, encouraging and easy to follow, and designed to lead the reader to the secret of success. The moment that secret is realised the reader is asked to turn over a glass, for that occasion is said to mark the most important turning-point in their life. A well-thumbed copy of *Think and Grow Rich* rests in the BIL library in Wellington.

This and other testimonies of successful men are the only books Brierley appears to have read, though he is an avid reader of newspapers. Bob Jones remembers pressing him to buy a copy of Joseph Heller's *Catch-22* in a bookshop. Brierley picked up the paperback, studied the cover, read the back blurb, pondered it for a while, then put it back. 'You miserable bugger,' said Jones. 'Why don't you just buy it?' Brierley looked at him and asked with genuine confusion, 'But what on earth would I do with it after I've finished?'

He could, however, see the point of harbouring a copy of *Think and Grow Rich*, and in this he was not alone. Stars of the capitalist firmament such as John D. Rockefeller and E. M. Statler, who founded the Great Hotel System, had read and endorsed it. Would-be capitalist Ron Brierley read it, joined the Napoleon Hill Club and even went to the trouble of meeting a disciple of Hill who came to New Zealand. Brierley declared that his meeting with the president of the Combined Insurance Company of America, W. Clement Stone, was momentous.

Today he is a little embarrassed and cynical about his involvement with the Napoleon Hill Club. The club attracted the usual assorted odd-bods, dreamers and losers who needed booster shots of courage, optimism and common sense in equal doses, and Brierley hoped he was out of place there. He recalls: 'The club involved telling each other they were getting better and better, with everybody looking at each other and smiling and telling themselves they were good fellows and were going to get there. I suspect that I was the only one that ever got anything out of it in terms of doing something.'

However, he admits it did clarify for him a basic philosophy of self-confidence, determination and the importance of setting goals. 'I think that's the most important aspect of it, because a lot of people set out without any idea of what they are seeking to achieve.'

So far all Brierley knew was that he wanted to make money and the way to do that was to have greater involvement in the money market itself. But how best to achieve this and not lose his shirt? He could become a stockbroker, of course, but he wanted to be his own man.

The ingenious scheme he finally came up with was inspired by a business venture of his second employer, E. E. ('Mac') McCurdy, whose firm distributed magazines and books. Brierley did the accounts for McCurdy and now admits that, while he would have made a good accountant, he was a little lax in terms of routine accounting assignments. Within a year of his starting work there the firm was in receivership. For a time Brierley tried to run the business himself, but it was futile — he found the books were being imported at a loss.

Always eager to turn a loss into a gain, Brierley declares the experience at McCurdy's to be tremendously chastening and educational. He says that seeing everything from go to whoa impressed on him how not to run a business. One of McCurdy's activities also planted in Brierley's mind the germ of an idea for his own publication.

While he was in business, McCurdy owned a racing tipsheet called *Turf Newsletter*, which he had bought from Alex Smith, a well-known racing reporter. McCurdy knew nothing at all about horse racing and relied on correspondents for the copy. But after a few weeks of ownership, McCurdy sacked the correspondents and did the job himself, learning as he went, and when he was away Brierley filled in for him.

Gradually it dawned on Brierley that if he was capable of putting out a racing tipsheet knowing nothing and caring little for racing, surely he could write a financial tipsheet. All he had to do was blend some well-known facts with a smattering of original research and a whiff of tantalising market gossip. He calculated this would only take a few days at most.

First he tested the market by inserting a tiny advertisement for the tipsheet in the local newspaper. He had already decided to abandon the project if no one replied, but to his delight five cheques came in for £1 10s, totalling £7 10s, roughly the cost of producing the first month's issue. Suddenly a cold wave of responsibility began to wash over him. He realised that he didn't want to put out any old rag. It had to be good, and that required hard work.

As Brierley threw himself into the project, working long hours into the night, he cursed his own untempered enthusiasm. If he had known how much work it was going to be, he would never have bothered. It would cause him to say ever after that a daily deadline must be one of the greatest burdens a man can work under.

The first issue of *New Zealand Stocks and Shares*, in November 1956, was a long way from the expert analysis that later issues would contain, but there was nothing else like it on the market. Its six small pages of advice touched on everything from the way the Middle East crisis would affect insurance to Whakatane Board Mills Ltd's prospects, and even an 'old favourite of ours', Tekau Knitwear.

The newsletter also gave him his first opportunity to indulge in a little self-promotion. He was a natural. From the beginning he assumed the tone of a chirrupy, eager salesman and he was clearly not restrained by modesty. The newsletter was subtitled 'The Leading Investment Journal' and Brierley promised readers that investing with him would be lucrative. *New Zealand Stocks and Shares* was also said to have special features such as an advisory bureau and another section called 'Our Experts' Report'. The 'northern correspondent' introduced his recommendations with the sweeping 'We think'.

A reader could have been forgiven for believing the journal had pooled the energy and talents of a rare group of specialists, but in fact, nineteen-year-old Ron Brierley was writing the newsletter, folding the finished product and licking the envelopes himself. These days, just remembering he went to such trouble gives him pause for thought.

Although he had only half a dozen subscribers in the beginning, Brierley always printed at least a thousand copies of *New Zealand Stocks and Shares* and sent one to every listed public company in New Zealand. He reasoned that if he did this for six months and then billed them they would probably pay up because they had become accustomed to the newsletter.

Brierley remembers vividly how he and Trevor Beyer looked forward to clearing his post office box every day. There was a frisson of excitement when they discovered it was crammed with mail. Having emptied the box, they would carry their trophies back to a coffee bar and sift through the replies.

About one in four paid up, and Ron privately savoured each one, thinking to himself, 'Seventeen and six — not bad for a day's work.'

The replies sometimes began, 'Dear Sir, we did not order this. Please do not continue to bill us.'

'Bastards,' Brierley would say, picking up another envelope.

Overleaf: *Pages from the first issue of* New Zealand Stocks and Shares

New Zealand Stocks and Shares

"The Leading Investment Journal"

Published on the first day of each month by National Investments, P.O. Box 1520, Wellington, New Zealand.

Subscription 30/- per annum. November, 1956

We welcome you to "New Zealand Stocks and Shares" with the hope that your association with us will be a long and profitable one. We hope also that you will appreciate the format of this journal which has been designed to eliminate all surplus material and to bring forward in a clear and concise manner only those facts which the investor will find relevant and important

We feel, from the information which is being published in this journal, not only will you be able to save many pounds from our timely warnings but even more important you will find that your investments will be come more and more lucrative. The success of "New Zealand Stocks and Shares" rests upon the quality of this information, and in this results will bear us out, in our claim to being "the Leading Investment Journal".

ADVISORY BUREAU

We intend to make this one of our leading features. Just send in any queries you have and they will be dealt with in this section. By taking advantage of this you can pay your subscription from the saving in search fees alone!

BELOW PAR BUYING CAN BE PROFITABLE

We publish below a list of 33 companies whose shares are now selling below par. When share values drop, the prices for some shares fall more than the circumstances really warrant and in these instances there may exist a good chance to make a profitable investment.

Name of Company	*Par Value*	*High 1955 1955*	*High 1955 1956*	*Low Price 1956*	*Current Price*
Auckland Laundry	20/-	14/-	14/6	14/-	14/6
Avon Metal Industries	20/-	9/6	—	—	—
Canterbury Farmers	35/-	30/9	35/-	33/3	34/-*
Consolidated Brick & Pipe	20/-	14/-	13/8	11/9	12/-
Courtaulds (Aust.) †	16/2	15/-	16/3	15/4	15/9
General Finance	20/-	13/-	—	—	—
Gisborne Gas	20/-	10/-	11/-	11/-	13/6*
Hadfields †	16/2	15/9	14/4	14/4	14/5
Holeproof Industries	20/-	18/6	15/-	11/-	12/9
Hugh J. Kearns	20/-	19/-	—	—	19/6*
Invincible Building	100/-	92/6	93/6	93/6	93/6
M.C.P.	5/-	6/-	5/9	4/6	4/6
Matheson Minster	10/-	9/6	—	—	8/6*
Morts Dock †	16/2	17/4	13/9	13/9	12/6*
Napier Gas	200/-	—	—	—	90/-*
National Pictures	20/-	—	11/6	11/6	11/6*
N.Z. & River Plate	20/-	8/11	—	—	5/-*

SELECTED SHARES

Each month we intend presenting to our subscribers a short survey on the shares of a company, which we and our expert consultants believe is worth close attention from the point of view of sound and lucrative investment.

This month we have selected the ordinary shares of Denhard Bakeries Ltd., Wellington. There are 70,000 of these and although quoted reasonably regularly on the Stock Exchange they do not change hands very often,being fairly tightly held. At the moment they can be obtained at around the 26/- mark and investors who purchase at this figure are certain to make a profit in the fairly near future.

Profits of this company have been rising steadily the past few years and for the year ended April 30th, 1956 the dividend rate on ordinary shares was lifted from 6% to 8%. From information received from a very reliable source, we can assure our readers that not only will this higher rate of dividend be maintained but there is every chance of a further rise in dividend at the end of next April (Paid in June). An interim dividend of 4% is forecast for December of this year.

We think we can say that with profits rising as they are there is a definite likelihood of further capital being required within two or three years or even sooner if suitable market conditions prevail. Denhard Bakeries do not appear to have been affected by the credit squeeze nearly as much as many other firms. Reports received by us to date continue to be increasingly optimistic, stating that the Co's main difficulties are staff problems and the rising costs of production.

In conclusion, "New Zealand Stocks and Shares" makes the recommendation to all investors to seriously consider these shares at 26/- each, keeping in mind the chance of capital appreciation combined with an attractive dividend yield.

Slight downward trend of Insurance shares last week was probably on account of the Middle East crisis. A large proportion of the business of South British and New Zealand Insurance is done overseas. Standard appear to be steady at 22/-.

OUR EXPERTS REPORT......

Dominion Builders Supplies (Ch'ch) Ltd. have for the last four years been paying practically all profits out in dividends at a steady rate of 7%. Profits for year ended April 30th, 1957 are expected to be substantially lower with a corresponding drop in dividend. The 10/- shares can currently be bought at 10/3.

Many shareholders of Aulsebrook & Co. Ltd. are unhappy with the management of the Co. Previous to 1955 the Co. was paying an 8% dividend but net losses for the past two years have exceeded the £50,000 mark. Full advantage has been taken of special depreciation allowances and a considerable saving in income tax has resulted, but many shareholders appear to be a little uneasy over the whole position. This is a firm which could conceivably profit from modernisation and a more alive approach to the marketing of their products. Aulsebrooks are operating in a field where the percentage of profit on each article sold is very high, but competition is very stiff indeed and the volume of sales depends largely on the amount of money freely circulating in the community.

But it did not stop there. Those who declined received another letter saying, 'We're very disappointed in your attitude and we are billing you 17s 6d for the issues you have had.' And if that did not work, his final letter usually made a stronger impact. The opening paragraph read, 'We are extremely disappointed in view of the fact that we are writing an article on your organisation.'

Very few held out against this barrage of demands, but even the refusals were devoured by Ron. He examined the letterhead, the tone of the letter and even the kind of paper. Like a bloodhound sniffing a telling item of clothing, Brierley examined every detail for clues. He said that these letters gave him a feel for each company. Brierley was like a new father with his subscribers, at once proud and sentimental, and he mourned any losses. Losing a subscriber, he said, was like losing a member of the family.

At this stage the publication was still put out under the name of National Investments, a title that concealed as much as it revealed. No one knew that Ron Brierley, a young unqualified accountant, was behind it and this oversight was deliberate. Brierley knew the facts might alter readers' appreciation of the product.

In fact, one of the first five cheques to arrive was from George Chapman, later president of the National Party and a director of the Bank of New Zealand. Ron knew him slightly and said to him one day, 'Thanks very much for sending me the cheque.'

'What do you mean?' asked Chapman.

'For *New Zealand Stocks and Shares*. I put that out,' said Brierley with sly satisfaction.

'Is that you?' exclaimed Chapman. 'I'll cancel it immediately.'

Soon after that Brierley told stockbroker Eric Nathan from Hamilton Buckleton & Nathan that he was responsible for the newsletter. Nathan was shocked to discover that their friendly young investor was responsible for the publication that had upset so many of his clients. He told Brierley he felt it was inappropriate for it to remain anonymous, so in July 1957 Brierley put his name to *New Zealand Stocks and Shares* for the first time.

By 1962, *New Zealand Stocks and Shares* had progressed from an amateurish, six-page document to a well-known, A4, ten-page newsletter. Brierley wrote about reserves companies did not want disclosed, recommended paying bonuses to shareholders and at times commented adversely on the market for companies' products. With its unabashed criticism and the wry and sarcastic wit which developed later, the newsletter was refreshingly bold and was soon known as *New Zealand Shocks and Stares*.

The attention it gained, however, was not always congratulatory. In 1959 the journal was drawn to the attention of one James Fletcher by his colleague C. M. Richwhite, who alerted him to an article on the sad state of the local cement industry. Brierley's comments stung both men, who had substantial interests in the industry, and Fletcher told a staff member to find out who the publisher was.

New Zealand Stocks and Shares was doing well, but not well enough to support its senior writer, and, unbeknown to Fletcher, Brierley was working for Fletchers Hardware Ltd in Kaiwharawhara, north of Wellington. When Fletcher discovered that the publisher was actually working for him, he offered Brierley a job in head office in Auckland. Brierley refused and at about the same time Fletchers discovered the accounts Brierley was working on weren't exactly up to accounting copy-book standard. Needless to say, his decision not to take the job suited everyone.

Brierley's accounting might not have been first-rate, but his analysis was improving. There had been a few errors of judgment, such as recommending the disastrous Hauraki Whaling Company and the Standard Insurance Co. Ltd (which crashed shortly after his promotion), but investors were given a number of good tips.

He even got the occasional scoop, such as the time he was invited by a shareholder to a Rubber Distributors Ltd annual meeting that was barred to the press. Initial optimism for this speculative stock had taken a battering and its pound shares had fallen to 7 shillings when their meeting was held in August 1957. The meeting turned out to be highly contentious, with angry shareholders demanding explanations. Brierley knew he had a hot story on his hands and after its publication Rubber Distributors was forced to send out a circular explaining why things had gone awry.

But *New Zealand Stocks and Shares* was not his only interest, for these were years of opportunism and experimentation. He was prepared to try anything in his search for capital. For a while he was even a salesman for a superannuation scheme, but he soon decided there must be an easier way to make money.

He also attempted to enter politics, which seems extraordinary since he is now totally unmoved by the machinations of politics unless they directly affect his world. His friend Bob Jones enjoys political discussion but has never been able to engage Brierley in debate. He has discovered that Brierley regards political or economic debate as the ultimate futility. His attitude is that of a philosophical anarchist, and Jones believes he would willingly subscribe to the doctrines of Ayn Rand if he had ever heard of her.

But in 1959 Brierley went along to a meeting of the United Independents and, since they were short of candidates, obligingly put his name forward for the local body elections. The United Independents party comprised a group of disparate, idiosyncratic individuals and was spectacularly unsuccessful. It was led by Saul Goldsmith, who then had the largest chain of jewellery and souvenir stores in the country. He was a cranky, irrepressible man who buzzed hopelessly around the corridors of power, as much an individualist as his more successful cousin Sir Dove-Myer Robinson, for many years the mayor of Auckland. One of United Independents' recurrent platforms was to bring back the trams, which were phased out of Wellington in 1964.

Brierley stood for the United Independents in 1959, 1962 and 1965. He had shed his glasses almost as soon as contact lenses were introduced, and his clean-shaven, youthful visage appeared in the paper under banners like 'The council is big business. It must be run on businesslike lines' and 'Let's have the trams back'. For a man whose natural inclination is 'I' over 'we' and who has no political interests, it was a strange move. What was he thinking of?

The perks, quips his mother cynically. She points out that he never rode the trams anyway, preferring to travel by car and amass mountains of unpaid parking tickets.

Brierley's friends were even more taken aback when he invited them to hear him speak at a meeting to select the National Party representative for Island Bay in 1960. They saw him as a quirky, gnomic figure who gave their circle a worldly business air. They took him to dinner and parties and didn't mind when he fell asleep by ten o'clock. He slept so soundly they sometimes rearranged his limbs like a rag doll or put a flower in his mouth. He astonished and amused them with the contrast between his shy demeanour and brazen behaviour.

In any event, he was not selected and, typically, was unwilling to accept the decision of the panel. Why was he passed over, he demanded to know. John Meadowcroft, the chairman of the Wellington division of the National Party, Dominion president and businessman, looked at him with distaste. We don't have to give reasons, he said truthfully.

Later Meadowcroft asked Goldsmith who Brierley was and he called him 'a funny sort of chap who has been attacking a lot of businesses lately'.

There was no doubt that *New Zealand Stocks and Shares* was making waves. No stockbroking newsletter or financial journal gave opinions as baldly as it did. By the time Brierley started his own company in 1961, the view of many who read his publication was that he was brilliant and would either go broke, go to jail or narrowly avoid both and become a multimillionaire.

Brierley relishes any role that casts him as an outsider. He likes being noticed, being different and being annoying, and *New Zealand Stocks and Shares* was the perfect vehicle for his rebellious, irreverent instinct. It had all the illicit crackle of a pirate radio broadcast and Brierley loved it. He never worried about defamation. On the contrary, he was thrilled to receive a written threat, for it meant he had upset someone and anyway nothing ever came of the threats of legal action.

'I was conscious of the fact that if one wrote offensive untruths it would be possible to be sued for large sums of money, so one tried to write offensive truths. But really, what seemed offensive in those days is now innocuous. Winstones used to hate me writing about their reserves, so you couldn't even make people happy praising them,' he says.

As he researched the New Zealand business scene a picture began to slowly emerge. What struck Brierley time and time again was the large number of companies dominated by elderly board members who preferred to sit on under-performing assets and tuck away profits into reserves earning little for shareholders. He could see businesses whose existence had outlived their function, and others whose size and capital structure meant they were no longer viable.

As far as he could see, this situation was likely to continue, since there appeared to be nothing to threaten this cosy set-up. Two world wars had robbed New Zealand of many energetic, well-educated young men who might have stepped in to revitalise these companies. Instead, an older, entrenched generation held the nation's assets in a firm grip. During the 1940s, '50s and '60s many companies were run by men in their eighties. Consequently, throughout this period of growing prosperity there were surprisingly few takeovers and new enterprises of any kind.

The same thing had happened in Britain after the Second World War. Unable or unwilling to spend profits hoarded during the war years, or acquired as compensation for war damage, companies kept their assets liquid in order to replace premises and equipment. And the increase in the value of the assets the company still had often also added to its vulnerability to takeovers. Companies that failed to revalue their assets regularly risked attracting the attentions of people like businessman Charles Clore who recognised their true worth.

Brierley was a fan of Clore and he saw in New Zealand an echo of the British scenario of the 1940s. New Zealand business was sluggish and smug. He imagined the ageing directors, dozy and distant in the wood-panelled dimness of their boardrooms, recovering from a heavy luncheon at the club. Goodness knows, there was no need for them to be on full alert. It was their game and generally they found everyone played fair.

Brierley saw these directors drugged with complacency, and the picture in his mind grew clearer and clearer. There was room here for someone like him, someone concerned with purity and efficiency in business. It was simply a question of how it could be achieved.

He decided it was probably time to put his theories to the test, to expose himself to a little risk. In 1958 he became something of an agitator over the Wellington Loan and Investment Co. Ltd, publishing a series of critical statements and comments which he today says were 'a lot of fun'. When a second offer pushed the price up, the local newspaper credited Brierley with the rise.

He then cast a watery-blue eye on the men's clothing retailer, Hallensteins, based in Dunedin. Hallensteins had already heard of Brierley — indeed it was hard to forget a person who had described the company as 'fairly mediocre, short on earnings but flush with reserves' in his newsletter. He had gone on to say that the property portfolio was undervalued but with dynamic management could produce excellent income. He clearly didn't think much of the company's management and even went so far as to warn them to protect the company's vulnerability by producing a bonus, better profit or a dividend.

Four days before the annual meeting on 27 September 1960, Colin Nicholson, a director of Hallensteins, was rung by his sister, who asked if he had got the circular from Brierley with its proxy forms, critique of the company and request that shareholders support his nomination to the board? 'It says here,' she said, 'that he thinks the company is so mismanaged they should consider selling technical equipment, not clothing.'

Nicholson was alarmed and immediately rang the chairman, Peter Fels. He thought Brierley had a 'darn cheek and went about things in a nasty way'. Fels decided to rewrite his speech, denying all Brierley's charges and asking shareholders for their loyalty.

Although it was a cold night, more shareholders than expected turned up and the meeting had to be moved to a bigger venue. To his chagrin, Brierley found his attention to detail had slipped up. His nomination did not come within the time-frame required, so the directors declared with relief that it was invalid.

However, the board decided to increase the dividend that year and Brierley felt a glow of satisfaction. That was his doing, surely. Nicholson scoffs at the suggestion. He says it would have happened anyway, that the company was just coming out of a lean period.

But in case Hallensteins thought they had outsmarted Brierley, he had one last weapon left in his armoury — the pen. When he got back to Wellington he sat down and wrote about the meeting for *New Zealand Stocks and Shares*. The resulting article is bristling with understated sarcasm. 'The meeting,' he wrote, 'heard a long tale of the terrible difficulties which had been faced over the past ten years. But just in case anyone felt inclined to ease the burden with changes at board level, this fortunately had happened to be the year in which everything has come right.'

Brierley had failed to get board representation, but he had learned a valuable lesson. Corporate muscle was imperative if he were to succeed. An individual shareholder was powerless, lacking capital and clout. Brierley wanted both.

THREE

Real Adventure

'NOW YOU CAN HAVE Real Adventure on the stock market even if you've never owned a share in your life!' With this advertisement Ronald Alfred Brierley publicly proclaimed the intentions of his new company, R. A. Brierley Investments Ltd, incorporated on 30 March 1961.

'R. A. Brierley Investments Limited is modelled on the successful techniques of the new overseas school of enterprising financiers — the takeover men — the merger experts — the 'corporate raiders'. You've read the amazing stories of these millionaires . . . the same opportunities are right here in New Zealand.

'Now — even if you've never owned a share in your life — you can join in the secret and dramatic planned assaults on sleepy public companies . . . Mail the coupon below — today — for a free copy of the prospectus.'

Brierley put in a number of other similarly audacious advertisements with headlines like, 'Want to Get the Most Action into Your Investment Programme?' or 'Shareholder in a Public Company?'

Each one was blatant and boyish, brimful of wonder and urgency. It is the salesman with the miracle hair cure speaking, enthusiastic but not entirely believable. Brierley says himself that the sort of people who did believe him were the very people usually destined to lose their money.

Newspapers were more suspicious than investors, and some even refused to run his advertisements. The stock exchange was equally alarmed. Brierley's brand of roll-up, roll-up promotion was unheard of in the financial sector. Although his first advertisements had been small and discreet, he was later encouraged by an advertising executive to conduct a more sensational campaign if he wanted to be noticed. What people wanted, said the executive, was some real adventure.

Brierley says with undisguised pleasure that stock exchange members nearly died on their feet at the result, and the only thing he regrets now is that the campaign was not cost-effective.

In every other respect the launching of R. A. Brierley Investments

Ltd had gone as he had planned. For example, the name was a critical choice for Brierley. He had wanted to call the company R. A. Brierley Investments Corporation Ltd, rather like the Australian real estate company he so admired, L. J. Hooker Investment Corporation Ltd. But the registrar of companies refused pointblank. He said the word corporation sounded too official and people might think it was part of the Reserve Bank.

Corporation or not, Brierley decided the company had to be named after him, in part to satisfy his ego but primarily to assist the fusion of his personal and corporate identity. He wanted the two to become inseparable and interchangeable, hoping this would also reinforce his commitment to the task. Brierley had already decided the task he had set himself demanded total commitment or it was not worth pursuing.

Brierley then sent out personal invitations to his former school friends and *New Zealand Stocks and Shares* subscribers. The first offer to the public was really an underwriting agreement, since teething problems with the prospectus meant its publication was delayed. In the meantime an underwriting arrangement provided an unintended loophole allowing him to seek subscriptions from the public without a prospectus. Few accepted the initial offer, and the official prospectus followed some months later.

The prospectus was a thin document, bound in blue, and looking rather like an ancient schoolbook. But inside it contained some of the most radical analysis and claims the market had ever faced. Brierley's journals, advertisements and his prospectus are now classics, not only for their style and immodesty, but for his prescience about future trends in corporate history.

He wrote that his company had five objectives. It would take over other companies and reorganise their finances, selling off surplus assets and reinvesting the funds for the more useful development of an existing business. It would invest in industries where mergers were inevitable, and it would participate in private companies. Many of these companies were not expanding because they were conserving cash for death duty purposes, but a share exchange with a progressive private company such as R. A. Brierley Investments would provide the necessary cash. The company would also form a property arm, and it would invest some funds in leading stock exchange securities for short- and medium-term appreciation.

New Zealand business needed this approach, he wrote. It was already supporting enough 'dead' companies and, since it was a growing country with a high standard of living, there would be opportunities galore for the resourceful and the enterprising. The same applied to Australia.

To back up his claims he offered newspaper quotes about Charles Clore and another on the benefits of taking over the Bank of NSW. This latter claim really raised eyebrows. Taking over a bank was no laughing matter, and although the article was taken from the *Australian Financial Review*, the lasting impression was that Brierley ought to be watched.

Finally, he inserted an extract from a book by Edward Westropp, financial editor of the *Sunday Express*, called *The Way to Fortune*, which outlined the takeover technique perfected by Clore and Isaac Wolfson in the 1950s. In essence, it amounted to 'buy cheaply and sell at a profit'. Today, any amateur investment analyst could give you Brierley's analysis, but in 1961, from a twenty-three-year-old, it was revolutionary and challenging stuff.

To investors the most remarkable aspect was the stated aim that R. A. Brierley Investments Ltd would pay a 10 per cent dividend on the first full year of operation. In those days government stock was paying only 5 to 6 per cent, while savings banks rewarded depositors with a mere 3 per cent.

It all sounded rather impressive, and although R. A. Brierley Investments Ltd had no profits, losses, assets, liabilities or dividends, some people were persuaded that it was a grand concern. Brierley recalls that not long after the prospectus was issued they were involved in negotiations to buy a privately owned company called The Jones Timber Co. Nothing came of it, but during the discussions Jones told Brierley frankly that, 'You people are running a large public company whereas I'm only running a small family business.'

R. A. Brierley Investments' first acquisition was *New Zealand Stocks and Shares*, which was bought for £4,000 and continued to be published until 1963. He also bought *Turf Newsletter*, with McCurdy as its correspondent, but Brierley found it difficult to produce and later sold the newsletter back to McCurdy. Brierley Investments' first bid for a company was for the Dunedin company Otago Farmers Co-operative Association of New Zealand Ltd. Otago Farmers was on the unofficial list of the New Zealand stock exchanges, meaning that it had not complied with official listing requirements. Detecting 'odd-bod' companies on the unofficial list became a Brierley speciality. They were usually companies that had been overlooked, with poor earnings but often with attractive assets.

Brierley made a bid for Otago Farmers in July 1961, hoping this would attract shareholders to BIL. He felt he needed to do something provocative and there was just the faintest of hopes that he might actually get control. His approach, however, was not warmly received. Only half a dozen shareholders accepted the scrip exchange, and some wrote highly abusive notes on the share transfer forms they had been sent and returned them in the reply-paid envelopes. They doubtless thought they were anonymous, but Brierley had written their names in pencil on the back of the share transfers so he knew exactly who had responded. He still chuckles thinking how mortified these highly respectable Otago gentlemen would have been if they knew he had identified them.

Better still, following Brierley's offer, the directors of Otago Farmers changed their policy on shareholders' discounts, which had the effect of raising the market value of the shares.

But what Brierley remembers most about these early takeover attempts is the laboriousness of the task. He still seems impressed that he personally folded the sales pitch, acceptance form and share transfer into the handwritten envelopes and then licked each one himself. He solemnly calls it 'grinding out every £100'.

The second takeover tilt was at Auckland-based Southern Cross Building and Banking Society Ltd, in November 1961. Southern Cross's earnings were poor, but its balance sheet was rich in liquidity and undervalued properties. It also had a savings bank, although there was a limit on the funds that could be taken.

Brierley made three offers in all, each one rejected by the dismayed board, who said they were undervalued and unrealistic. He first offered 15 shillings cash a share or 20 shillings a share over three years. The offer was conditional on acceptance of 51 per cent of the share capital by December 1961.

The directors felt deeply aggrieved. In the first place, Brierley had ignored the convention which decreed that a prospective purchaser should first approach the directors and arrange for an approved deal. Nor did he proceed through the stock exchange or get a stockbroker to buy the shares. He went straight to shareholders.

The fact that he had found out who the shareholders were was another transgression. Southern Cross was not a company, but a building society governed by a special Act. As such, the society did not have to make their shareholders' list available to the public. But Brierley had unwittingly hired a disreputable agent who bought the list for £5 from a former employee. He didn't use the agent again, but he did use the list.

Then there was the matter of timing. Coming as it did just before Christmas was a 'damn nuisance' says the chairman, Howard Sexton.

He believes Brierley was trying to catch them unawares, and he was probably right.

Brierley's bare-faced cheek went further still. The layout of his offer was decidedly questionable. The offers were headed, 'memorandum to the members of Southern Cross', and at the bottom he put his name and address. Coincidentally, his office was in the Southern Cross building, and not surprisingly many shareholders thought his message came from Southern Cross itself.

The letters exchanged by both parties at this time are a study in cheek and desperation. In one letter Brierley noted, 'If their statement is meant to imply that the shares are worth more than 20 shillings each, this seems strange in view of the fact that the society itself has arranged a number of sales over the past few years around the 12-shilling mark, and the directors themselves have purchased shares at this level without previously having felt compelled to advise members they were worth more.'

In March 1962 the society announced a one-for-four bonus issue. They said it was an opportune time to demonstrate the strength of the society's structure by bringing its balance sheet more in line with its assets position. The share price was also going up, and the next year the society revalued its land and buildings at almost double the 1961 book value.

Brierley's role in their decision was recognised by many, and the *Evening Post* wrote that he was approaching the status of the radio personality 'The Man Called Shepherd'. Says Brierley: 'It was a vintage example of an organisation selling at vastly less than its value which all of a sudden discovers it can reward shareholders as never before in its history.'

The volley of terse letters between Brierley and Southern Cross directors continued well into June 1962, and people who had accepted Brierley's offer began to feel uneasy. Some even issued legal proceedings to recover their share certificates from him. One law clerk attempting to retrieve a certificate was Hugh Rennie, who later became chairman of the Broadcasting Corporation. He remembers visiting Brierley in his office and talking to him. Brierley eventually gave in and handed over the desired certificate. In great triumph Rennie went back to the office brandishing the documents.

However, in the meantime the society decided it could issue new certificates to investors who had had second thoughts since Brierley's offer had been unsuccessful. Ever since, Rennie has wondered whether Brierley knew this on the day he ceremoniously handed the certificate to him.

There is no doubt that Brierley's 'real adventure' corporate-raiding technique was a shock to the business world. The fact that he was able to make his offer without being required to publish company accounts showing any profits, losses, assets and liabilities and without any recourse to stockbrokers or the stock exchange suggested to many that changes were needed to the Companies Act. The society had already sent their protest to the Minister of Justice, the Law and Accountants' Societies and the police. In fact, legislation was later passed which required a predatory company to inform its victim and the stock exchange of the terms of an offer.

However, Brierley's attack in April 1962 on two unit trusts which had been launched by Wellington's leading stockbroker, Daysh Renouf, made a far greater impact on the financial scene.

Unit trusts, new to this country, were set up along overseas lines as the small person's avenue to stock exchange investment. But since they were established during the peak of the share boom in the very early 1960s, the only way they could have moved was down. The two trusts Brierley was interested in, the First New Zealand Unit Trust and New Zealand Income Trust, were selling below issue price when he made his share-swap offer.

Those who accepted felt they had little to lose, but the directors were furious. The directors were Establishment with a gold-plated capital 'E' and included people such as (Sir) Bernard O'Connell, a director of New Zealand Breweries Ltd, and (Sir) Clifford Plimmer, who sat on the boards of AMP Society, Cable Price Downer Ltd and Wright Stephenson & Co. Ltd. The chairman, (Sir) Frank Renouf, was not Establishment but he was a keen contender.

The timing of the bid particularly irked them. Brierley sent out his circular the Thursday before Easter, knowing that traditionally stockbrokers, lawyers and many public accountants' offices were closed for ten days over this period. He hoped anyone who could have poured cold water on this offer would be out of town.

The directors knew, too, that Brierley would be able to redeem any units he acquired for cash. Under their trust deeds, unit trusts are obliged to buy back their own units at market valuation. All Brierley had to do was issue more of his own shares for the units and then sell the units back to the trusts concerned. So a holder of 200 New Zealand Income Trust five-shilling units could swap their holding for 180 five-shilling Brierley shares. He could then sell them for £45 in hard cash.

Brierley's sly tactics had changed little since his attack on Southern Cross. Once again his circular to unitholders was damned as misleading, since it featured the name of the trust at the top and less prominence was given to the Brierley name below.

It was legitimate, but Renouf thought his approach cunning and cowardly. Brierley had already written an article about Renouf in his journal detailing how he had made £650,000 in six moves, and Renouf was beginning to dislike him immensely.

Newspapers were equally critical and advised readers not to sell, but observers were less moved by Renouf's plight than they might otherwise have been. Renouf was a New Zealander but London-educated, and most of the time he behaved as if he was still in Britain. His bowler hat, rolled silk umbrella and aristocratic manner did little to endear him to the locals. At 6 foot 5 inches, when Frank Renouf looked down on someone, it was a long distance indeed. He was blackballed from one club and equally unwelcome at others, but it did not stop him setting up the unit trusts nor promoting the first merchant bank in the country, the New Zealand United Corporation. Jack Radford, a partner in his firm Daysh Renouf, says the financial establishment had not really supported the unit trust movement nor Renouf. Their attitude to his being attacked by Brierley was more one of 'Serve you right, mate' than sympathy.

Renouf could not abide Brierley for years after this incident, and it was not until the mid-1970s that relations between the two men warmed. Renouf made a personal effort then to understand Brierley's company and eventually became an ardent convert to his business philosophy.

The incident had a dramatic effect on Brierley director Colin Beyer. A photograph of Beyer, a recent law graduate, appeared in *New Zealand Truth* under a headline which both Brierley and Beyer can recite word for word today — 'Brierley Boys' Brigade Looks for the Loopholes'. The photograph showed Beyer looking very young in his capping outfit and the article pointed out the little-known fact that Brierley, like his co-directors, was still in his twenties.

That picture, and a statement in Brierley's prospectus, cost Beyer his job. He was working for a firm of solicitors, Robieson & Olphert, who, the prospectus said, were Brierley's solicitors. The firm had no idea it was supposed to be acting for Brierley and did not like finding this out just when Brierley was gaining notoriety.

Beyer then went into business on his own and retired from Brierley's board in 1963. By that time Alistair Hutchison, the company secretary, had been replaced by a new accountant, John Lawrey.

Brierley had found it difficult to get an accountant to act as his company secretary. Many professionals felt that anyone working for Brierley deserved odium money, a premium often paid to reporters on scurrilous newspapers for the loss of reputation they would suffer as a result. Lawrey, however, needed the work. He had just begun practising on his own account and his only client was the Wellington Boxing Association. After numerous rejections from other accountants, Brierley noticed Lawrey had just hung out his shingle and deduced that he would be needing work.

Brierley makes the first encounter with Lawrey sound like something out of an old black-and-white movie script. He, all of twenty-three years old and with a doubtful reputation, walked into John Lawrey's office and outlined the position thus: 'Mr John Lawrey, we are looking for a company secretary. We have a number of people in mind but you've been strongly recommended. I'd like you to consider accepting the position of accountant and company secretary for R. A. Brierley Investments Ltd.'

Although there was little other work competing for John Lawrey's time, he solemnly considered his work commitments and finally allowed that he could fit Brierley into his schedule.

Upon hearing this, Brierley rewarded him with a directorship and to celebrate the auspicious occasion Lawrey produced a bottle of whisky. Although Brierley doesn't drink whisky, he realised it was only right he should toast the liaison, and so the two raised their glasses and wished themselves the brightest of futures.

After Brierley had left the office Lawrey popped in to see a friend in the same building. Dennis McGrath was a Wellington solicitor, deputy mayor and chairman of the Wellington branch of the National Party. Lawrey told him of the visit and asked, 'What do you think?'

'Well,' said McGrath thoughtfully, 'I've been a subscriber to *New Zealand Stocks and Shares* since it was set up and I've got shares in his company. The guy's brilliant. I read his stuff avidly every month. But he'll either become a multimillionaire or go broke. Unfortunately, I favour the latter.'

Lawrey says McGrath was probably weighing up the power of the Establishment when he made that assessment.

Brierley himself was feeling typically sanguine about his future. He says after *New Zealand Stocks and Shares*, the 'Real Adventure' advertisements, the share exchange offers, the unit trust offer and a 'few fiddles in terms of issuing shares to myself for *New Zealand Stocks and Shares* rights', R. A. Brierley Investments Ltd had 144,000 five-shilling shares and about 200 shareholders.

'For the cost and effort it was barely a success. On the other hand it wasn't everyone who was walking around with about £36,000, after costs say £30,000, to invest,' he says.

And the first successful takeover was just around the corner. After three bitterly resisted and failed bids, this one was so very, very easy. Brierley's bid, in early 1963, for a company on the unofficial list called Billiards Ltd in Wellington was hailed by all. The company directors happily recommended shareholders accept the offer and the elderly chairman of the board welcomed Brierley with relief. He was at a loss at what to do with the decaying company. Brierley quickly received acceptances for 51 per cent of the shares.

Billiards Ltd, as its name suggests, owned a billiards table factory, but ten-pin bowling had temporarily jostled snooker to the sidelines. The company was showing poor returns, but the acre of company land nestled between a Catholic church and a parish school in Newtown had access from three streets and was worth nearly twice its book value.

Despite this, the bank was not impressed by Brierley's move and refused to lend the £30,000 he had been counting on to pay for the shares. Typically, Brierley was phlegmatic about the setback and he went back to his office to think. 'I wasn't worried. I knew I would get the money, somehow,' he says.

Fortunately, his old friend Andrew Hamilton was acting for the trustees of the Catholic Church and he approached Brierley. The Church trustees had heard a rumour that Brierley planned to build a bowling centre on the land and were worried that it might distract parishioners. Besides, they thought they might need the land later themselves. Although he didn't have the money to actually pay for his purchase, Brierley was reluctant to sell but the Church finally made him an offer he couldn't refuse. They paid him an extra shilling a share plus £500. The two trustees of the Church then owned all of the capital of Billiards Ltd, the Church took the land and Brierley had a profit of £1,000.

Oddly, this very first takeover, smooth and amicable though it was, has remained contentious to this day. The current managing director of Billiards Ltd, Jim Couper, denies it ever took place and usually demands a public retraction when the story is repeated. Couper, who has been associated with the company since 1934, claims that Brierley only had options on the shares but did not own shares in the company.

Couper's sensitivity probably has something to do with the fact that Brierley's name affected his company's reputation for some time afterwards. For at least half a dozen years following Brierley's alleged involvement, Couper said his ability to pick up contracts was limited and he was forever explaining that, no, R. A. Brierley Investments did not have a holding in his company.

Brierley's certainty is unshakable and he repeats a phrase he uses often: 'You will find my version is absolutely correct.' He believes that Couper owns a different company than the one he took over.

Nevertheless, despite this small win, the first year of operations for R. A. Brierley Investments was disappointing. The balance sheet for June 1962 was released ten months late and appeared in June 1963. It showed a loss of £2,950, and Brierley also fell short of honouring his promise of a 10 per cent dividend. However, he paid 6 per cent with a 3 per cent tax-free element instead, a rate better than most organisations were offering at the time.

Brierley's faith in his vision, however, was implacable. He promised better things for the succeeding year, the results of which were to be released in three months' time. As predicted, the 1963 results were much healthier and he was able to distribute a dividend of 10 per cent.

Although for years Brierley was ill at ease at company meetings, stammering and faltering, his comments never betrayed doubt. Even at his first meeting, when announcing his first loss, he had no hesitation in saying that his portfolio was irreplaceable and worth a great deal more than market value. He also affirmed a philosophy he would often have to defend in his own group, which was that the company would not trade long-term prospects for short-term gain.

The press understandably took a dim view of the first year's result and said it made poor reading compared with the glowing prospectus issued eighteen months earlier. What happened to the dividend, the reshuffle of directors, and the short-term capital appreciation that had been promised, they asked. Instead of the £43,570 sought in the prospectus, Brierley's actual paid-up capital was only £33,647, and not enough details were given explaining what had happened. For example, they wanted to know exactly how many shares were issued in exchange for the unit trusts. But these were not issues that concerned shareholders. Instead, when one person expressed confidence in the company and offered congratulations, others cried 'hear, hear' in approval.

Brierley is not an obviously charismatic figure, but his conviction and commitment are compelling. As one shareholder put it at the time, 'Whenever I ring Mr Brierley, whether it is Saturday or Sunday, night or day, he is always in the office working. I know he is doing his best for us.'

The only good news Brierley had to offer at the meeting was the company's acquisition of the Finance Corporation of New Zealand Ltd. He knew it was a real find and he now rates this acquisition as the first turning-point for R. A. Brierley Investments Ltd. Not only did it raise large sums of money for the company, but the Finance Corporation catapulted them into what Brierley describes as a 'necessary ordeal'.

FOUR

Kicking the Establishment

THE FINANCE CORPORATION of New Zealand — the name conjured up images of dependability, nationalism and stature. It was a 'lovely name', says Ron Brierley and he wanted it. He was first alerted to the company in the newspaper and he noticed they shared the same auditor. From that he concluded that there couldn't be too much wrong with the company and, besides, the name had to have a financial value all its own.

The origins of the grandly titled company were actually quite mundane. The Finance Corporation of New Zealand was founded in 1952 to finance the hire purchase of radios. When its parent, Radio Corporation of New Zealand Ltd, was taken over by AWA Ltd, the Finance Corporation became something of an orphan. In the eleven years since its formation it had earned a total profit of £19,232.

Brierley beat off another bidder for the company and at once went to work to test his faith in the potency of the name. In September 1963 he issued a prospectus to raise £100,000 in 10 per cent registered, unsecured, interest-bearing deposit notes, each of £1 par value and repayable in five years.

The Finance Corporation's value was quickly grasped by the press. One financial editor wrote that many innocent investors might be forgiven for supposing that the company was a government or semi-state organisation operating a national money market, instead of being an obscure little hire purchase concern.

They worried, too, about Brierley's ability to pay the promised 10 per cent interest, which was substantially higher than the current rate. But Brierley was convinced he could get a better return than that, so in his view, even at 10 per cent it was still cheap money. He said the difference between paying 10 per cent and, say, 6 per cent on £100,000 was only £4,000 a year or, in other words, the cost of a secretary plus expenses. Brierley saw no difficulty in raising the extra £4,000.

He also knew the public would ignore the criticisms. 'I knew the 10 per cent would be criticised, but I also knew there was a certain proportion of the population whose greed would cause them to take a high rate of interest regardless of what critics were saying.'

Brierley was right. The issue was considerably oversubscribed and by October 1964, £265,965 had been raised. But the criticism ran on unabated. His most ardent critic was the financial editor of the *Auckland Star*, Adrian Sturman. Sturman believed the 'go broke or go to jail' maxim about Brierley, and he was the first person to highlight a misstatement in the prospectus. He noticed that Brierley had promised his funds would be further augmented following an offer to shareholders of the First and Second New Zealand Acceptance Companies. But Brierley's offer was unsuccessful and another company had taken over these companies.

Other financial pundits correctly pointed out that although money raised from the Finance Corporation issue sounded as if it was going to fund a range of investments, it was, in fact, all going to R. A. Brierley Investments Ltd. Brierley had created a façade under which he was raising debt and hoping to avoid any taint of association with himself.

Brierley eventually made three offers for unsecured deposit notes, all of which were hugely successful. His first issue raised £1 million and ran for over a year, although usually such issues ended after a few weeks.

Brierley was by this time becoming the sort of person people talked about in hushed undertones. It was one thing to kick the Establishment in a newsletter, but he had gone on to make a number of audacious takeover bids, publish cheeky advertisements and, to top it all, he had now issued a dubious prospectus raising money from the public.

In his private life, too, he would flaunt rules he thought had no merit, and his particular fetish was parking fines. Brierley had first owned a car long before his friends had. His grandmother bought him his first car, a Morris Minor, and by 1963 he was driving a leased Jaguar. But although he likes driving good-quality cars, he treats his vehicles with a devastating nonchalance and has been known to calmly walk away from a car that has broken down in the middle of the road.

However, his biggest bugbear was the parking meter. They were introduced to Wellington in 1954, and from the outset Brierley refused to recognise their existence. He would park anywhere — on corners, no-stopping zones, yellow lines, or in front of expired meters. A deluge of tickets did nothing to modify his behaviour. In fact, he rather enjoyed outfoxing the traffic officers.

On one occasion they visited him in his office and requested he accompany them to the traffic department. He agreed and walked downstairs with them. When they reached the officers' car, Brierley told them he had forgotten something and asked if he could just pop upstairs and get it. But he never came back and an hour later the officers were still waiting. Upstairs, Brierley kept on working, no doubt smiling cleverly to himself.

By December 1963 he had been fined 25 guineas for speeding, and he and his company were facing another twenty-four traffic charges. *New Zealand Truth* reported that Brierley was an 'elusive customer'. His name had been called four times in court recently and always the same reply was given: 'The defendant is not present, Your Worship.' He clearly frustrated a great number of people, for when they heard again that he was overseas, 'the groan that went round the court was just audible and the small army of traffic officers and meter maids looked almost dejected'.

Brierley still refuses to pay traffic fines, regarding them as an infringement of his inalienable right to do what he likes. In the end, Trevor or Colin Beyer paid them all.

So the rumours and doubts about 'that Brierley' gained momentum. Before long the city's grapevine was lurching like a live wire. His name had even reached the ears of the politicians, who seized upon his 10 per cent offer as a dangerously high figure. Halfway through 1964 a warning was sounded in Parliament by the Minister of Justice, Ralph Hanan. In October the MP for Waitakere, Dr Martin Finlay, had more questions, and when a full-page advertisement for the Finance Corporation appeared in the paper the next day it was viewed as deliberately provocative and requiring further enquiry. The advertisement shouted in bold letters, 'Heavily Over-Subscribed. 10% Deposit Notes Issue Definitely Closing Next Thursday'. By November that year the advertisement had been referred to the Solicitor-General for an opinion.

In the midst of this boiling sea of distrust and innuendo, Ron Brierley waited calmly. He knew what was coming and he welcomed its advent. He knew the politicians and financial pundits needed a public inquiry for their own purposes, but he also believed a public scrutiny and clean bill of health would assist his progress.

The inquiry everyone was waiting for turned out to be a court case charging both himself and John Lawrey. John Lawrey is something of a Mr Magoo figure in the Brierley empire, comical, popular and often bewildered. Brierley remembers telling Lawrey that he had a court case pending and Lawrey said he was sorry to hear that. As

Brierley left the room, he added, 'Oh, by the way, you're named too.' It is the sort of parting shot Brierley loves, and he particularly enjoyed doing it to Lawrey. 'John wasn't too upset. People have been telling him things like that all his life,' Brierley says.

Nevertheless Brierley has never forgotten Lawrey's loyalty to him throughout this difficult period. In February 1965 the pair faced four charges in the Wellington Magistrate's Court. Three of the four charges were dismissed on the first morning. The only charge to be considered, that of making a misleading statement about the two companies he had bid for earlier, was heard in March. The Crown's case was that Brierley's claim that this takeover would augment funds was misleading, since funds were only increased by £210.

The sole Crown witness was public accountant John Tipping. He spent some time in Brierley's office inspecting the books and it would amuse Lawrey and Brierley that when they were out Tipping would take messages and look after the premises for them. That year they also presented the best set of accounts ever, he said; Tipping had done them and they were spot-on.

It took the senior magistrate only two days of hearing evidence before he came to a decision. He dismissed the charges, saying that no one could tell him what 'augmented further' meant.

But the case did not rest there. In a move that surprised many observers, the Crown appealed. In April 1965 Brierley faced the court again. His lawyer, Herbert Taylor, told Mr Justice Hutchison in the Supreme Court that 'there were political overtones and undertones lurking in the background'.

The case stimulated speculation that the Establishment was goading the Government to do something about the Brierley phenomenon. Brierley himself was convinced that the Solicitor-General, Dick Wild, had a vendetta against him, and he said this thought became obsessive during those years.

Certainly Brierley's barristers were worried about their chances, given their client's reputation, but when they saw him in court all their misgivings were dispelled. Brierley charmed the judge with a disarming frankness and his counsel, Dick Collins, declared he was 'honest almost to the point of naiveté, the antithesis of the scheming bandit'. These judgments are a tribute to Brierley's manner, rather than an accurate assessment of his character.

On 31 May 1965, Mr Justice Hutchison dismissed the charges for the last time. The Crown was defeated. It decided that the only course of action left was to change the law itself and it began to draft the Companies Amendment Bill. The Bill stated that if a prospectus contains an untrue statement, it cannot continue to be distributed without an amendment.

To prove the prosecution was designed to hurt Brierley rather than an impartial application of the law, Colin Beyer was pursuing another company whose prospectus contained an untrue statement. The solicitors acting for that company were from Dr Martin Finlay's old firm. Beyer decided to try to embarrass Finlay and contacted Solicitor-General Dick Wild to discuss the matter. But after one acrimonious conversation with Wild he was told nothing would be done about it.

Later the Minister of Justice, Ralph Hanan, tried to make an appointment to see Brierley, who was out of the country, and by the time he was available Hanan had died. Brierley never found out why Hanan called and he now wonders if it was a peace offering.

In the meantime the Finance Corporation was once again asking for subscriptions to an issue of unsecured notes and they offered free life insurance in return. Brierley had paid Colonial Mutual Life Insurance Company a premium for a bulk life insurance policy. The scheme is understood to be one of the first of its kind to be offered in New Zealand or Australia.

Such generosity, however, was seen as suspicious. Dr Finlay fired a volley of questions in Parliament in July 1966 about this latest issue. When was legislation coming in to control this type of financing? Did the advertisement for the issue comply with the provisions of the Companies Act 1955, and did the life insurance proposals referred in it comply with the provisions of the Life Insurance Act 1908?

The Minister of Finance, Harry Lake, told him about the pending legislation. A few days later another group of MPs, including Norman Kirk, were asking more questions. Would this affect Government borrowings and for what purpose was the money likely to be used?

Dr Finlay was unconvinced by the replies to his questions: '. . . is the Minister satisfied that the results of their takeover business enables them steadily and continually to pay a dividend of 10 per cent?' he asked.

Lake said that Brierley's company had made profits and had been 'able to pay its dividends without any great difficulty . . . it would be quite unfair and unkind to say that there is anything wrong with this group'.

Paying the dividends, however, was not as easy as Lake made it seem. Former BIL director and accountant Don McDonald said they often sweated trying to get the money. 'To be quite frank, I did not agree to become an official director until 1971 because I was so concerned about the fragile capital structure of BIL in the 1960s. The unsecured notes raised through the Finance Corporation were a scary feature of that period. Many of the notes had rolled over and were virtually demand notes. Had there been a run on them, it could well have been curtains for BIL because they represented such a high proportion of the capital — indeed often more than the capital and reserves combined. Much of that money had been invested in shares that would have been slow to realise at short notice.'

Brierley would think McDonald's qualms barely worth a mention. After all, he did pay the dividend, didn't he? He was right in the end, wasn't he?

He was, however, deeply irritated by Adrian Sturman's sustained attack on him. Brierley is generally sympathetic to journalists, and he says that in a way he prefers criticism, usually from 'left-wing types. It's more interesting.' But he felt Sturman's writing went too far, and in 1964 he filed an action for £10,000 damages against New Zealand Newspapers Ltd, the publishers of the *Auckland Star*, and Adrian Sturman. He said Sturman's articles made it sound as if he and his company were making untrue statements, deliberately misleading the public and that he was unscrupulous and not to be trusted.

As is often the case, the suit acted as a 'gagging writ' and ensured Sturman and the *Star* did not reopen the debate for at least three years until the claim was dropped.

Brierley continued to find it hard to get his advertisements printed, and he cites the *Auckland Star* and the *New Zealand Herald* as the most obstructive, thanks to Sturman's influence. Sturman was also a key trustee in the New Zealand Newspapers superannuation fund, which had a large portfolio of shares. It is said that he opposed the fund's buying Brierley shares for years. However, to be fair, Sturman was really only reflecting the views of many financiers, stockbrokers and top company executives.

On the whole, though, Brierley was satisfied with developments. Everything had gone pretty much as planned. The public airing had been successful, and though many people's minds were still fogged with suspicion, Brierley now had the support of the Minister of Finance and the backing of the country's legal system. Even having an Act of Parliament introduced in response to his activities could be seen as a victory of a sort. Not many could make that claim.

Besides, he had more to worry about than politicians and his public image. For the next five years the real adventure for R. A. Brierley Investments Ltd would be simply one of survival.

FIVE

An Australian Education

ON SATURDAY NIGHTS around midnight, after they had left the pub, and the party after that was wearing thin, Ron Brierley's friends would often drive past his office. Spying a gleam upstairs, they would bang on the door, wait until he unlocked it and then play cards with him until one or two in the morning. It became as much a ritual as their regular lunch meetings at coffee bars.

His friends knew there was little point dragging Brierley to the parties, for he simply fell asleep at ten o'clock for a few hours, woke up and then went back to work. He seemed to be constantly working, though his pace was always measured. Ron Brierley reminded them of an industrious ant doing his homework by the light of the harvest moon.

Brierley is a great believer in the maxim that knowledge is power. His work, then and now, involves detailed research, generally gleaned from libraries. In the early days, the stock exchange library in London and in Sydney acted as his unofficial office. Brierley loves libraries, having discovered early on that they are great value for money, and he has always been one of the heaviest users of his own libraries, especially in Australia.

The research habit was first ingrained in him during the *New Zealand Stocks and Shares* days and it has stood him in good stead throughout his career. He is a meticulous researcher and used to say that by the time he had finished studying a company he knew more about it than its own directors. Occasionally he would even turn up assets the company had forgotten it owned.

Brierley's self-discipline and thorough research have formed the backbone of his enterprise over the years. They both maximise his control of a situation and minimise risk, so that by the time he is ready to move on a company he is completely confident he has made the correct judgment.

His choice of targets has also distinguished him from many others in the takeover and acquisition business. He prefers what he calls 'bricks and mortar' companies, with easily identifiable assets producing a relatively simple product, and he has deliberately steered away from companies involved in technology, because he does not understand them.

Brierley's favourite hunting ground is among the down-at-heel and dispossessed. Bob Jones calls him the bag-lady of business, but he should more properly be called the redeemer of trash. He goes down among the rejected of the earth and returns with the sort of treasures no one would have given a second glance. But under his control their true value is revealed for all the world to see.

His quest started with unlisted public companies, which he redeemed from virtual oblivion. Before Brierley came along, there was no market for unlisted companies and they were in poor shape. Brierley's intervention lifted their value and shareholders were rewarded with the best price they had had in years.

Brierley was also particularly fond of unlisted companies that had been so neglected their own shareholders had consigned them to the rubbish bin. Some of the companies had shown such disappointing returns that many investors in the 1950s and '60s had simply forgotten they owned shares. These people were affectionately known by Brierley as GNAs or Gone, No Address, and they could comprise up to 30 per cent of a share register.

Brierley quickly realised that a generous proportion of GNAs in any company meant he could gain control without having to pay for 50 per cent of the shares. Sometimes a stray certificate tucked behind the kitchen clock or uncovered in a deceased estate might surface and payment would be made, but generally the GNAs were gone for good.

Forestry companies in New Zealand were particularly susceptible to harbouring a host of GNAs. Many of these forestry companies harked back to the 1930s, when share-hawkers went door to door selling bonds in the companies and promising that investments would grow with the forests. But time and inflation made liars of them. When the forests were felled some thirty years later, the hapless investors had lost interest, lost value and often forgotten they even had shares. By this time, however, they actually had shares in something of value. In many cases these companies had disposed of their assets in a one-off sale and overnight they had become valuable cash boxes.

Ron Brierley had become something of a specialist in forestry companies through his research for *New Zealand Stocks and Shares* and he was eager now for closer involvement. His chance came with a company called Mamaku Forests Ltd. As its name implies, this company had forests near Mamaku, north of Rotorua, but it was in bad shape thanks to indifferent maintenance and a lack of pruning. As yet there was no local market for sub-standard trees, so the company had decided to become a property-owning and investment operation.

By the time Brierley was on its trail, Mamaku Forests had some properties in Auckland, a few clumps of forest and debts owed to it from large organisations who had bought their forests. To gather more information about the company, Brierley visited the Mamaku Forests office in Auckland, where he met the company secretary, Don McDonald. At first McDonald was suspicious, demanding to know who Brierley was and what he was doing, but his suspicion turned to support once Brierley told him. He, too, had been unhappy with the way business was run in New Zealand and he was particularly disturbed by the actions of the Mamaku directors, who were buying the shares at absurdly low prices. McDonald gave Brierley all the information he wanted and promised to forward any available shares to him.

The shares were then selling at about 7 shillings, although Brierley calculated they were worth 25 shillings. When Brierley came to bid for the company, Don McDonald advised him that 17 shillings was likely to be acceptable to the board.

Although another bidder emerged who was prepared to pay more for the shares than Brierley was, the board honourably stuck to its agreement and the counter-bidder withdrew meekly from the field. Brierley was amazed by their compliance, knowing that in the same position he would never have given in so easily. 'I would have gone ahead and made an unwelcome counter-bid anyway.'

More than 70 per cent of the shareholders accepted the offer and Mamaku Forests was soon his. Brierley marks it as yet another turning-point on his road to success. He had achieved a respectable takeover of a sizeable public company with shareholders' funds of more than £20,000, a substantial leverage thanks to the GNAs, and steadily improving profits.

He had also met a man with whom he would have a lifelong association. McDonald was already a senior partner in an accounting practice in Auckland and a well-known identity in sporting and racing circles when he met Brierley. He later served on the Auckland Regional Authority. In the early days his support lent a veneer of respectability and authority to Brierley's operations. Although McDonald's partners in his firm often queried his involvement with 'that man Brierley', he remained a staunch ally.

Brierley liked McDonald immediately. At first glance McDonald appears imposing, with his dark eyes and thick eyebrows, but his winning smile quickly dispels any doubts about his warmth and humanity. He is also a man of strong views and acute perception. It has been said of McDonald that he is often right even if it is for the wrong reasons. As soon as McDonald met Brierley he could see he had outstanding ability and he resolved to do his utmost to assist him in pursuing what McDonald regarded as laudable goals.

His contribution to the company has been immense. For years the paternal McDonald has worried and watched over Brierley, often with little thanks and with no thought of personal reward.

Though he continued with his accountancy practice, he was largely responsible for the running of the Auckland operation, which had Mamaku as the holding company for interests as diverse as shipping, quarrying, wholesale merchandising, property and warehouses. Mamaku Forests then constituted the bulk of the group's commercial and industrial trading in New Zealand.

Like Brierley, McDonald had also become something of an expert in forestry companies. One of his responsibilities was to prepare the accounts for a company called Putaruru Pine Products Ltd. Putaruru was a Sydney-based holding company with an operating company, Putaruru Pine and Pulp (NZ) Ltd, in New Zealand. Two-thirds of the 2,400 shareholders were Australian and the rest were New Zealanders who had been with the company one, if not two, generations. Some, of course, conveniently for Brierley, had forgotten they were with the company at all.

McDonald thought Putaruru was a a better buy than Mamaku Forests, so at his prompting, and intrigued by the Australian link, Brierley began buying Putaruru shares at the same time as he was accumulating a holding in Mamaku Forests.

Brierley was probably the first New Zealander to exploit Australia's commercial potential as our closest neighbour. Australia had an exotic appeal for Brierley, but his corporate ambitions were first whetted by the 1961 takeover of Huddart Parker Ltd by Boral Ltd in that country. Until that time Huddart Parker had been regarded as virtually impregnable and the takeover of such a substantial company astonished observers. Brierley says he couldn't see something like that happening without wanting to be part of it.

Brierley was so certain his ambition would succeed he had already adjusted his company's reporting date to comply with Australian requirements. The Australian reporting date was 30 June, so R. A. Brierley Investments followed suit, though in New Zealand most companies reported at the end of March.

Putaruru was not his only Australian investment, and by the time he made his first visit to Sydney in November 1963 to research Putaruru further, he had bought shares in a few Australian companies. His research into Putaruru showed the company was giving a return to shareholders by progressive reductions in capital, but since it was a public unlisted company there was no real market for the shares.

What surprised Brierley the most, however, was the positive response of Putaruru's directors to his advances. Their enthusiasm aroused his suspicions and when he saw that one of the directors was buying Putaruru shares, worth at least 15 shillings, for only 3 shillings each, Brierley assumed he was using his position for personal gain. He confronted the offending director, company secretary Doug Wylie, who shrugged and said he was only buying them to help out shareholders. Brierley was welcome to them.

R. A. Brierley Investments bid for the company early in 1964, hoping fervently the bid would not become public. The principal asset of the New Zealand subsidiary was a debt by Putaruru Timberyards Ltd, and Brierley reasoned that if they heard about the bid they would be keen to make a takeover themselves, thus buying their debt back at a discount. So Brierley quietly bought shares and made a public announcement only when he had 50.1 per cent of the shares and thus control of the company.

As soon as the news of the takeover broke, horrified Putaruru Timberyards directors rang Sydney, wanting to make an offer, but it was too late.

As well as this debt, Putaruru had other less apparent but equally important attributes. Since the holding company was Australian, when Timberyards made its annual debt payments to the New Zealand subsidiary, it was able to remit funds to Australia. The severe exchange controls operating at the time meant that there was a big premium for overseas funds through the fringe market. Brierley was quick to use this to his advantage, though he knew he was, in all likelihood, breaching the regulations. He admits there was really no reason to remit funds to Australia because they were only remitting to themselves.

Putaruru Pine Products also provided him with two new directors — accountants Doug Wylie and Doug Sutherland (who later became the Lord Mayor of Sydney). Both directors went on the IEL board later and stayed there for twenty-two years.

On that first trip to Australia, Brierley also met the man who was to play a major role in the development of his Australian enterprise. He placed an advertisement in the *Australian Financial Review* explaining his aims and asking people knowing of 'special situations' to come forward. Although he received only two serious responses, one of them was from an investment analyst, Robert Blackburn, who had once employed Brierley in New Zealand as an insurance salesman.

In 1959 Blackburn and Christchurch stockbroker Jack Hindin had put together the first lump-sum superannuation scheme in the country and called it Superannuation Investments Ltd. The company enjoyed considerable success and when it advertised for salespeople Brierley responded. Alas, although Brierley did the week-long training course, he proved to be ineffectual. After a few months of inactivity, Blackburn came to visit his Wellington representative and both agreed that Brierley's appointment should cease.

Now Blackburn was in Sydney working as an investment analyst for Niel and Partridge. Brierley and Blackburn quickly struck up a friendship and, as a result, Brierley began to place his business with Niel and Partridge. Their premises became his unofficial office in Sydney, and within a short time Blackburn was his unofficial agent in Australia. Contrary to the gloomy predictions of the experts that Australia had already been picked over, Brierley did not find the opportunities in Australia to be exhausted. But it was a hard market and he had much to learn.

The Australian enterprise started promisingly enough with an investment in a West Australian company called Kalgoorlie Goldfields Petroleum NL. It was a speculative company which had evaporated 80 per cent of its funds, but it still held a parcel of Ampol Petroleum shares worth about £35,000. After two offers were rejected, Brierley gained full control in January 1965.

His most significant early acquisition was the purchase of Citizens and Graziers Life Assurance Company Ltd in December 1964. Brierley read about the company in a letter published in the *Australian Financial Review*. Someone wanted to know how much their shares in this unlisted public company were worth. The reply gave the history of Citizens and Graziers and mentioned it had not paid a dividend for thirty years and that it had just sold its life assurance business.

Brierley saw at once it was a valuable company with cash in the bank, so he instructed Blackburn to buy shares for him. The board repelled his advances, but finally Brierley decided to make a first-come first-served bid for Citizens, which Blackburn believes was the first bid of this type in Australia. The directors had intended to convert the company into an investment operation, but that required approval by 75 per cent of the shareholders and Brierley held 25 per cent of the shares. Finally the board conceded defeat and agreed to recommend his takeover offer to shareholders.

Citizens and Graziers then became the vehicle for other Australian purchases and investments, the most important of which was the takeover of Industrial Equity Ltd in 1966.

But the successes were dwarfed by the disasters of his early trans-Tasman investments, which brought R. A. Brierley Investments Ltd to the brink of insolvency. Brierley now calls these experiences lessons and says Australia was a fantastic education. For one thing it gave him an insight into Australia's con-men.

The education began with an investment in a company called Video Box Ltd which marketed a new coin-operated machine playing popular songs to video images. Brierley thought it would be a good idea to buy a batch of the machines, put them in pubs and collect the money.

But the scheme never worked. Some of the machines were not delivered, there were problems with the coin mechanism and when recompense was sought from the vendor it was found that he had had a nervous breakdown and had booked himself into a private hospital. Brierley was unable to contact him and later the man left the country.

Brierley estimates he lost about £50,000 cash, which in the 1960s was a small fortune. The loss delivered a 'mortal blow' to Brierley and preyed heavily on his mind. After much thought he decided he had been tempted by greed into a diversionary activity and he resolved to stick to the path he had mapped out in his prospectus.

However, there were still more expensive lessons in store for the young entrepreneur. In 1965 he bid for a New South Wales company that had once generated electricity for the local authority but had since sold all its plant. Hawkesbury Development Company Ltd took its name from the Hawkesbury River on the outskirts of Sydney, where it had once had its electricity grid. By 1963 it had only cash and liquid assets, and two years later its $1.50 shares had a net asset backing of $2.40.

But at the same time Brierley put in a bid for the company, a rival bid at the same price appeared by a Sydney investment company, Palgrave Corporation. Palgrave was headed by Alexander Barton, a Hungarian Jew who later fled to South America as a result of his dealings in the mining boom of the 1970s. He later returned to Australia to face the music, but in 1965 he was busy cornering Ron Brierley.

Barton was the first to acquire 51 per cent and Brierley found himself locked in with 49 per cent. If ever he needed a lesson on the importance of gaining an extra 2 per cent, Barton was about to give him one. Once Barton announced his success to the stock exchange, the money in the Hawkesbury till was siphoned over to him, some £245,000. Brierley lost £100,000 and all efforts to retrieve the money failed.

Blackburn now wonders whether Barton ever had 51 per cent, though he did have the complete support of the directors. According to Blackburn, this might have been because they thought anyone would be better than a corporate raider. In the 1960s corporate raiders were as reviled in Australia as they were in New Zealand. A few people, such as Boris Ganke of Brinds Ltd and Sir John Dunlop of Colonial Sugar Refinery Ltd, were dabbling in the field, but Brierley was the most public and determined of them all.

The final lemon in the Australian basket was an investment in Castlemain Woollen Co. Ltd, a woollen and worsted company located near Melbourne. Brierley thought he had bought the company at about one-third net asset backing, but he soon learned the asset backing was largely illusory.

The setbacks left Brierley feeling bitter and depressed. His entry into Australia had been riddled with unknown pitfalls. He realised that he had not handled it well, and in the long run the move had been of questionable wisdom because it had simply dispersed his business risks over a greater area. 'There was a feeling that we shouldn't be buggering round in Australia and should have been getting New Zealand right first.'

R. A. Brierley Investments in New Zealand had also had its ups and downs during this period. It had bought and sold small investments such as South Wellington Pictures and Investment Co. Ltd. It also bought Redwood Forests, the only survivor of the land-development companies floated in the 1930s. Redwood Forests had never paid a dividend and its principal attractions were shares in New Zealand Forest Products Ltd, commercial property and its missing shareholders. Brierley's bid for John Chambers and Son Ltd was repelled by the family who owned the company, but he later emerged as the largest shareholder in the engineering company Andrews and Beaven Ltd, after it merged with John Chambers.

In 1966 he also made a futile bid for what he said was the most antiquated family company he had ever seen. A. J. Entrican Sims & Co. Ltd was a living museum piece, says Brierley, and as such it encapsulated and exaggerated some of the worst aspects of this period. Entrican Sims was an Auckland grocery and general merchant company with 75 per cent of the shares held by two families, Entrican and Sims.

It had been a household name at the turn of the century with its Beehive stores scattered throughout New Zealand. For years the company had imported goods for retailers, but later they began importing their own goods and the wholesale food business dwindled. By 1965 Entrican Sims was showing trading losses but the ageing family members of the board were not acting to save the company.

The only outside director, Alan Gray, recalls an incident that perfectly illustrates how the board worked. At a meeting where he put forward proposals for change for board approval, Gray asked Entrican senior what he thought of his ideas. The old man thought, looked at him and said, 'You know, Mr Gray, I've always thought Mr Wakka was offside.' He was referring to the outcome of a rugby match some ten years earlier and hadn't heard a word Gray had said.

Brierley tried to wind up the company, but the board easily defeated him and sold it instead to L. D. Nathan, who were friends of the family.

Despite Brierley's later reputation as a ruthless asset-stripper, his colleagues say he did not often advocate winding up companies as a solution. For example, in 1965, when he took over Barton Ginger & Co. Ltd in Wellington, he hoped he could revive the ailing customs and cartage business. Barton Ginger was founded by a prominent Wellington city councillor and was a highly reputable company. News that it was in receivership was greeted with dismay in the city and was even mentioned in newspapers overseas. Brierley, who knew the second generation Barton-Gingers, was invited to assist.

It was an opportunity too good to miss. Here was an old-established firm with a solid reputation and all he had to do to gain control was to inject funds into the business. Brierley accepted gladly but quickly learned the industry was highly capital intensive with a low return on assets. The company had no shareholders' funds and the money put into it was borrowed through the Finance Corporation's issue, which cost interest.

The company was finally sold in 1969 at three times the value of the shares, but John Lawrey says while R. A. Brierley Investments owned Barton Ginger a lot of work was put into expanding it. 'Selling a company was always a second choice for Brierley. His ideal was to better utilise the assets for an improved financial return.

'He genuinely believed that younger staff were restricted by old boards and his first ambition was to let people have their heads, back them up, and only if they failed would he look for the stripping situation. I don't think he was a good manager of people or assets, but through his willingness to sponsor the ambitions of people and the respect and fear people had of his efficiency a company would improve.'

The disasters of that period shook R. A. Brierley Investments Ltd to its foundations and caused the company to come close to insolvency. Preparation of the 1966 accounts caused such difficulties that an arbitrator was appointed to decide whether losses incurred in Australia, particularly Hawkesbury, should be included in that balance sheet or carried forward. The arbitrator was their old foe John Tipping and he found in their favour. The losses were carried forward, for which Don McDonald was greatly relieved. He firmly believes that if the company had posted a loss that year, this would have led to a run on the unsecured notes and finally insolvency.

Investors should have been alerted that trouble was afoot when the accounts for 30 June 1966 did not appear at the usual time. In fact, they were not signed until March 1967, and the annual meeting was held a month later, ten months after the balance date.

Although the accounts showed a profit of £22,870 to the holding company, R. A. Brierley Investments, the auditors, Feil Morrison and Connolly, were clearly unhappy. In the notes to the accounts they point out that a £13,208 loss had, in fact, been incurred. Brierley had been able to record a profit only because he did not present consolidated accounts and instead presented the accounts for each subsidiary and associate company separately. The auditors argued that this was just a smokescreen obscuring the loss.

Feil Morrison and Connolly resigned after this and the talk then was that the accounts were offered all around town until at last a small firm, David Markham & Co., took them up. Ironically, that firm was later bought by Peat Marwick Mitchell & Co., the same company that bought FMC. So the very people who refused to handle Brierley's accounts ended up in a firm that proudly held the account.

The company, however, could not hide 1967's loss of $56,742, though that figure appeared in the middle of the page and required some investigation to find. Had the reader glanced at the bottom of the consolidated revenue statement, they would have seen a healthy profit of $56,271. Takeovers had been temporarily suspended that year, so there was no major activity to report and the loss was attributed to Barton Ginger and heavy expenditure overseas, including the Hawkesbury loss.

By now financial commentators and professional accountants had begun to scrutinise Brierley's accounts carefully. His accounting methods are discussed in a later chapter, but there is one matter worth noting here. Until the mid-1980s moving money out of New Zealand was hampered by tough exchange controls imposed in 1938. Before 1966 one way of moving money out of the country was to buy overseas shares on the local market and resell them on the Australian market for Australian dollars. There was even a premium of up to 25 per cent attached to those shares when they were sold in New Zealand, which Brierley wrote into his accounts.

Although 1966 Budget measures placed restrictions on these shares, there was still a premium attached to them. In fact, as the restrictions took effect and the pool of shares diminished, the premium climbed.

The proceeds of the sale of these shares could also be used for an import licence, and most people imported new cars with the money, since new cars were scarce. But Brierley used these overseas securities to develop his Australian base. A former chief cashier of the Reserve Bank, Ray Hardie, said Brierley was almost unique in New Zealand in the 1960s and '70s because he used his foreign funds for entrepreneurial purposes, while others used them to buy consumer goods.

Brierley also took the unusual step of including the premium in his accounts instead of the standard stock exchange rate for the overseas shares. The 1967 *Accountant's Journal* took issue with this practice and asked if Brierley knew something they didn't.

Brierley believed he did. He was confident no one would pay a premium unless the funds were worth it, and that the New Zealand dollar had to come into line with its true value. His confidence was rewarded when New Zealand devalued its dollar in 1967, lifting the value of his Australian investments considerably.

'I remember turning on the radio in the car in the morning and the first item was that the United Kingdom had devalued. I felt a quiet sense of elation because I knew that immediately they did, we would,' Brierley says.

Australia did not devalue immediately and the value of his Australian investments appreciated by $116,380 overnight. Devaluation was a turning-point for the company.

So far Brierley had been learning some hard lessons in business. R. A. Brierley Investments had made a loss in the first year of operation and then again in 1966 and 1967. So for three of the first six years of operation he was losing money, largely because of his Australian ventures. But despite the obstacles he was not about to give up on Australia. He already had the company that would become his major vehicle of investment there.

Industrial Equity Ltd was a non-operating company formed in 1964 to issue options on shares it had bought. Although $360,000 had been raised in issued capital by IEL at the time of float, the stock option business had turned sour. Its shares had declined to a point where a decision was made to wind up the company.

Brierley was looking for a back-door listing to the Australian stock market and he acquired IEL through Citizens and Graziers in 1966. Showing his financial inventiveness, he issued IEL shares to other partly owned Brierley subsidiaries such as Kalgoorlie Goldfields and Putaruru Pine Products Ltd, instead of paying cash on the liquidation. With these holders and the IEL employees who stayed with the company, sufficient spread was obtained for the IEL listing to be retained. So now he had his Australian base with himself as chairman and Bob Blackburn as managing director.

Yet even though his operating base in Australia was listed on the stock exchange and he had investments in several other Australian listed companies, R. A. Brierley Investments was still unlisted in his home country. But that was not for want of trying.

SIX

Big Fleas Have Little Fleas

FROM THE MID-1960S UNTIL 1970, Ron Brierley virtually abandoned the New Zealand market in favour of Australia. There the sharemarket was buoyant and the opportunities for a listed investment company were greater than in New Zealand, where R. A. Brierley Investments was still languishing on the unofficial list.

The New Zealand financial establishment and the Government did not understand the Brierley phenomenon, and until they did, they wanted to keep him at arm's length. His ambitions were unusual, he respected no convention, his progress to date had been unremarkable and his accounts were some of the most complicated ever presented. *New Zealand Truth* commented in 1968 that the accounts could provide a searching two-hour test for advanced accountancy students.

Several applications to list the company were turned down because Brierley clearly failed the all-important test of respectability. His friend Bob Jones was encountering the same prejudice, and he believes that no one under forty years of age was considered respectable in those days. The pair used to compare notes on the difficulties they had employing good accountants and professionals.

But Brierley attracted more than the usual scepticism reserved for the *arriviste*, and in part that was due to his defiance of all restrictions. Brierley loves detecting a loophole in the law, and in 1968 he found one just big enough to wedge himself through and embarrassing enough to upset the Government.

Legislation to prevent a public company such as the Finance Corporation of New Zealand raising money via unsecured deposit notes was being introduced into Parliament in 1968, but Brierley realised that there was no restriction on individuals raising money. He decided to capitalise on the fact that, in the public's mind, he had become indistinguishable from R. A. Brierley Investments Ltd. He became the public borrower himself, with the issue managed by the Finance

Corporation. The two identities had merged just as he intended.

The Government at once recognised this was simply an attempt to circumvent the regulations, and questions were raised in Parliament in October 1968 about Brierley's personal flotation of an issue of $1 million in negative unsecured 10 per cent deposit notes. In response, the Minister of Finance, Robert Muldoon, explained that Treasury was already investigating the matter and so far Mr Brierley had not been forthcoming with information.

The story made headlines, with Muldoon later describing Brierley as 'at best unhelpful and at worst evasive'. Brierley retaliated with the accusation that Muldoon and George Gair, the North Shore MP who had been asking the questions in Parliament, had engineered a political stunt. He denied refusing to produce information for the Treasury and said that he had tried to contact Muldoon the previous week after being told by a Treasury official that there would be a 'blow-up' when Muldoon returned from overseas. But instead of contacting him on his return, Muldoon 'had taken advantage of my absence [Brierley was now in Sydney] to launch an unwarranted attack'.

While in Sydney, Brierley rang Muldoon, but this resulted only in a terse exchange between the two men. It was Don McDonald who finally arranged a meeting. He had watched the unfolding events with trepidation because he was convinced that, if Muldoon stopped the issue, this would stimulate a panic run on the deposit notes and Brierley Investments would be in grave danger of going under.

By the time McDonald and Brierley walked up the steps of Parliament to speak to Muldoon, McDonald was taut with worry. When the pair entered Muldoon's office, McDonald's antennae, as alert to signs of hostility as a spider to the vibrations of its web, detected immediately that the atmosphere was hostile. In front of him sat the stony-faced bulk of Muldoon flanked by a phalanx of Treasury officials.

At first the warring parties traded accusations of who had said what, with little agreement. Brierley claimed to have gained an agreement from Treasury weeks before, but this was hotly denied. Then Brierley suddenly remembered that when a Treasury official gave him this approval he indicated that he was simply following orders, repeating a modified quotation from Jonathan Swift — '. . . a flea hath smaller fleas that on him prey, and these have smaller fleas to bite 'em, and so proceed *ad infinitum*.' The official blushed at once, recognising his turn of phrase, and from then on it was obvious to all present whose recollection was the most accurate.

Muldoon quickly appraised the situation and said that they should use his office and press secretary and dictate an appropriate press release. He then countersigned it and Brierley released the statement to the press in October 1968. In it both parties regretted their heated accusations and Brierley assured Muldoon that no income would go to himself.

Brierley said he also asked Muldoon why he was under parliamentary scrutiny so often and claims that, following this discussion, the next time a question was raised in Parliament Muldoon defended him, saying it was not fair to put an emphasis on particular individuals.

Subsequent legislation prevented Brierley from repeating the personal flotation. The Protection of Depositors Bill, introduced that year to curtail his other deposit note issues, was amended to include individuals and came into effect in 1969. By then Brierley was able to get money from more conventional sources, but the deposit notes had harnessed vast sums of money for the practising corporate raider.

The same year Brierley was summoned to the Prime Minister's office he found his company under threat from a first-come, first-served bid for 15 per cent of Brierley Investments. Bids of 15 per cent were popular then, since a holding of this size prevented a full takeover. Brierley was shocked to find that the bid came from two of his own friends — Peter Heginbotham, an optometrist, and Bill Hallam-Eames, a quantity surveyor. They believed that, at 44 cents each, Brierley shares were grossly undervalued, especially as they were also relatively scarce on the market. The bid was intended simply to boost the price and their personal holding in the company.

They did not get 15 per cent but believe that their overall aims were achieved. By the end of 1968 the price moved to $5 per share, and Heginbotham credits their intervention for some of the movement.

Neither Brierley nor McDonald, however, would thank them for their trouble. They regarded the bid as disloyal, and doubly so since Brierley was in London at the time. Hallam-Eames recalls that Brierley did not speak to him for almost a year.

Whether the 15 per cent bid helped the company or not, antipathy towards Ron Brierley was slowly starting to weaken. The next time he was turned down for listing by the New Zealand stock exchange the decision was greeted with cries of indignation and outrage. This was the sixth time Brierley had been rejected for listing, though by then, November 1969, he had almost 500 shareholders and four listed subsidiaries in Australia. The chairman of the Wellington exchange said there was a 'violent reaction against the decision' from brokers who wished to meet their clients' desires to buy and sell Brierley shares. Moreover, the unofficial list penalised shareholders because its brokerage was double the rate of the official list. Even more worrying was the fact that the unofficial list was about to end in April that year.

Brierley had, in fact, only narrowly missed being listed. The results of the vote from all the exchanges had revealed a tie, so the president of the New Zealand stock exchange, Fred Knox, of Invercargill, used his casting vote.

Knox explains why he blocked Brierley: 'There was a general unhappiness about what he was doing, and I was conscious of the fact that listing a company confers status. People wanted to understand his accounts. I don't know that people fully understand them to this day. With so much doubt about him, I voted to preserve the status quo, which was the normal thing to do in this situation.'

Despite this rejection, Brierley forged ahead with his vision of an international investment company. His early setbacks in Australia were disappointing, but instead of abandoning the world beyond New Zealand, he decided to try further afield. In 1967 he began to dabble in the British market. He had first visited London in 1965 and had been impressed by the size and complexity of the market. He says it was a hope, rather than a vision, that he would invest there some time.

In 1967 he bought in Britain a controlling share in a poorly regarded South African gas company called Grahamstown Gas and Coke Company Ltd, which led to his only two visits to that country. Later Brierley would show no interest in visiting his assets, but in those days he wanted to see what his money had bought. It had, in fact, bought a dud, and in 1970 he sold his shares at a small margin over original cost. His only other British investment, Ampat (Sumatra) Rubber Estates Ltd in Indonesia, had also not fared well, and in the end Brierley had to meet losses incurred by the former owners.

His total investment in the United Kingdom at that time was £14,000 and had required enormously complex financing, much of it done on deferred terms. At the end of it all Brierley had to admit both investments were a mistake. Once again he found himself on the fringe, without the necessary resources or the contacts in the City of London to assist him. 'I had failed to conquer the world,' he says sardonically.

His early lessons in the Australian market, however, were beginning to pay off. By 1971 he had interests there in companies as diverse as Australia's first lawn cemetery (Pine Grove Memorial Park

Ltd), an electrical contractor and manufacturer (Colmax Electric Pty Ltd), a printing and publishing concern (Shipping Newspapers Ltd), and a company Brierley was particularly fond of — Woodley Wines Ltd of Adelaide. The company was founded in 1853 and was well known for its Three Roses sherry and Queen Adelaide claret. Annual meetings were often toasted with the company's products. Brierley has a special affection for red wine and he used to say he would never sell Woodley Wines.

While Brierley does not become overtly attached to the people around him, he does have a sentimental fondness for some of the companies in his portfolio, particularly those with established and respected products. New Redhead Estate & Coal Co. Ltd was a perfect example. It dated back to 1895 and its main activity was operating the smallest railway in Australia, a sixteen-kilometre line between Belmont and Newcastle in New South Wales. The company's major customer was BHP, and New Redhead had the distinction of actually carrying coals to Newcastle.

It was the classic undervalued company, with complacent directors, low dividends, and a portfolio worth over $1 million at market values. New Redhead received income from the railway line and owned valuable tracts of land. Shares quoted on the market in 1968 at $2.50 had a net worth of about $3.40. The company was, in fact, larger than IEL at the time.

But New Redhead did not welcome intruders. The company's articles of association included a sliding scale of voting which deterred would-be bidders by limiting the second hundred shares to fifty votes and, above that, twenty-five votes per hundred. So a company could have 51 per cent of the shares and not have voting control. This method of repelling raiders was not uncommon in New Zealand and Australia then, and Brierley enjoyed working out ways to defeat such restrictions.

Brierley had been buying New Redhead shares since 1964, and by the time he was ready to bid publicly for the company in 1968, he knew exactly what to do. IEL distributed its New Redhead shares in parcels of 200 among 600 friends and associates of the IEL directors, who had signed over the power of attorney and proxies to IEL.

The New Redhead directors were unconvinced. They employed an expert to see if the handwriting on the original transfers was the same as the signatures on the proxies. The expert declared that the twenty he examined were forgeries, which Blackburn vehemently denied. He admits now that he had, in fact, forged a few signatures, having lost some proxies, but claims that these forgeries were not in the pile studied by the expert.

About 160 IEL proxies were disallowed at New Redhead's annual meeting, thus dashing all hopes of getting a seat on the board. The matter was later carried to the Equity Court in Sydney, but IEL outmanoeuvred a rival bidder and continued buying New Redhead shares until it won control in early 1969.

The acquisition of New Redhead gave IEL access to the working capital it needed when it was being shunned by the banking system. Blackburn found that simply getting a bank loan to buy New Redhead was hard enough. He remembers spying one bank manager's notes which said IEL was a poor risk.

Brierley's attachment to New Redhead lasted until he sold IEL in 1989, and a photograph of the famous train often appeared in IEL annual reports.

Not long after Brierley won New Redhead, IEL acquired the remaining capital of Minerva Centre Ltd. Minerva was a property investor, although it had once owned a number of theatres and cinemas. These had been sold or destroyed and, as a result, its 51 per cent subsidiary, Tivoli Freeholds, had $1.4 million available for investment. Brierley saw these funds as a great resource for his corporate ambitions, but a minority Tivoli shareholder, the Herald and Weekly Times, objected in a court action in 1971.

Brierley's *modus operandi* was closely examined by Judge Menhennit, who began the case knowing little about corporate raiding but ended with an almost romantic appreciation of his activities. 'You mean,' he asked Brierley, 'that there's just *one big pool* of assets available for use in corporate raiding?'

Brierley quietly replied, 'Yes,' and the description was repeated in the judgment.

Brierley is superb in court. His understated, unsophisticated manner and his accurate recall of facts suggest a painfully honest individual who is being unjustly accused. But Brierley is not so naive. When arguing his case, whether in court or in the boardroom, he employs tactical skills his colleagues claim are so crafty and compellingly logical that he can win over opponents to the most absurd propositions.

On this occasion Blackburn noticed how Brierley would concede points to the opposing lawyer, who would then be temporarily disarmed by him. But on proceeding further, the lawyer would discover that he had walked into a trap.

The judge was charmed. He declared Brierley a 'very impressive witness' and went on to give him what amounted to a testimony of good character. He said he was a person of 'marked ability with a wide comprehension of what is involved in running a company and its business and of the value of a business and its assets'. He was 'completely candid and honest with an outstandingly good memory for facts, figures and details and a marked capacity to make quick calculations'. Furthermore, the judge decided that where there was a conflict of evidence between Brierley and the respondent he would accept Brierley's evidence.

The lawyers, too, were impressed. Brierley presented his own case and the QCs referred to him as 'my learned friend' rather than the usual 'defendant'. His friend (and a lawyer himself) Colin Beyer rates Brierley as one of the best corporate lawyers in Australasia.

SEVEN

Brierley's Accounting

ACCOUNTING IS PROBABLY the only profession in the world where the word 'creative' carries pejorative connotations. It usually means that the accounts present a view of a company that owes more to the imagination than reality. So to call the self-taught Ron Brierley the father of creative accounting in New Zealand is not the same as handing him a prize awarded by the New Zealand Society of Accountants. Nevertheless, it is a fair description of his impact on accounting procedures in this country.

From the beginning he took the view that if something was not legally enforceable, it had passed the Brierley road-worthiness test. So whenever his auditors told him his suggestions were in breach of the Society of Accountants' standards, he would invariably reply, 'Where does it say that in the Companies Act?' The answer was, of course, nowhere, but that did not comfort accountants and auditors throughout the country.

Brierley's own auditors in New Zealand and Australia frequently had raging arguments with him. He was a dogmatic opponent who held fast to his position, which he had usually worked out fastidiously on the back of an envelope.

Geoff Harris, who was first involved in auditing the IEL accounts at Bowie Wilson Miles & Co. in Sydney, recalls the disputes with wry affection, and regards some as particularly memorable. For instance, there was one incident in 1971 when new regulations had just been brought in to ensure the difference between what was paid in tax and the figure appearing in the accounts was explained. But Brierley already knew what he was going to do.

'Ron said we are talking about a 15 per cent figure against nothing, so we'll have to do nothing. That's the way he thinks. I made an appointment to see him and said, "We have to have this out." It was 9.30 in the morning and I started to talk about it, then it went into a discussion and then into an argument which took forty minutes.

'I was telling Brierley he was wrong and he was telling me I was wrong. He said, "Obviously you are wrong, just go away and think about it,'' but I just sat there and we didn't say anything for an hour. I started to work on some papers and he started to do some work and then I said, ''Look, Ron, this is ridiculous.'' And he said, ''You agree I'm right then?'' I said, ''No, but I tell you what, we'll get a legal opinion on it.'' He said, ''Fine, you draw up a brief and get a QC.'''

Harris grimaces. 'I drew up the brief and went off to the QC, who told me Ron was right.' Over the many years he has worked with Brierley, Harris reckons he has only caught him out on a handful of occasions.

'I have a great respect for his accounting ability. He used to sit down and go through a hundred sets of accounts and he would do them all himself in a couple of days. We would spend weeks doing the same thing.'

Up until the 1980s Brierley was closely involved in writing the annual report and he was always extremely particular about its layout. He insisted that the balance sheet should be in the middle of the report and he agonised over his grammar and choice of words in his own report.

In the first ten years of BIL's existence he used standard consolidated accounting — albeit with his own significant variations, particularly in 1966 — and then in 1972 BIL became the first company in New Zealand to adopt equity accounting, again with Brierley's own variations.

These Brierley-inspired variations drew him constantly to the attention of financial commentators, and he achieved headlines as jaunty as 'Whoopee on the Fruit Machine' and as sinister as 'It's What They Don't Tell That Counts'. As far as conventional accountants were concerned, Brierley's idiosyncratic approach had the effect of exaggeration and obfuscation. In other words, his accounts looked good but accountants were not always certain what they really meant.

In the beginning it usually meant that Brierley was simply trying to keep the company afloat. Until listing in 1970, BIL was in an extremely precarious state, and it will be recalled that for three of the first six years of operation he lost money.

His accounts during the 1960s were sprinkled with quirky variations to standard accounting practices. For example, in 1968 the profit of $64,883 had been boosted by $30,000 because of interest expense that had been capitalised. Brierley had paid this interest on an investment and, though it was really an expense, he added this to the book value of the investment in the balance sheet. Although this never happened again, it illustrates Brierley's fondness for a little exaggeration.

On other occasions he might calculate the earnings rate to capital to his own advantage. Instead of measuring the profit against the paid capital plus the reserves, he ignored the reserves and came up with a ratio much higher than the true return on shareholders' funds. So in 1965 a profit of £17,000 on a paid capital of £100,000 resulted in a publicised earnings rate of 17.1 per cent. But he should have added reserves of £62,000 to the £100,000, making a true return of only 9.5 per cent. Or he might state, as he did in 1969, that group profit before tax and minority interests exceeded $1 million for the first time. However, the profit attributable to BIL was only $145,511.

Brierley clearly knew the value of good public relations. But these departures alone, however misleading and unorthodox, would not have raised the hackles of the Society of Accountants. They were concerned with what they saw as more serious misdemeanours, such as his surplus on acquisition, miscellaneous contingencies provision and equity accounting Brierley-style.

Surplus on acquisition is the difference between what Brierley paid for a company and what he thinks it is worth. So if he paid $100 for a company he believed to be worth at least $150, he would take the $50 difference to the surplus on acquisition. This then went into the profit of the company for the year. But Brierley's surplus on acquisition violated a deeply entrenched article of accountants' faith: that a profit has to be made from a completed transaction before it can be considered profit. What Brierley was doing with the surplus on acquisition was to take to profit an unrealised gain that might be made from the sale of the company in due course.

The resistance to this approach dates back to the 1929 Wall Street crash when it was discovered that many companies had inflated their profits with unrealised profits on overvalued assets. They had borrowed heavily against these overblown profits and when the crunch came there was nothing there to pay the debts. After 1929, accountants worldwide agreed that the only profits that mattered were those that had already been made from completed transactions, because the future was unknown.

Surplus on acquisition first appears in Brierley's accounts in 1972, though as far back as 1964 there was an item in the revenue statement called profit on sale and revaluation of investments. In some years, like 1972 and 1977, if Brierley had not included surplus on acquisition in his profit statement the company would have made a loss. In other years it would have seriously diminished the size of the profit. But a large profit sent soothing waves of confidence out into the market and the share price responded sympathetically.

The miscellaneous contingencies provision is related to surplus on acquisition, and it first appears in 1967's accounts at $24,939. Ten years later it was a $10 million provision and ten years after that, in 1987, it had grown to a mammoth $123 million. An adequate explanation of this provision was never given, probably in part because its character changed over the years. It was really a form of secret reserve to allow for losses and expenses that may be incurred in the future; a sophisticated rainy-day fund.

So in the previous example, where Brierley has bought a company for $100 which he values at $150, leaving a $50 unrealised profit, he might choose to put $40 of that sum into the surplus on acquisition and the remaining $10 into the miscellaneous contingencies provision, where it locks away value for the future.

If he has overestimated the value of the company, he is protected to some extent because he has put $10 into the provision. If it is sold later for $200, he can take $60 to profit, remembering that he had already taken $40 when he first bought it.

Both the surplus and miscellaneous contingencies were profit-smoothing devices. If Brierley Investments had shown its profit conventionally, the company would have shown a choppier growth pattern. But it was more reassuring for investors to witness a smooth upward curve than the sort of line normally seen on an electrocardiograph. These devices were later used to deliberately underplay some enormous one-off profits.

BIL's shares are best valued on their break-up value. The company's use of the investment fluctuation reserve has greatly assisted investors when estimating this figure. This reserve resulted from an annual revaluation of BIL investments to market value. In this case, the change in value was not placed in the profit statement of the balance sheet but in the investment fluctuation reserve. Although unique to BIL, this procedure was generally welcomed by the accounting profession.

In his defence Brierley argued, convincingly enough for his auditors to agree, that his business was quite unlike most other businesses. He was not manufacturing and selling a product, he was trading shares and selling assets, and that required special treatment. His profits depended on his ability to buy assets at bargain prices and it was more realistic, therefore, for BIL to counts the gains as profit at the time the valuation increases became apparent. He was probably right while inflation and a buoyant market jollied things along on an ever-increasing climb, but accountants worried what would happen if the good fortune ran out.

So BIL's profit and earnings are almost irrelevant statistics when assessing value in the company. Every year the company gives the market what it expects, although it does play some part in influencing analysts' expectations, either upwards or downwards.

It is also worth remembering that BIL's profit in any year is usually related to acquisitions made in earlier years. An acquisition this year at a favourable price locks away profit for the future, while the sale of an asset purchased years before provides the profit for that year. So a good profit is not necessarily an indicator of the company's present performance (except for the impact of the surplus on acquisition accounting procedure as previously described). The profit may simply relate to a smart buy several years ago.

The same year surplus on acquisition was introduced, Brierley also changed his accounting procedure. He gave up standard consolidated accounting and took up a unique form of equity accounting, which enabled him to take his portion of the assets, liabilities and profit of a company he had substantial shares in to his accounts. Equity accounting is possible when you own between 20 and 50 per cent of a company. A holding of this level makes the company an associate, while a bigger holding means it is called a subsidiary.

Using standard consolidated accounting, he could include only the assets, liabilities and profits of a company once he had control of 50 per cent. Equity accounting acknowledged that with a 30 per cent holding it was possible to control a company. It suited Brierley, who had a number of smaller holdings in companies, and it was a more accurate portrayal of his dealings.

When he adopted this procedure in 1972, it was still relatively new worldwide and it was not until 1974 that the New Zealand Society of Accountants put out a statement of standard accounting practice known as SSAP No. 2 on equity accounting. Brierley was even invited to speak to Wellington members of the society on the topic in 1972. But once again Brierley had put his own idiosyncratic stamp on equity accounting, and when the SSAP No. 2 statement was published it was clear he was again in breach of conventional accounting procedure.

It was really only a simple case of window-dressing, which did not affect the profit. In the balance sheet Brierley took 100 per cent of the assets and liabilities of the associate company, and in a balancing item called 'outside interests' he would record the majority portion of the company he did not own. By picking up all the assets of a company the size of Dominion Breweries, BIL looked enormous.

In the profit and loss account he put in 100 per cent of the profit from associates and took out the portion he didn't own elsewhere, so the final figure was correct. Equity accounting did not overstate the profit; the size of the company just ballooned in the balance sheet.

The conventional way to show the item in the balance sheet is as a 'one-line item'. This means only including your percentage of the net amount of assets and liabilities in a single figure on one line. Fortunately for BIL, the Companies Act was silent on equity accounting and there was little the Society of Accountants could do.

Brierley's reports were often tagged by his auditors, and the year he introduced equity accounting and surplus on acquisition was no exception. The auditor's report highlighted nine qualifications, two on the new departures. Conventional accountants only accepted innovative measures where there was substantial authoritative support. There was none for anything Brierley was doing, so his auditors knew they were putting themselves on the line. They pointed out these innovations in the first year but accepted them in the years after that.

The first time the Society of Accountants hauled BIL over the coals was in 1975, when two BIL directors faced the society's professional standards committee. The directors were adamant they were showing the true and fair picture of the group. A year later Brierley's auditors were brought before the same committee, but there was little they could do to force BIL to toe their line. Ironically, Brierley's auditor, Bob Pope, became president of the society in 1980.

In the 1979 auditor's report Markham and Partners noted that BIL's accounts were at variance with two accounting standards, notably those of the surplus on acquisition and equity accounting. However, they stated that they agreed with the methods adopted.

Brierley deeply resented any qualifications and, in an outburst in his chairman's report that year, he deplored the trend towards 'accounting authoritarianism'. The next year he aired his views on equity accounting in his chairman's report and stated unequivocally that it is only a matter of time before 'our method is not merely endorsed but insisted upon by responsible professional bodies'.

It never happened, and nor has his surplus on acquisition and miscellaneous contingencies ever been well accepted. In the end Brierley's innovations have not contributed to any change in accounting policy in New Zealand.

Brierley's accounting made less of an impact in Australia, where the Institute of Chartered Accountants left him alone. Generally, IEL operated on the same principles as BIL, though Australia's legal requirements meant IEL had to show more detail in the accounts than did BIL.

Since 1986 BIL has fallen into line with conventional accounting. Equity accounting is now done on a one-line basis, and surplus on acquisition is no longer put into the profit. But these concessions do not indicate a change of heart, rather a new appreciation of where his self-interest lies: BIL needs the support of the international banking and financial community, and accounting variations are not viewed sympathetically. The company is also now large enough not to need these devices. Profit-smoothing occurs of its own accord, since the volume of transactions is now so much greater than in the early days.

It is fair to say, though, that Brierley's creative accounting paved the way for an even greater artistry in the field. When the floodgates of finance opened in 1984 and a new group of entrepreneurial companies came to the fore, Brierley suddenly seemed timid and conservative in comparison. Like the younger child emboldened by her elder brother's cheek, this new breed dared to push beyond the limits. Some leaders in the Society of Accountants were appalled, but many of their number were happy enough with the new trend. They were lining up to sign the accounts.

EIGHT

Take-off

BRIERLEY LOOKS BACK on the 1970s as the golden era of BIL and IEL. He says conditions were perfect for the two companies, which by then had amassed enough credibility and cash to enable them to become more active. New Zealand and Australia were littered with middle-sized companies struggling to survive. Many were substantial companies, but often were no longer economically viable.

For example, once-prosperous retail companies like DIC found they were competing with large stores or small, exclusive boutiques. In Wellington, DIC was also housed in a building deemed an earthquake risk, so further expense was inevitable. Companies in this position either had to be small, large or extremely well managed to avoid collapse.

Although it would have sounded absurd at the time, every one of these middle-sized companies had a 'hidden number', which was the year of their ultimate bankruptcy, says Brierley. If nothing had happened in the market, they would have all gone broke.

Brierley sensed change was in the air and his role was to hasten the inevitable. He saw himself not just as an acquirer but as a catalyst in a process that would eventually transform the New Zealand and Australian economies. BIL could act as an economic enema, flushing out the waste in the system.

He remembers the 1970s with nostalgia. He says the company had all the advantages of size and substance and none of the disadvantages of leadership responsibility necessary in the 1980s and beyond. The day-to-day company operations were within his grasp, and the future was still uncertain enough to thrill him. He was constantly aware that one fatal mistake could bring the whole edifice tumbling down. We could go broke or we could conquer the world, he says with a grin.

The take-off year was 1970. R. A. Brierley Investments was finally listed on 2 March 1970 (the R. A. was dropped in 1971), and IEL was doing so well its shares were trading at $13. Shareholders were happy and the *Dominion* newspaper in Wellington noted that

BIL's annual meetings were among the most popular in the country.

BIL also received a glowing review from a broking firm, R. A. Jarden & Co., which had been regarded as a maverick in the broking world during the 1960s. Ron Jarden set up office in 1960, dealing in odd lots (incomplete marketable parcels) on a capital of £2,000. In three years his savings had dwindled to £86. Just when it looked as though the axe might fall, business picked up and the firm grew, eventually becoming one of the largest sharebroking concerns in the country.

In the late 1960s, Jardens invited a number of British and European brokers to examine investment prospects in New Zealand. The brokers were unimpressed by the Establishment companies but took a keen interest in BIL, which was still on the unofficial list.

Jardens followed this visit with an investment review predicting rapid growth for the company. It was also careful to point out the difference between BIL and a conglomerate. It said Brierley's use of cash in takeovers prevented watering down the capital and also avoided artificial growth through an inflated earnings rate. This was a danger with a share swap, which depended on the difference between the company's own share price and that of the company being acquired, and it had been the main problem of conglomerates overseas. In tougher economic times they could not get enough income from subsidiaries to maintain the earnings rate on rapidly increasing capital.

By then, Ron Jarden and Ron Brierley were friends as well as business associates, and it was Jarden who urged Brierley to form a mining company in 1970. He was confident the public was ready for this type of investment, and he was right: the creation of Australasian Mining and Oil Investments Ltd was a masterstroke. This public company was set up just in time to cash in on the new heightened interest in oil and gold. AMOIL was formed to invest in mining shares, fund exploration and engage in underwriting and investment banking in mining and oil. BIL held a 20 per cent share in the company, and Ron Jarden was one of the directors.

The move marked a bold return to the New Zealand market after a long dormant period and it highlighted the absurdity of the refusal to list BIL. AMOIL was floated the same month BIL was finally admitted to the stock exchange. The float raised $1 million, although $250,000 was subscribed by BIL, in a matter of months. Brierley could scarcely believe his good fortune and now says it was a signpost marking the end of one era and the beginning of the next.

In New Zealand, AMOIL's best-known investment was the Kanieri gold dredge on the West Coast. The gold dredge was essential to the welfare of the region, a fact BIL cunningly pointed out to the Government when it wanted assistance. In 1975 the Government loaned AMOIL $475,000 to keep the dredge afloat. Ironically, that Swiss franc loan turned sour in 1978 and AMOIL faced currency losses of almost $300,000 on the advance.

In 1976 BIL again went to the Government asking them to prop up the gold price, which was falling internationally. The Government obliged, much to the chagrin of jewellers and dentists.

The gold dredge had a number of indifferent years and it was finally sold in 1978 for a dollar under $1 million to avoid the necessity of getting Government approval under the Trade Practices Act.

But AMOIL's mining discoveries were not restricted to precious metals. In 1974 its coffers were boosted with a chance find at the bottom of a swamp. For years Brierley had had an investment in a public unlisted company called New Zealand Pulping Mills Ltd. It was a typically obscure Brierley choice — New Zealand Pulping Mills was another old Depression company, set up to grow flax and pulp it for paper. As with many of these companies, its claims far outweighed the reality. Flax still grew in its swamp but the company no longer made paper when Brierley discovered it. The company had been inert for some thirty years but was kept afloat because underneath the swamp lay two million tonnes of coal.

BIL finally gained control of the company in 1973 and soon afterwards New Zealand suffered its first oil shock. The New Zealand Co-operative Dairy Company was adjacent to the swamp and when the prices for fuel began to sky-rocket they panicked. They had been buying blocks of land for coal when needed, but with BIL as the ultimate owner they knew the price from then on would be high. The Dairy Co-operative desperately wanted to secure alternative sources of energy, so they decided to buy the swamp, offering to pay New Zealand Pulping Mills $800,000 for their black gold.

Brierley had forty-eight hours to mull over whether this sum could be bettered or whether he should take the money. He took the money, thereby securing the best deal in the history of BIL.

By 1971 the company's stature had grown considerably. BIL shares had rocketed from below par in 1968 to eight times par two years later (thanks to AMOIL) and it felt confident enough to bid for a company by using an unusual issue of its own shares. However, the directors of the Northern Steam Ship Co. were not impressed. They regarded the share issue from a speculative company as a major obstacle to the success of his bid.

Prior to Brierley, no one had used nominees to ambush a company. Brierley used them extensively, first gaining a toehold, often promising not to go beyond a set limit, and sitting there for years before finally making a bid. With Northern Steam Ship the agreed limit was 25 per cent, but at the time he agreed to this Brierley already owned 28 per cent of the company. The board was unhappy with his use of nominees, but Brierley refused to disclose who they were and signed an affidavit agreeing to the 25 per cent threshold instead. In effect, Northern Steam Ship had an agreement with Brierley that was impossible to monitor.

A competing bid from a rival bidder in 1975 released Brierley from his 25 per cent obligation and he started buying on the market again. Eventually he cornered the bidder and emerged having paid $1.1 million for a company worth $1.6 million.

But if any takeover illustrates the Brierley technique to full advantage, and the reaction of a resistant board in those days, it was the battle for Geo. H. Scales Ltd in 1971.

Geo. H. Scales was formed in the late nineteenth century to beat the shipping monopoly enjoyed by the British Conference lines. Since incorporation in 1912 the company had been instrumental in having freight rates reduced, and by 1971 it operated several charter ships and had two lucrative agencies. Although it was a public company, only sheepfarmers could own shares in Scales.

Brierley had been stalking the company since the early 1960s, buying shares by using farming acquaintances as nominees. By 1971 BIL claimed to be the single largest shareholder, and when he finally bid for the company, irate shareholders rang the farmer nominees demanding an explanation.

Brierley's bid was deliberate and well planned. He had gone over and over the details in his mind to an almost obsessive extent. He even calculated the time advantage to be gained by sending letters from particular post offices. Scales was something of a dynastic family company, with names like Riddiford and Beetham peppering the share register. It was also one of the most prosperous companies Brierley had ever encountered and he did not want anything to go wrong.

For its part, Scales suspected Brierley was up to something and queried some of the new names on the share register, particularly farmers who were not well off. But it was a sharebroker's oversight that gave the game away. A box number on a share register alerted Scales' registrar, and it did not take long to work out that the beneficial shareholder was BIL.

The impact of Brierley's bid on Scales was enormous. Brierley was later told that, after hearing the news, the chairman's wife suggested her husband sit down, then she poured him a port and asked if he was comfortable, because she had something shocking to tell him: Brierley was trying to take over his company.

By this time the company secretary, Lily Hyslop, had also heard the news and was trying frantically to contact her general manager. When she was unsuccessful, she said she became 'pretty hysterical'.

But the company moved fast. Brierley's letter to shareholders arrived on a Friday, and by midday the following day Scales had sent out a 'don't sell' notice.

'That took quite some doing, since we were a very little company and everything had to be done manually. Some of the shareholders got our letter before they got the Brierley offer, because of the way rural delivery worked. We knew more about the mail than they did,' says Hyslop.

Scales worried with some justification that Brierley would asset-strip the company, for it had a share portfolio worth $1.7 million and substantial cash reserves. Directors travelled around New Zealand persuading shareholders not to sell and explaining that, since shipping was a very uncertain trade, their large financial buffer was necessary.

The bid also prompted Scales to attempt to alter its articles of association in order to limit the number of votes a shareholder could exercise. It also wanted to ban votes for non-sheepfarmers and to ensure that nominees had to disclose the beneficial owner of shares.

Brierley wrote another letter to shareholders, claiming that his company would lift the restrictions on membership and use the assets more effectively. He then sought an interim injunction to stop Scales carrying out its proposed changes. The changes were passed at a shareholders' meeting, but the company had agreed not to implement them pending a further order of the court. In the meantime BIL sold its shares to a group of farmers at $10 a share, $3 more than the shares were selling for earlier that year.

Later the articles were changed, but it is interesting to note that Brierley's suggestions were also adopted. The share portfolio was sold and shareholders were paid $5 a share. The company was restructured into a holding company and reserves were severely cut.

The regional manager of Scales in Wellington, Michael Christie, remembers the incident and acknowledges that Brierley's criticisms were valid. But he said that had the bid been successful, Brierley would have had a rude shock. All BIL would have got was the share portfolio and a couple of desks. Scales directors and their lawyers were working on slipping the shipping interests into another company before Brierley could get control, and this measure was actually taken after BIL's departure.

By 1989 Scales was still in business, even if it was struggling. Two failed investments left the company sinking under a mammoth debt burden and it had to be rescued by the Dairy Board and a Scales shareholder.

Brierley's return to the New Zealand market was short-lived. By 1970 he was spending 75 per cent of his time in Australia, where the opportunities for investment were much greater. Almost half of the industrial companies listed on the stock exchange were selling at prices below their disclosed net worth. Many industries were suffering from the effects of over-competition, namely over-capacity, idle capacity costs and paper-thin margins.

Mergers were inevitable, and nowhere was rationalisation more badly needed than in the motor vehicle dealers' industry. Brierley saw that each one of these companies was going to be taken over, because vehicle manufacturers wanted entrepreneurs, not stuffy, bureaucratic, family-based dealers, to sell their cars. The industry had a number of appealing features to Brierley: easily saleable stock, clean premises and well-situated land, or, in the parlance of the raider, cash, liquid stock and real estate.

His roving eye first alighted on the Sydney-based General Motors Holden dealer Stack & Co. Ltd in 1967. Twenty years earlier, a Holden dealership was tantamount to having a licence to print money. Queues of people waited outside the dealer's door for cars to come off the production line. However, one by one, the four original Holden companies in Sydney had faced intense competition, and rising land values in the 1960s pushed their asset values higher than their share price. The Holden share of the Australian car market was also declining. All in all, it was a classic break-up proposition.

Stack successfully opposed Brierley's bid, but by 1972 he had control of two Brisbane-based Ford dealers — Cossey Investment and Finance Co. Ltd and Coachcraft Ltd. Ford was quick to see the attraction of Cossey to Brierley, and a senior executive visited him offering $500,000 if he dropped his bid and handed over the shares. Brierley estimates that $500,000 as equivalent to $50 million today. In fact $500,000 is worth about $2 million today, not the massive $50 million he cites, but this exaggerated claim shows the value of the takeover in his own mind. He was stunned. 'It was the first time anyone had come into my office and offered me so much money, and it was from Ford, not some tin-pot organisation.' But because he calculated there was an even larger margin still in Cossey, he turned the offer down. Even so, it was not an easy decision, he said.

That year IEL also bid for NSW General Motors Holden dealer Boyded Pty Ltd, a move that flushed out rival bidders for the company. But in the end it was action from another quarter that thwarted IEL's plans.

A month earlier the Government had announced it would police foreign takeovers of Australian companies. Under new legislation, foreign control by a single company was limited to 15 per cent of the voting power, and total overseas interests to 40 per cent voting power.

IEL was the first major company to be tested under this legislation. It was clearly foreign-controlled, since BIL held 95 per cent of Citizens and Graziers, which in turn owned 52 per cent of IEL. The Government declared IEL foreign and froze the Boyded bid. Brierley was appalled and suggested, facetiously perhaps, that the Government should study IEL's bid for Watson Victor Holdings. They did and that bid was also frozen.

Undaunted, Brierley announced IEL's plans at its 1972 annual meeting as if nothing, not even the Government, could stand in its way. But in early 1973, when IEL bid for NSW coal-miner and brick-maker Muswellbrook Industries Ltd, the Government again froze the bid for three months (a move that allowed rival bidders to take control of each of the companies virtually unchallenged).

By April, Blackburn was making statements that indicated he was worried about the freeze. IEL might not be able to survive indefinitely in its present form, and the rapid growth rate of the last six years had come to a halt.

The moves only hardened Brierley's innate resistance to authority, and when the Australian stock exchange demanded statistics from IEL to comply with listing requirements he refused. They wanted the percentage moves in turnover and profit for the six months to December, and Blackburn wrote to the stock exchange explaining why IEL did not keep these figures. But the exchange was adamant and promptly delisted IEL the same month the company had its third bid frozen by the Government.

Suddenly the figures materialised. A few weeks after delisting, IEL announced that profit for that period rose by 3.27 per cent and gross income by 5.39 per cent.

A shareholders' watchdog group, the Australian Shareholders' Association, applauded the stock exchange's victory and issued a statement saying they supported its efforts to enforce the listing requirements. The chairman of this group was also the managing director of IEL, one Bob Blackburn. It was an unusual situation, with Blackburn's quotes appearing in the same newspaper report as the representative of organisations on opposite sides of the debate.

Blackburn saw no conflict of interest in this, but his boss had no trouble spotting it. Brierley found the stance of his managing director ludicrous and irritating. He has little sympathy for watchdog organisations, believing that they obstruct what should happen and usually does happen over time.

Blackburn was also less than happy with Brierley's public statements. After he told the stock exchange that the statistics they required did not exist, he was rung by the general manager of the exchange, who told him the figures had just been telexed to him from Wellington.

Blackburn said Brierley later explained that he had been walking to lunch, wondering what to do about this problem, when he popped into the post office and sent the first figures that came into his head. Blackburn felt foolish and was annoyed that Brierley appeared to have made a liar out of him when, in fact, he believed Brierley was lying.

IEL's golden run of success appeared to have become a little tarnished. All was clearly not well at home or abroad. The company's shares dropped that year from $3.70 to $1.95, and Brierley predicted in May 1973 that the 1972/73 year would be one of consolidation, 'partly planned and partly accidental'.

The company was still trying to find a way out of its bind with the foreign takeover legislation, and that month let it be known that IEL was going to sponsor a new all-Australian company owned by the IEL Staff Superannuation Fund, which could be listed in two years' time, offering equity to current IEL shareholders.

In the same news item in the *Sydney Morning Herald*, the company announced that Bob Blackburn would be leaving the following month. He claimed the need for independence and time to see his family. The media assured people that the other half of the 'dynamic duo' would still be a force at IEL, at increased fees and within his own hours. They were right, in a sense, but only loosely.

NINE

Feud's Corner

FROM THE BEGINNING, Industrial Equity Ltd was Ron Brierley's company. Although BIL carried his name and was the parent company, it was less active than IEL in the early 1970s and Brierley was content to leave the running to someone else. It was IEL that claimed his loyalty and increasingly his attention. He was spending more and more time in Australia, and he ruled there, as in New Zealand, with unquestioned authority. It was understood by everyone that his word was final.

However, during his absence Bob Blackburn had taken the helm. This worked well while Brierley was in New Zealand harassing Scales, the Northern Steam Ship Co. and sundry politicians, but when he began to devote his energies to Australian business, tensions between the two men began to surface.

Robert James Blackburn is a tall man with penetrating eyes and a manner reflecting a background he says was hammered out in the school of hard knocks. Fifteen years older than Brierley, he is a street fighter by nature, and at times this has applied to him both literally and metaphorically, for he loved an argument and would pursue an action to the bitter end. He could also be intolerant and at times betrayed an arrogant streak.

Blackburn was brought up in Christchurch and studied part-time for a commerce degree while working at the State Advances Corporation as a cadet. His study was interrupted at the age of nineteen when he joined the Royal New Zealand Navy to become a Fleet Air Arm pilot in the Second World War.

After the war he returned to the State Advances Corporation, assisting with ex-servicemen's loans. One of his jobs was to take the projects to Jack Hindin, an accountant, for evaluation. Hindin impressed Blackburn and their association led to the pair forming Superannuation Investment Funds. Hindin planned the scheme while Blackburn marketed it.

Blackburn's career has been varied. He again volunteered for the Navy during the Korean War, and on returning to Christchurch, he became half-owner and manager of a plastics manufacturing firm that made, among other things, fibreglass boats and sports cars.

Blackburn loved boats and cars and raced competitively in both fields. As a racing driver, he won New Zealand's first 100-mile road race in 1954. In Australia he took part in two America's Cup challenges, first as a member of the training crew on *Gretel I* in 1967 and as a deputy navigator on *Gretel II* in 1970.

By 1962 he was living in Australia. His marriage had broken up and he wanted a fresh start. There he completed a securities industry apprenticeship with broking firm Niel and Partridge, and he stayed with them until 1966, when he became the managing director of IEL.

He and Brierley had much in common when they met. Like Brierley, Blackburn was an adventurous, independent thinker. He, too, had read about Charles Clore and was familiar with the concept of investing in undervalued assets. As a broker he advised people to deviate occasionally from the old maxim that a portfolio without BHP was like a yacht without a keel. He felt that second-class stocks would provide a better yield and were likely to be taken over, so boosting the share price.

Thus he was comfortable with IEL's ambitions and the pair were soon referred to as the 'Brierley-Blackburn team' or the 'dynamic duo'. Both loved scouring articles of association for errors and omissions, and both relished the boardroom battles. Blackburn calls them the best unscripted theatre in town. He was a loner like Brierley, not unhappy with his role as unwanted agitator and unwelcome acquirer.

In many ways his aims and techniques were not dissimilar to those of his boss and they appeared to be compatible. But there were differences in style which were magnified as time wore on. Blackburn's boardroom battles were inevitably public and brawling, while Brierley engaged in a long, silent war of attrition. Bob Blackburn allowed himself to become emotionally involved and took the outcome of each case personally. Brierley rarely made that mistake.

For instance, in 1972 Blackburn was IEL's representative on the board of a Queensland company called Industrial Sales & Service (Qld) Ltd (ISAS). Blackburn queried the proxies and demanded eleven polls on issues such as acceptance of the accounts, the election of each of the eight candidates and the appointment of auditors. His persistence wore everyone down and the meeting, which had begun at 3.15 p.m., finally ended at 10.45 p.m. When the ISAS annual report appeared in December it revealed that Blackburn had put in a minority report.

At first Brierley approved of such behaviour. It was spirited and annoying and suited IEL's reputation as the gadfly of the boardroom. They called meetings and disrupted them, researched legal loopholes and, as he describes it, 'we thoroughly enjoyed being militant'. But Brierley's appetite for militancy eventually deserted him. Brierley's explanation for this is that, as the company grew, those tactics were no longer appropriate, yet it is ironic that BIL and IEL executives have levelled the same charges at him over the succeeding years.

Brierley's main concern was probably Blackburn's involvement with the Australian Shareholders' Association, of which he was a member from 1964 to 1980 and chairman from 1968 for three years. Once again, in the early days Brierley had approved of such stirring, but he felt the righteous indignation and moralising should stop once they had become a company of some substance. To his horror, he discovered that Blackburn appeared to take the organisation seriously. As an ardent individualist whose sole concern is capital acquisition, Brierley could not understand Blackburn's commitment to the association.

It is true, too, that the competing roles of corporate raider and shareholders' watchdog sat uneasily next to one another. There was a conflict of interest that Blackburn was blind to, and when the press pointed it out, he took legal action. He says making that accusation cost *The Australian* $20,000 in defamation costs because, he believes, it was untrue, unfair and malicious, although *The Australian* cannot confirm this payment today.

For Brierley, however, Blackburn's interest in the ASA was a potent symbol of their increasing divergence, and trouble at a subsidiary, Swans Ltd, did little to endear Blackburn to Brierley. IEL took over the Sydney builders' supplier in 1968, but its performance declined under Blackburn's stewardship and in the 1973 IEL accounts $520,000 had to be written off for Swans. Some within IEL blamed Blackburn's manner as much as his managerial ability for the result.

Blackburn, too, had his complaints. He resented Brierley's tendency to make unilateral decisions without informing him. The incident with the stock exchange over the percentage figures illustrates this. On another occasion Brierley allowed Blackburn to make a representation to a member of the Foreign Investment Review Board regarding IEL's status as a foreign company. Later, outside the room, Brierley told him he had changed everything anyway and the case Blackburn had presented was complete nonsense.

But the most humiliating defeat for Blackburn came at a meeting of Offshore Oil NL. IEL bought a stake in the mining company in

1969, which, when it was sold, provided the working capital of IEL for a number of years. The profit doubled IEL's capital base, giving it enough money to expand.

Although IEL had sold its shares, Brierley and Blackburn remained on the board. Since Offshore Oil had lent IEL money, Brierley was more than happy to retain a formal association. In the days when banks handled IEL with caution, this was an important consideration. So in 1971, when Blackburn questioned a deal by an Offshore Oil director and accused the directors of mismanagement of the company's funds, Brierley did not leap to his support. Blackburn put his alternative director's report on the table, and still Brierley refused to endorse his stance. Blackburn was embarrassed and felt betrayed by his boss. As managing director he expected the unequivocal support of his chairman.

However, Brierley's yardstick of morality has always been limited to how a decision affects BIL or IEL. Using this criterion, Blackburn's actions failed to measure up. Brierley believed he was acting against the commercial interests of the company.

After the Offshore Oil defeat, Blackburn said he offered his resignation. He said Brierley turned it down, saying it was not convenient at the moment. Blackburn wondered what he meant.

It was evident to everyone at IEL that the relationship between the two men had disintegrated into thinly veiled hostility. At board meetings the atmosphere was often poisonous with ill-will and resentment. At the end of these meetings everyone resolved to do better, but inevitably arguments would break out again next time. It was rather like a marriage reconciliation, says Brierley drily.

Whatever residual support Bob Blackburn had, evaporated overnight after another Offshore Oil meeting in January 1972. Brierley's memory of that meeting begins with manoeuvring himself to sit next to the chairman, his old hero Sir Les Hooker. Hooker was not a strong chairman and Brierley said it was well understood that whoever sat next to him could effectively control the meeting. Bob Blackburn, who was also supposed to be sitting at the board table, was nowhere to be seen.

As Brierley tells it, just as he began prompting the chairman with, 'Les, we'd better start the meeting now,' a high-pitched cry of panic could be heard above the crowd, 'Mr Chairman, Mr Chairman, stop the meeting. Mr Blackburn has just knocked out Mr Hetherton.'

The chairman duly adjourned the meeting and Boris Ganke, chairman of Brinds Ltd, and a friend of Brierley, took the microphone and announced, 'Ladies and gentlemen, a director of this company has been punched.' The press rose as a single body and ran to see what had happened while bystanders shouted 'Call the police!' and 'Is there a doctor in the house?'

It transpired that Frank Hetherton, also a director of Offshore Oil and an associate of Boris Ganke, had attempted to bar the entry of a man he believed to be an IEL associate. An argument had developed with Blackburn and others over his right of entry, but when Blackburn was called to the board table, he invited the man inside with him. Hetherton then barred the doorway and a scuffle broke out. A few seconds later Hetherton found himself on the floor, with a sore head and looking at his broken watch.

It was a shocking development but, far from looking remorseful, Brierley remembers Blackburn wore a maniacal gleam of triumph.

Les Hooker looked at his friend dolefully and said, 'Oh Ron, how embarrassing for you.' Brierley could only nod in agreement, knowing the worst was yet to come.

The Offshore Oil meeting had taken place in the morning. In the afternoon Brierley attended sensitive negotiations with a company IEL was intending to take over. The raid on Pitt, Son and Badgery, an old Sydney-based wool and produce broker, was IEL's first move into the Establishment and Brierley was keen to make a good impression. The meeting went well and Brierley departed feeling rather pleased with his performance. And then he saw the billboard. 'Company Director KO'd,' shouted the *Daily Mirror*.

'The person I was with, our auditor, said, "Good gracious me, dear, oh dear, oh dear." I thought, "Oh God, I know what that is." So what do you do, hope they won't see it, realise it's you? I said, "Actually, Bill, I think that's Bob Blackburn, a most unfortunate incident."'

The incident did not affect IEL's bid for Pitt, Son and Badgery and in the end IEL joined forces with a rival bidder, the 130-year-old British-owned pastoral company Scottish Australian Co. Ltd, and their $3.20 per share, $3.5 million bid succeeded. But it had sealed Blackburn's fate. Brierley already had a replacement in mind: Bill Loewenthal, who had left New Zealand a year before to take up a position in the Jeffs brothers' ill-fated empire JBL. Loewenthal knew working for JBL was a risk but he wanted a change from his work as general manager at T. W. Young, a subsidiary of Dominion Breweries, and JBL was prepared to pay for him, his wife and their three children to move to Australia.

The JBL group collapsed in July 1972 and soon afterwards Brierley employed Loewenthal. Bill Loewenthal was the antithesis of

Bob Blackburn. He was a genial man with shrewd, twinkling eyes, wavy hair and enough sense to know that it would not be wise to threaten Brierley's position as king of the heap. His role in the company was one of the tolerant peace-maker, but though he would later affectionately be nicknamed 'Uncle Bill', this did not mean he was slow to make hard decisions. At the time of his appointment as general manager he had no idea he was being groomed to take over from Blackburn, who was the managing director, but in June 1973 Brierley decided the time for Blackburn's resignation was now convenient.

McDonald learned that Bob Blackburn was not easily dismissed. He recalls that he, Brierley, Beyer and another IEL director, Gordon Moffat, spent a whole day trying to convince him to resign, but Blackburn was determined to stay. The following day Beyer and Moffat were not available, so the task fell to McDonald and Brierley. McDonald recalls that Brierley was devastating in his criticisms. He catalogued precisely all his deficiencies and Blackburn retaliated by trying to defend himself.

Finally Brierley decided that if he did not offer to resign, he would announce to the staff at 2 p.m. that Blackburn was leaving the company. At 2 p.m. Blackburn was still there and Brierley made the announcement.

So Blackburn was forced to resign, but the protracted argument had served one useful purpose. It had won him a farewell package that included $70,000 cash, use of a car for a year and 35,000 shares.

It was a generous settlement but, according to Blackburn, there was one more clause in the agreement. He claimed that Brierley promised to buy his shares, then selling at $1.70, in twelve months' time at $2.

But Brierley never replied to Blackburn's requests to redeem the shares and, since he had nothing in writing, there was little he could do. Indeed, he concedes it was just as well he kept the shares, since in subsequent years, with bonus and rights issues, they provided him with a regular income.

Blackburn's departure was viewed as a great loss to IEL by observers who knew nothing of the internal dissent. He had a high profile and was seen to be crucial to the company's success. When he left, many business people asked Brierley, 'What are you going to do now that Blackburn has gone? I understand he's the inspiration for all you've been doing.'

One person who particularly admired Bob Blackburn was Sydney property developer Sidney Londish, who had worked alongside him as joint controlling director of a company called Tulloch Ltd. Tulloch was an ailing company with little hope of recovery, but while he was on the board with Blackburn, Londish was mightily impressed by his energy, commitment and imagination. He listened eagerly to Blackburn's talk of how money could be made through takeovers and how they were executed.

As far back as the early 1960s Londish had singled out Ron Brierley as an innovative entrepreneur, and when he heard Blackburn was leaving IEL, he invited him to join the board of a recent acquisition, Loloma Mining Corporation NL. Blackburn was the managing director of Loloma for twelve months and helped clean up the company.

Londish also helped set him up in business as a corporate consultant along with another businessman, Bob Hodge. Blackburn quickly got to work marketing his speciality — IEL.

One of his first consultancy tasks was to offer IEL a parcel of shares in Southern Farmers, which had recently altered its status from a co-operative to a company. The change had gone largely unnoticed and the shares were selling at bargain prices when Ron Brierley spied its attraction.

Blackburn knew IEL would be interested in boosting its strategic holding in the company and he told them the Southern Farmers parcel had been offered to him by Robert Holmes à Court. He suggested a joint venture in Southern Farmers with IEL, and in his scheme IEL would have had a modest share.

Naturally Brierley and his team were appalled by his proposal. Here was the man they had just ousted in a bitter dispute daring to offer them a deal based on information he had gleaned while working for the company. They had no hesitation in turning him down. The Southern Farmers shares then went into the Loloma portfolio. IEL later bought these shares from Loloma and then initiated legal action against Loloma and Londish for the resale profit of those shares. Blackburn applied for the action to be dismissed with costs to him. Since he did not profit from the sale of the Southern Farmers shares, the exercise had cost him dearly.

It was not long before Brierley realised Blackburn was attempting to frustrate his initiatives by going to opposing companies and offering to tell them all about IEL. For example, in April 1974, when IEL bid for Sydney earthmoving and construction equipments group Conquip Ltd, Blackburn made a counter-bid on behalf of a company he was advising. But Conquip favoured IEL's straight cash offer over Blackburn's cash-and-share bid, even though it was theoretically worth more.

It was a good deal for IEL, and its subsequent sale of Conquip assets provided the profit for that year.

That takeover was IEL's first as an Australian company. To qualify, it had reconstructed its voting scale to lower the foreign element, and plans for a new company to take over IEL were abandoned. Instead, since BIL owned 95 per cent of Citizens and Graziers, which owned 50 per cent of IEL anyway, Citizens' directors simply consented to reduce their voting power from 50 per cent to 14.9 per cent, thus satisfying Australian regulatory requirements and avoiding the need for shareholder approval.

Blackburn immediately detected an apparent vulnerability in this scheme and set about exploiting it. It was clear to him that as there was no other major shareholder, the 14.9 per cent voting restriction meant that anyone cornering 16 per cent of the shares could get 51 per cent voting control. He put the proposal to his much wealthier friend Sid Londish and top corporate lawyer Aleco Vrisakis, his associate.

Londish had known nothing of the dynamic duo's divorce when Blackburn joined him, but the intensity of Blackburn's bitterness towards Brierley was now painfully obvious. Blackburn was depressed, inconsolable. Although he was making barely enough money to keep his head above water, all he could think about was sweet, corrosive revenge. Londish refused to take part initially, but he could see that Blackburn was obsessed with his vendetta. So to appease him a company, Blackrod Pty Ltd, was formed in April 1974 with the purpose of taking over IEL. (The company took its name from a tradition in the British Parliament. The door to Parliament is opened by an officer known as Black Rod, who knocks on the door three times with a black rod before entry is allowed.)

Blackburn knew, of course, that a threat to Brierley's favourite company would stimulate a reaction. IEL was practically Brierley's nerve centre; certainly it was his identity, and Blackburn was publicly making a play for his domain. But while this would be the public perception, in reality both Blackburn and Brierley knew his bid had little chance of succeeding.

In April 1975 Blackrod announced it was offering $3 a share for up to 49 per cent of IEL's capital, even though the market price was currently $1.60. The net asset backing, however, was a healthier $2.59. The offer finally came out in May, but Blackrod had until 30 September to decide whether it would purchase the shares.

Blackburn claimed the motivation behind his bid was to restore the growth rate IEL had enjoyed before it was classified as a foreign company. He said IEL had chosen to limit the voting rights of its shares instead of selling equity to Australians. IEL's actions put the company in a sensitive position in relation to Government policy.

He also admitted his aim was to establish the true nature of IEL. If his bid revealed that control of IEL lay in the hands of overseas shareholders, the Australian shareholders knew they had been deprived of the benefits of selling their shares at well above the market price.

At first glance it appeared the new voting structure gave Blackrod a strong advantage. Since IEL shares, other than BIL and its associates, held 1.9 per cent of the votes for every 1 per cent of the issued capital, this meant Blackrod needed only 8 per cent of IEL's issued capital to outvote BIL, and 27 per cent of IEL to control 51 per cent of the voting structure.

However, it was recognised that BIL would probably transfer the shares to other hands, which would return to the holder full voting powers and would show that IEL was not sincere in restricting New Zealand's voting rights.

So there was more than an element of mischief to Blackburn's plans, and he admits today that he was stirring.

The marketplace guessed this was the case. Although IEL shares initially jumped to $2.30 after Blackburn's offer was finally announced, they fell quickly back to $2.06 and commentators noted that the market clearly did not rate Blackburn's chances highly. Brierley was also certain that Blackburn would fail and he was quick to condemn the raid as futile and a farce.

But Blackburn's raid did prompt an exchange of catty remarks. When Blackburn claimed he had run IEL like a one-man band where he played all the instruments, Brierley spat back, 'He sounded more like a trumpet solo and a badly tuned one at that.' He snidely added that IEL had not needed to replace Blackburn, not mentioning that Loewenthal had been hired for this very purpose.

Brierley also revealed that Blackburn had tried to sell his IEL stake for $2 per share barely a month before Blackrod had implemented a takeover scheme for $3 per share, casting 'further grave doubts on the credibility of the proposal'.

By August, Blackburn held the power of attorney over the statutory 10 per cent of the voting capital necessary to call an extraordinary general meeting. Although IEL disputed the validity of Blackburn's power of attorney, the meeting was finally held in late September.

Blackrod suffered a resounding defeat. Blackburn's motions to the board were knocked out by just over 1,000,000 votes to 248,000 and Brierley revealed that Blackrod had made an embarrassing error. Vrisakis had forgotten to send in a signed declaration of the three Blackrod directors' willingness to stand for office. Brierley quietly explained what had happened to the assembled throng at the meeting.

Two months later, at IEL's 1974 annual meeting, Blackburn and Londish once again failed to gain board representation, but Blackburn had some news to impart that he hoped would stimulate a reaction. He revealed that on the day of the extraordinary meeting Brierley had transferred 21 per cent of the capital of IEL to a nominee company, Simsa Nominees Pty Ltd, so that when the vote was cast against Blackrod, IEL was actually foreign-owned. Brierley's response to that was 'So what?' and the shareholders seemed to agree. His revelation sank without a trace.

Londish decided then and there to pull the plug on the takeover. It saddened him to see Blackburn becoming more and more twisted with bitterness and he began to regret his support of the whole nasty, doomed episode. He realised that even if Blackburn could win control, the success of IEL was inextricably linked with its leader, Ron Brierley, and so he started turning down IEL shares offered to him.

'Quite frankly it was a half-hearted bid as far as I was concerned. After all, Brierley made the business and he is the business. I regret the incident altogether. Blackburn had all the right facts and all the wrong reasons. It's not our scene and I should never have let him do it in the first place. If he had just concentrated on doing other things, he would never have looked back. It is a great tragedy,' Londish says.

After Blackrod was dissolved, Londish never saw Blackburn again, but in 1975 he appeared at a meeting of VIA Ltd where Brierley was attempting to gain board representation for the second time. Blackburn had become a shareholder the week before, having paid high prices for his shares. He stood up and slated IEL, the company he had helped mould. Brierley retaliated and the clashes made news once again.

Perhaps the saddest outcome of Blackrod and the ongoing vendetta was that the feud had become a public brawl, and Blackburn, in the eyes of many observers, was being beaten to a pulp. The meetings were being recommended for people who had missed out on the clash between George Foreman and Muhammad Ali. So far, according to one magazine, the score was Brierley 5, Blackburn minus 2.

In 1976 the score lifted in Blackburn's favour, although it was a victory at the expense of IEL shareholders. IEL wanted to distribute shares in its property development subsidiary Minerva Centre to its shareholders. It was meant to be a gift — IEL shareholders were effectively getting these shares at half their intrinsic value. But small shareholders and Citizens and Graziers, which owned 58 per cent of IEL, received cash to the tune of $360,000 instead of scrip.

Blackburn decided to challenge this on the grounds that there was not enough profit at 30 June to pay such a dividend. He was technically correct, although IEL planned to revalue its assets and create an asset revaluation reserve to prove the company had enough potential profit to cover the distribution. Brierley had made a mistake and Blackburn was keen to show him up and demonstrate his own skills at the same time.

Blackburn won the first round in court. Brierley appealed, but in 1977 the Court of Appeal upheld the earlier Equity Court judgment. IEL took the case to the High Court and was rejected once again.

In the end the Minerva shares were recovered from all IEL shareholders, who received nothing in return. The case made legal history in Australia and is studied closely at law schools today, but it was regarded by people like Bill Loewenthal as nothing more than a Pyrrhic victory. Blackburn might have beaten Brierley, but he had certainly lost any goodwill he had with shareholders. Furthermore, he had thought it would cost him about $5,000 and take three months. In fact, it cost him close to $50,000 and took three years.

Bob Blackburn was to become a familiar figure to IEL shareholders. Since 1974 he had turned up at every annual meeting with a list of questions and objections. His participation alone tended to boost attendance figures, and he was a living example of his own theory that company meetings were the best unscripted theatre in town. An air of expectancy pervaded those meetings, with shareholders as eager to hear the flying insults as the profit figures for the year.

At one memorable meeting, Blackburn stood up and started to badger Brierley with a predictable list of questions. Brierley was unresponsive, so Blackburn demanded an answer.

Brierley replied wanly, 'Read them all out and I will answer your questions.'

Blackburn obliged, Brierley thanked him, and invited him to sit down.

'But you haven't answered my questions,' protested Blackburn.

'I might answer them at the end of the meeting depending on how you behave,' came the reply. Then he added, 'You are the managing director of Horizon Pacific, aren't you?'

'Yes, I am.'

'You haven't put in your half-yearly reports yet,' said Brierley, who then carried on with the business of the meeting.

At the end of the meeting Blackburn stood up again and said, 'Mr Chairman, you haven't answered my questions.'

Brierley stared hard at him and said, 'No, you haven't behaved and I'm not going to. You hurry back to work and put out your half-yearly report.'

By now the Brierley camp was starting to respond to Blackburn's jibes and accusations. Don McDonald remembers that he and Trevor Beyer had the job of shouting down Bob Blackburn every time he stood up to speak at the annual meetings, and the constant niggling was beginning to eat away at even Brierley's studied indifference. Instead of greeting each criticism with silence, he began to retaliate. In his words, he was becoming 'seduced into pursuing this feud'.

In 1977, when the ASA questioned Brierley about his involvement in Acmex Holdings Ltd, Brierley responded with a fourteen-point questionnaire about the activities and purpose of the ASA. It was a tart missive with sly references to Blackburn. He asked what the ASA was doing about losses incurred by shares of three companies Blackburn had been associated with, and was it interested in contributing to an appeal he was sponsoring for 'failed and embittered directors of unsuccessful public companies'?

Brierley turned up with his old friend Boris Ganke at a Horizon Pacific meeting and, true to what was fast becoming a ritual, he behaved badly. Then, under an anonymous byline, he descended to writing a humorous, deprecating article on Horizon Pacific. Brierley says the article appeared in *The Bulletin*, in an altered form, although they can find no record of its publication.

In the latter part of the article a proxyholder is closely questioning Blackburn about an Arab oil company, Ajman Petroleum:

> However, Mr Blackburn, about whom it can be observed with the greatest respect, that throughout these proceedings his knowledge of the company was somewhat less than encyclopaedic, clearly indicated his view of the significance of Ajman. The resolute proxyholder was on his feet. And — *sacré bleu*! — he was questioning, none too politely, the very existence of Ajman Petroleum Industries Co. Ltd (Incorporated in Ajman). Is it real? Fact or fiction? Michael Kulakowski [the managing director of Ajman] or Lewis Carroll?
>
> Mr Blackburn was quietly reassuring. He was fairly sure that Ajman *did* exist, because he had once spotted a copy of the Memorandum and Articles of Association and, anyway, on a visit to Dubai he had seen the company's very large Head Office building.
>
> 'How large is large? How many storeys? What activities were they engaged in there?'

At this point the chairman became somewhat querulous. He didn't know how many storeys. He hadn't counted them. 'We only have 5 per cent of this company so I didn't go around counting the door knobs and door handles. If you owned 5 per cent of BHP you wouldn't go around counting all the nuts and bolts, would you?'

Oh dear, oh dear. Was this really happening? Your correspondent felt a warm glow. The resolute proxyholder looked very dissatisfied. The meeting swept on.

There was more to come. The resolute proxyholder was always worth listening to but had to risk the impairment of his own faculties in this regard when former Horizon chairman Mr George Crutchley sensed a slight on his integrity and threatened to 'thump him on the bloody ear!' (Shades of Offshore Oil). Mr Blackburn rather primly intervened and order was restored.

Blackburn's appetite for revenge was still unsatisfied. His next step was to prompt an investigation by the NSW Corporate Affairs Commission into IEL. The first IEL knew about it was when Bill Loewenthal and IEL company secretary Barry Holmes received summonses alleging that they had been responsible four and a half years earlier for breaching Section 67 of the Companies Act, which says that a company should not finance the purchase of its own shares. In order to raise the company's holdings in IEL, and since share prices were low, BIL had bought shares through Citizens and Graziers in IEL and debited them to C and G's account, which was in credit, but all the Corporate Affairs Commission saw was that IEL had bought shares in IEL. In fact, C and G had money on deposit with IEL, and IEL just paid money on C and G's instructions to the broker concerned.

The investigation started late in 1978 and ended some nine months later, during which time CAC staff were frequent visitors at IEL. But a week before the case was due to come to trial, the CAC suddenly realised what had happened, dropped the case and paid the two men $3,000 each in compensation.

Blackburn did not give up on the commission, however. He told it that IEL had a number of discrepancies on its register. The CAC probably realised this was the inevitable outcome of a fast-growing company and so ignored his complaint.

Today, Blackburn is a yacht broker living in Queensland. His dreams of becoming a corporate consultant faded over the years and he now says the feud was unnecessary. But the grudges he harboured against Brierley remain with him. In his view, Brierley lit the match that started the fire by refusing to buy his shares and by taking action over the Holmes à Court share parcel.

Brierley, on the other hand, sees his former friend and colleague as a pitiable creature. Here was a man at the pinnacle of his career, known and respected, striking out on his own. Instead of capitalising on his good points, he exposed himself to the world as a man lacking depth and wisdom. Had Blackburn not pursued this self-destructive path, Brierley believes he could have been a forerunner of today's merchant bankers.

Other IEL directors are less charitable. They believe that had Blackburn stayed with the company IEL would no longer exist. He was a good analyst but a poor manager with an unfortunate manner.

After Blackburn was fired, the two men saw each other only to do battle at company meetings, and for twelve years, until March 1989, Brierley had not seen Blackburn at all. So when I told Brierley that I was scheduled to visit Blackburn in Sanctuary Cove the following week, he kindly offered me a seat on his plane. His mother lived in Southport, seventy kilometres south of Brisbane, and he was visiting her at the same time.

Sanctuary Cove was further from Southport than we realised, and by the time the IEL limousine had driven us there he was reluctant to let the opportunity pass. Dressed as ever in a grey suit on that hot Queensland day, he was unusually helpful in trying to locate Blackburn's boat, called *Strictly Business*. When we spotted the yacht in the distance, I thanked Brierley for his kindness, but he did not get back into the grey car and drive off as he normally would. I realised then something more was required and I asked him to accompany me to the boat. In the event of problems, I promised to say that he was simply helping me find the yacht.

As we approached the yacht, Bob Blackburn's partner, Heather, came striding toward us. She smiled brightly and guessed whom we had come to see. Bob Blackburn was resting below, she told us. We clambered onto the yacht and waited for him to emerge.

Blackburn was sixty-six years old by now and the most noticeable change from the newspaper photographs was his shock of grey hair. Brierley, who was fifty-one, has probably always seemed old. That tentative manner conveying fragility, together with his soft, underground pallor, was doubtless a Brierley characteristic even in his twenties. Blackburn seemed well, and Brierley opened the conversation by commending him for his lifestyle decision.

Blackburn was ill at ease. He would have settled for verbally circling Brierley, reluctant to face the past, which sat between them with its own guilty presence. But Brierley felt impish; he was enjoying Blackburn's discomfort and enjoying the difference in their positions.

Suddenly I heard myself being referred to as 'she'.

Brierley in 1970. Newspapers at the time noted his empire was already worth $10 million

NZ Herald

Above: *Don McDonald*

Above left: *Peter Elworthy, Federated Farmers and Ravensdown representative*
Fourth Estate

Left: *Bruce Judge*
Fourth Estate

Robert Muldoon, Minister of Finance in the early 1970s
Fourth Estate

Bob Blackburn (left) with Ron Brierley at IEL, 1972
Australian Photographic Agency

Bill Loewenthal, who took over from Bob Blackburn in 1973

BIL directors in 1978. From left: Selwyn Cushing, John Lawrey, Don McDonald, Trevor Beyer, Ron Brierley, Denis Kelly (secretary) and Bruce Judge

NZ Herald

'Well,' Brierley said, 'she is writing a book about me, as you know, and there were so many people willing to say nice things, I thought she should come and see you for a bit of acid.'

I felt somehow apologetic. It sounded as if I had simply come to record a few vicious comments for Brierley's amusement, although it must be said that I was waiting eagerly for Blackburn's response.

Blackburn gave an anaemic smile. 'Oh, my memory's fading now, Ron. It's not what it used to be. You forget the details,' he said, running one hand through his dishevelled hair.

After this brief meeting, Blackburn came outside to farewell Brierley. Blackburn enthusiastically questioned him about IEL's yacht. The replies showed that Ron took little notice of this aspect of his operation. Blackburn was obviously keen to present a positive image to Brierley, to leave him with the impression that he had not lost the capacity to take risks. Brierley, on the other hand, clearly showed he had nothing to prove.

'This is all tax-free,' said Bob Blackburn waving his arm in a wide arc. 'I've got it all organised so that I don't pay a cent in tax.'

Brierley smiled and said, 'I see we still have something in common, Bob.'

In my subsequent interview with Blackburn, I discovered he was an amiable host, but, in more ways than one, I could see he suited being the captain of his own ship. In his mind, the feud, albeit unnecessary, was not unjustified. There was no evidence of the alleged chip on the shoulder that I could see, though I am sure he was presenting a careful image of himself. The Bob Blackburn I saw was a fresh, unpredictable thinker, determined and solitary. My impression was that he counted his years at IEL as possibly the best in his life.

Months later I received a letter from Blackburn replying to my further queries. The letter confirmed, as I had suspected, that he had taken important clippings of the Offshore Oil debacle missing from the IEL file. Firstly he thanked me for bringing Ron on board and 'laying to rest an old ghost'.

Brierley's response to the reunion was to relive it with everyone who knew what had gone on. His account had gone round IEL before I returned from Brisbane a few days later.

TEN

Golden Opportunism

BLACKBURN'S MOTIVES and achievements may have been questionable, but his timing was perfect. When he launched his takeover of IEL, the company was at its lowest ebb, having been gradually dragged downward since the early 1970s by some poor investments. Swans Ltd and other lacklustre performers such as Barker Holdings Ltd and Frederick Ash Ltd absorbed a great deal of energy, and the question of foreign ownership continued to dog the company and dampen investor enthusiasm.

The balance sheet in 1973 showed that IEL's net profit fell by almost 10 per cent that year, although Brierley wrote confidently in the annual report that the company had since eliminated its unsatisfactory trading activities and reduced indebtedness.

The following year IEL would be severely tested by a recession precipitated by a worldwide stockmarket slump that left scores of collapsed companies in its wake. Australia was particularly hard-hit by the downturn. Although the nation had entered the decade on the crest of a mining boom, the boom had bust during 1971 and 1972. The cost of living began to soar and in 1972 unemployment reached its highest point for ten years.

But it was the credit squeeze, initiated by the Government, that really hurt IEL in 1974/75. Interest rates began to spiral upwards, and since IEL had no reserves, it had to sell assets to meet demands. Until the squeeze, IEL had been borrowing on a project-by-project basis, with its funding lines secured by shares. As the value of the shares went down, the bankers wanted more scrip or cash from selling assets to cover their loans.

For example, the funds for the takeover of the mechanical equipment company Conquip Ltd that year came from Partnership Pacific, an offshoot of Westpac Banking Corporation. IEL had been expecting interest rates of about 17 per cent, but by the time it drew down the line to buy Conquip shares, the rate had soared to 26 per cent. Mounting holding costs cast a heavy shadow over that deal, and in the end IEL had to sell major Conquip assets to pay Partnership Pacific.

IEL was also losing money on a number of its historically troubled investments, such as Swans Ltd, which some executives believe should have been sold years before.

Even today, IEL executives rate the 1974 credit squeeze as the toughest era in the company's history. The impact of the 1987 crash was more easily absorbed by a company as large and well lined as IEL was then, but in 1974 its resources were depleted. 'At least there was a lot of fat left in 1987. Back in 1974 there was hardly any fat at all,' recalls IEL's auditor, Geoff Harris.

IEL came perilously close to scraping the bottom of the barrel, providing a hard lesson for Brierley on the value of cash on deposit. He generally favoured an asset-based approach and tended to ignore the liabilities side of the balance sheet. But IEL's straitened circumstances showed the foolhardiness of this bias, and Brierley was appalled by the paucity of the company's reserves. He swore that from now on IEL would always have a large sum of money on deposit.

'I have always been aware of the value of liquidity, but that made me doubly, trebly conscious of the prudence and the eventual strategic value of having excess liquidity,' he says.

Although he was shocked by the predicament IEL found itself in, Brierley's reaction to the recession was rigorous and swift. After going through all the accounts, he came up with a list of about twenty items, in order of priority, that he thought should be tackled. That list formed the basis of IEL's activity for the coming years. It was the Bible at IEL, said Harris, and essentially it consisted of selling assets, rationalising others and adopting more prudent management practices, such as tightening borrowings and keeping tabs on the company's cash flow to ensure its survival.

However, the impact of the credit squeeze was even greater than observers could have imagined. Few knew that the grim financial times had also put an end to discussions that could have entirely reshaped the company. Just before the recession began to bite, IEL had been seriously considering merging with another company, Slater Walker Securities (Australia) Ltd.

Slater Walker UK was keen to sell its 35 per cent stake in its Australian counterpart. Discussions had started in London late in 1973 and continued early the following year in strictest secrecy. The two parties took the precaution of meeting in a hotel room at the Sheraton Wentworth in Sydney. Neither wanted to be linked to the other for fear of oiling the rumour machine. Since both were avowed corporate predators, rumours were likely, though Slater Walker was by far the better known of the two.

In its heyday Slater Walker was heralded as the most remarkable phenomenon of the British financial scene. It was the creation of two men — Tory politician Peter Walker and Jim Slater, who had become something of a star in the motor industry and had a small investment advisory business.

Slater Walker started off as a conglomerate in the go-go 1960s and, when that structure became unfashionable, it became an investment bank, spinning off satellite companies into which Slater fed acquisitions and financial services.

Slater's philosophy was similar to Brierley's, for he saw his operation as introducing a necessary stimulant to business — revving up lazy management and redistributing assets to more worthy owners. He soon became the torchbearer of a new style of capitalism applauded by the Tories. The Conservative Government of 1970–74 was even labelled the 'Slater Walker' Government.

Jim Slater had a hand in almost every takeover bid of the day, and his operations spread to Singapore, Australia, Hong Kong and, to a lesser extent, Canada. In 1968 Slater Walker Australia stunned the local financial community with its grand $28.6 million takeover of Drug Houses of Australia Ltd, one of the largest takeovers of the year.

In 1973 everything began to disintegrate, and by 1975 Slater's empire was in ruins, as was his promise of revolution in British management. He was chased from Singapore by Lee Kuan Yew, who talked of stamping out Slater's form of 'free-booting capitalism', and his deputy served four months in Changi Prison. A detailed investigation of his *modus operandi* by journalist Charles Raw later revealed how, throughout his entire career, Slater had manipulated the market for his own advantage.

The reverberations of the fall of the Slater empire shuddered through the financial world for years. Almost all the Slater companies collapsed in the mid-1970s, and the rest of the decade saw few new takeovers and hostile battles on the British corporate playing field.

So at the time IEL was considering merging with Slater Walker's Australian operation, its empire was already falling apart. The terms of the union were never finalised, but they had established that IEL would have to raise some $20 million to fund the merger. As the recession took hold, it quickly became apparent this was not feasible — IEL then had a market capitalisation of just over $4.5 million.

IEL executives, including Loewenthal and investment manager Geoff Pickles, believe that the company had a lucky escape. They are convinced that IEL would never have survived the merger, but this view is not shared by Brierley. He insists it is impossible to guess an outcome that depends heavily on the actions and judgments of the people involved, and suggests Slater Walker Australia's coal interests might have saved IEL during the energy crisis of the 1970s.

By the mid-1970s IEL was no longer alone on the takeover trail. Although the 1960s had not been without takeovers and mergers, the first of the new breed of takeover merchants began emerging around the late 1960s and early '70s. Like others of the time, they were capitalising on the stock exchange excitement of the resources, mining and nickel boom.

It was in 1972 that John Elliott took over the near-moribund jam company Henry Jones (IXL), and within a decade of that, he had executed a $202 million merger with Elder Smith Goldsborough Mort. At the beginning of the 1970s Robert Holmes à Court bought Western Australian Worsted and Woollen Mills, the cheapest stock on the West Australian exchange, and by 1974 he had control of Bell Bros. Then there was John Spalvins, who breathed new life into the conservative Adelaide Steamship Co. Ltd in the early 1970s; Alan Bond, who launched himself into the takeover arena in the late 1970s after years in property; and Larry Adler, whose original Fire and All Risks Insurance set the scene for a string of acquisitions in the 1960s and '70s.

Except for Elliott, the new boys were all immigrants to Australia, and this corroborates a finding by researchers Collins and Moore on entrepreneurs in Canada. Their 1970s study of 150 entrepreneurs revealed that on a per head of population basis the foreign-born were overly represented in this category.

Those entrepreneurs who survived the 1975 recession found that the range of takeover targets had widened to include most areas of Australian secondary industry, and the names Brierley, Spalvins, Elliott and Adler began to crop up in the news media with increasing frequency.

Their acquisitions covered a wide range of targets, but they were particularly attracted by the agricultural sector, which, with its numerous small companies, seemed to be crying out for rationalisation. In Australia most aspects of this industry had been traditionally dominated by the old pastoral business families. They operated in conjunction with the large international companies such as Heinz, Cadbury and Nabisco, who were drawn to Australia before and just after the Second World War.

But by the 1960s the pastoral companies that had not diversified out of the rural sector were competing with one another as well as facing competition from other products. For example, the wool industry was now in direct competition with the new synthetic fibres manufacturers. Australia's agricultural industry had become grossly inefficient, depending on subsidies for support and lacking modern marketing techniques. As one commentator on the Australian food industry noted, the agricultural sector was ripe for agribusiness.

In order to survive, many of the old families found themselves compelled to resort to mergers, share issues and takeovers simply to build up their size and market share. But they watered down their own stake at the same time and many sold out completely.

Brierley was quick to recognise that major adjustments in the rural economy were inevitable. So in the early 1970s IEL took positions in leading pastoral companies at a time when pastoral stocks were at their lowest ebb. The most significant of these investments was its holding in Southern Farmers Co-operative Ltd. Brierley was the first investor to notice that the eighty-five-year-old organisation had changed its status from a co-operative to a company, and in the 1970s he began buying shares for as little as $1.32 when the net worth of a share was $7.70. Southern Farmers was one of the most undervalued companies on the stock exchange, and Brierley discovered to his joy that it also had up to 1,600 missing shareholders.

When the directors of Southern Farmers realised Brierley was in pursuit, they hired an Australian merchant bank, the Development Finance Corporation Group, to advise them. Bob Seldon, the DFC representative studying the bid, was also a friend of Brierley, and his report led to the formation of a holding company to control Southern Farmers' trading activities and a $4.7 million payout to shareholders. As a major shareholder, IEL was one of the biggest beneficiaries of this generosity.

In 1974 Southern Farmers joined a consortium of pastoral companies, for which IEL received another large cash payment. The restructuring helped the company endure the rural recession in 1975, but it reduced Brierley's shareholding. It was not until Brierley purchased a Melbourne-based stock feed, milling and engineering group, Noske Ltd, in 1976, that he was able to boost his stake in Southern Farmers once again. Not for the first time that decade, his bid met fierce opposition from the Noske Board.

In the mid- to late 1970s, resistance to bids by Brierley was particularly high. He encountered widespread hostility and, to repel him, companies marshalled their defences with the speed and alarm of a group of bathers fending off a shark attack. In 1977 one newspaper noted there was an almost fanatical resolution to keep IEL at bay. That year Specialty Press brought in a large new shareholding simply to repel IEL. Carlton and United Breweries Ltd rejected IEl by buying shares in associated companies, and upon hearing of IEL's interest, William Haughton and Co. Ltd made sure its profit result improved after two years of poor returns and put in place an elaborate defensive arrangement with Dalgety Australia.

By this time Brierley's corporate manners had improved and he was careful to ring the chairman of Noske, George Bishop, to inform him of IEL's bid. He now felt it was a simple courtesy to let the chairman know of the bid, but he remembers it did not go exactly as planned. After he had finished his lengthy explanation, there was a pause and an embarrassed voice said, 'Look, there's been a mistake here. I'm Mr Bishop from the vehicle maintenance yard.'

Brierley's etiquette did not stop the Noske directors from appealing for protection. The Victorian Government then obligingly froze the bid by invoking previously unused legislation, claiming it could have an adverse effect on the economy of the state and Noske's employees. The legislation had been put in place three years earlier to prevent Thomas Nationwide Transport taking over Ansett Transport Industries, but it had never been used. Brierley says the action against IEL was the one and only time the Act was invoked.

But sometimes defensive mechanisms can subvert their original intentions. Following the Government's intervention, institutions began vigorously selling Noske shares. They sensed the Government might block the bid and were eager to obtain a high price. No alternative bidder for the company emerged, so when IEL increased its offer from 65 cents to 87 cents a share, the Noske directors had little choice but to recommend the bid, though they knew as well as IEL did that the net worth of the company was closer to $1.50 a share. Finally even the Government gave way and allowed the bid.

The bid for Noske was an important victory for IEL in 1976. It was a substantial company, adding a gilt edge to IEL's portfolio, and it also provided a door into Southern Farmers. In 1976 Southern Farmers bought Noske from IEL, thus boosting IEL's holding in Southern Farmers. This was quite a coup, as Southern Farmers was a venerable organisation with that ring of credibility Brierley loved. From time to time he would catch himself marvelling that he was even on the board at all.

Under IEL's guidance, Southern Farmers then gradually acquired related interests, and in 1978 it combined with another company, Bennett and Fisher Ltd, to become the third-largest pastoral group in Australia. Southern Farmers' total assets of $68 million represented one-third of the total assets in the Brierley group, and the question was now being asked whether IEL was trying to establish a pastoral base.

At the time, Brierley said he was more concerned with rationalisation than putting together a pastoral conglomerate, but today he says he saw IEL as the end-owner of a streamlined substantial wool and livestock house. Profits made through restructuring and selling assets would deliver this to them for nothing.

'That we should be the end-owner has always been my vision. I've never been attracted to businesses where the only intention was to sell them. That suggests you don't want to own them; if that's the case, you don't have the right to own them. It's true I might buy a company and later face the fact that the smarter move was to sell it to a more compatible company. Of course, opportunism is a big factor.'

Although Brierley can now explain clearly what the company was trying to do, those at IEL remember that at the time the picture was much more confused. They dispute Brierley's contention that he intended IEL to become the end-owner of a wool and livestock house. Opportunism was not just a big factor, it was everything. But it also created its own set of problems, which would occupy Brierley on and off for years.

One of IEL's most astute observers, special projects manager Ross Daniels, says IEL has tended to be a cyclical company, riding a number of troughs and peaks throughout its history. Periodically the company would stop and take stock of itself, setting in motion what Daniels calls a navel-gazing exercise, which could take up to a year or more to resolve.

1977 was such a year. Although the company had expanded as Brierley planned, he seemed to be weighed down by the demands of operating a public company whose profits came from opportunistic transactions. The short reporting cycles clashed with the long-term nature of their projects, and though Brierley could see the value quietly building up, shareholders expected to see the improvement reflected every year in the balance sheet. IEL had a ready-made buffer in the accounts with its miscellaneous contingency provision and investment fluctuation fund, but many of its projects did not reach fruition at convenient times.

Brierley became absorbed in trying to find ways of resolving these conflicting demands. A trust structure for IEL was looked at twice that decade, and other options, such as privatisation, were also considered, but nothing came of these and the reporting demands of a public company remained a vexed question for years.

That year the foreign-ownership devil appeared once again and, to IEL's relief, was exorcised for the last time. Although the rules had changed to take into account the total number of shares held by one party, not just the voting shares, IEL slipped through the net. A Government investigation into IEL revealed nothing and the problem never arose again. Bill Loewenthal says he later received a letter from the Government acknowledging the company was bona fide Australian.

But in the midst of all this uncertainty in 1977, Brierley did set a fresh course for the company. He decided IEL should undertake a massive clean-out of its uneconomic assets. Accordingly, it sold shares worth $20 million from its portfolio to give the company a $10 million cash surplus.

By 1978 IEL had the healthiest liquidity in its history and Brierley announced it was entering a 'new, more active phase of takeovers'. As if to emphasise his point, the company burst into the new year with two spectacular windfalls won with classic Brierley opportunism.

On both occasions Brierley launched a bid for a pastoral company and was bought out by a counter-bidder. His 10 per cent stake in the New South Wales flour and bread company Gillespie Brothers Holdings Ltd was sold to Allied Mills Ltd, and IEL's 15 per cent stake in Western Australian fertiliser company Cuming Smith and Co. Ltd went to Wesfarmers Co-operative Ltd.

For Brierley, IEL's enormous $28 million bid for Cuming Smith was a psychological milestone, but the courts took a dim view of how this was achieved. When the judge heard how IEL's use of another company to hold its Cuming Smith shares meant Wesfarmers could purchase their parcel without triggering the legal limit for a full takeover, or paying stamp duty and brokerage, he said, 'I do not think it does very much in the eyes of the public to inspire confidence in business, does it?' Nevertheless, Brierley kept the $2 million profit, which he estimates is probably worth some $100 million today.

IEL was now big enough to start annoying some of the doyens of Australian business. Brierley had already crossed swords with Sir Robert Southey, the chairman of William Haughton and past-president of the Liberal Party, and in 1978 he began to harass the redoubtable Sir Ian Potter. Seventy-five-year-old Potter had contacts in almost every business sphere in the country and probably sat on more boards than anyone else in Australia. His credentials were impeccable. After working in the Treasury in the 1930s, Potter set up a company that became the biggest stockbroking and underwriting firm in the country, launched into merchant banking and pioneered the official short-term money market.

When Brierley bid for Potter's 103-year-old shipping group, McIlwraith McEacharn Ltd, the *Australian Financial Review* dubbed it 'the boldest of any of Mr Brierley's corporate aggressions of the last decade'. He was clearly buying a fight with the Melbourne business establishment and one of the most influential figures in Australia's transport industry. Brierley reckons it was probably the first time Potter had had to face a raid of this kind.

Brierley's bid had a strong mischievous edge, for he had also launched an attack on Tricontinental Corporation Ltd, practically Potter's own merchant bank, and started to needle him about certain share transactions that seemed to favour Potter. Brierley turned up at Tricontinental's annual meeting in October 1978 and continued to goad Potter with his questions and an amendment expressing a loss of confidence in the directors.

His patience and tenacity were well rewarded. Bob Seldon remembers IEL executives urging Brierley to settle earlier for a fair profit, but Brierley refused. 'There's a premium here for the old Establishment pride,' he said. Finally, in October 1979, Brierley sold IEL's stake in McIlwraith McEacharn to Potter's white knight, TNT. The premium on pride must have been high, for IEL made $5 million on the deal, the largest profit it had made on a sale of shares until then.

But while Brierley was taking his profits where he found them in Australia, leaving New Zealand largely in the hands of his new general manager, Bruce Judge, and managing director Trevor Beyer, he was also putting in place what would become the international arm of his operation. The 1960s disasters of Ampat Sumatra and Grahamstown Gas and Coke had made his colleagues doubtful about the merits of international expansion, and some felt he should be concentrating on getting his domestic house in order. But the 1970s saw Brierley uncovering some of the most unlikely foreign companies BIL or IEL has ever owned.

Brierley's search for the old and unusual is never-ending. He travels everywhere with bags of newspapers, which he reads when he can. His reading often alerts him to a company that might warrant further investigation.

Bob Seldon remembers playing a game with Brierley modelled on Twenty Questions, where the aim of the interrogation was to guess a company, often of obscure or bizarre origins. It used to amaze Seldon how often Brierley came up with the correct answer, although given that locating corporate orphans is a Brierley speciality, this should not have been surprising.

On one of his sorties to London, Brierley happened to be looking through directories for 'interesting-sounding companies' when he spotted the Shanghai Electric Construction Co. Ltd. He learned the company had once run the municipal transport system in Shanghai before the Communists seized the assets of all imperial companies. Although Asian and British investors were still pursuing claims, their prospects of succeeding were slim. Brierley was immediately excited by the discovery of something with such rare and exotic origins.

'China was regarded as something out of Aladdin's cave. It was a mystery, a forbidden country thought to be on the brink of warfare,' says Brierley.

But Shanghai Electric had more than a romantic appeal; it had liquid assets, shares that were difficult to obtain and numerous missing shareholders. The share certificates were actually bearer notes, similar to our bank notes, and since there was no register, it was impossible to find the owners of the shares.

Before Brierley could take over Shanghai Electric in 1973, however, his proposal had to go through the British courts, where a scheme of arrangement was devised to accommodate the missing shareholders. The court ruled that if any of these shareholders turned up within twelve years of his takeover, they would have to be paid.

As the twelve-year period drew to a close, it seemed that Brierley's provision in the accounts for this purpose would be a windfall for the company. But with only months to go, a deluge of claims from China suddenly poured into BIL. There were more than 200 in all, totalling 25 per cent of the company's capital. A disappointed Brierley wondered how on earth these shareholders were all alerted to the deadline at the same time. Later he learned that an advertisement had been placed in a Chinese newspaper publicising the shareholders' rights, and he guesses it probably came from the Bank of China, eager to bring foreign exchange into the country.

Once he had discovered Shanghai Electric, however, Brierley realised there must be dozens of similar companies, and he set to work to find them. Most of his research was done in Hong Kong, where he uncovered gasworks, waterworks and housing estates, many of which had been registered in Shanghai. Since the war the registration of these corporate refugees had been transferred to Hong Kong, where they were controlled by companies such as Jardines Matheson from London.

Brierley was particularly interested in one company controlled by Jardines Matheson, Shanghai Dockyards, and he attended its annual meeting in Hong Kong, just after Christmas in 1972. Jardines directors were as surprised as he was to learn that his 8 per cent stake made him the largest shareholder in Shanghai Dockyards, and Brierley remembers he was the only shareholder present at the meeting.

It took two years and several visits to Hong Kong before Jardines relinquished control of the company, but Brierley eventually achieved his aim with only 25 per cent of the capital. This time there was no scheme of arrangement for the missing shareholders, but when Shanghai Dockyards announced cash issues in 1983, it brought howls of outrage from Chinese shareholders unable to take up their rights.

The company was a gem. Once the owner of one of the largest dockyard complexes in the world, it had assets well in excess of what Brierley paid for it. After Shanghai Dockyards was nationalised in 1952, it was left with $500,000 in cash and investments in the United States. American authorities retaliated by blocking the movement of the company's cash, but the money was able to be used as security for borrowings on the New York foreign exchange market. While this was a deterrent for some, Brierley was thrilled to have money in America.

So by the mid-1970s Brierley had a listed vehicle in Hong Kong, one in London and an investment in the United States. In 1977 Shanghai Dockyards changed its name to Industrial Equity (Pacific) Ltd and became the international arm of the BIL empire.

Once Brierley had the Shanghai companies, he continued to forage for other colonial remnants. Until the Second World War, British capital had sponsored companies all round the world, often with a utility emphasis, such as railways or waterworks. But by the 1960s and '70s, colonial power was waning and many of these companies were being confiscated, nationalised or sold, often to corporate raiders. Hence a large component of the London market was gradually disappearing.

Brierley considers he was too late to take real advantage of the bonanza, since it was winding down in the 1970s. But he did buy a fair smattering of this international grab-bag. He has, at various times, had investment in tramways in Portugal, electric light companies in India and barges in Brazil. They went by such storybook names as The Country Gentlemen's Association, Tjiwongie Tea Estates and the Corn Exchange.

Brierley has fond memories of them all. Their quirky history, quaint traditions and aura of respectability meant he could never let any one of them go without experiencing a pang of regret. But for

Brierley, the saddest loss of all was a concern he rates as one of the six most interesting companies he has ever stumbled upon.

The Antofagasta (Chile) and Bolivia Railway Co. Ltd belonged to the stable of Sir Denys Lowson, a former Lord Mayor of London and a noted financier, who had interests in companies spanning the British Empire. At about the time Brierley moved in on the company, Sir Denys was accused of defrauding his own company over a lengthy period. The emerging scandal added a piquancy to Antofagasta for Brierley, especially as Sir Denys was forced to sell his shares.

The company was a bargain. Its most distinctive asset was in South America, where it operated the highest railway in the world, running between Antofagasta, a south Chilean city, and La Paz, the capital of Bolivia. The railway was worth about £9 million and the company also had a £1.6 million portfolio of British shares. Brierley realised that the price of the shares was covered by Antofagasta's assets in London, so, effectively, the railway line came for nothing.

It was a steal, but no one would lend Brierley the £1 million necessary to secure Sir Denys's tranche. He said he scoured the world, but bankers were unable to understand how someone in Australia with a company in London would want to buy an operation in Chile.

'The Chilean thing was the last straw. I suppose I was asking for the equivalent of £100 million today, and the irony is that today I would have no trouble raising the money. The experience left me with a low opinion of the intelligence of bankers.

'In business you are either totally dedicated or not. Some are more than others. With me, there are no half-measures. So you can imagine how frustrated I was by my inability to raise £1 million. I had spelled it out in black and white and thought that surely someone would agree, but always I got that familiar blank look and sickly smile.

'My colleagues weren't exactly bursting with enthusiasm either, yet Antofagasta has been a very successful company over the past decade.'

In the end the Lowson shares were sold to another party, but Brierley refused to give in. He wanted involvement even if it was as a minority shareholder, and by 1978 he had 14 per cent of Antofagasta. Although he was unable to gain control, he did have the satisfaction of frustrating the intentions of the successful purchaser of Sir Denys's shares. Brierley then discovered that the board meetings of Antofagasta were conducted in Spanish, but his will to win was such that he promised to learn Spanish if he became a director.

Brierley later sold the shares for a considerable profit, but instead of being thrilled, it only reminded him how much larger the profit would have been had he been allowed to pursue his original intention.

The Antofagasta saga shows Brierley at his best. Identifying the unlikely, breaking down barriers that appear impenetrable and overcoming obstacles others would have baulked at long ago is unquestionably his forté.

Best of all, from Brierley's point of view, it was a solitary pursuit. He did not require the assistance of anyone, and he was answerable only to himself. Such glorious freedom was a quality of life Brierley was finding increasingly rare. He noted despondently that as the company grew, so did his obligations and, worse still, so did the public's annual expectations. He would have been even more dismayed if anyone had told him then that from the vantage point of the 1980s, the '70s would look very sweet indeed.

ELEVEN

A Millionaire and His Money

BY THE MID-1970s Ron Brierley had reached the pinnacle of the Island Bay Five's ambitions. The occasion was greeted with little fuss, although he did tell his friend Peter Heginbotham in an aside during dinner one evening: 'You know, Peter, I think I'm just about a millionaire.' Then he finished his meal and went back to work. It was 11 p.m.

Clearly, money had not diverted Brierley from his *raison d'être*; he appeared to have set himself a task without an end, and he was almost always working. It left him very little time for anything else but essentials such as sleeping. His unswerving commitment to his work is undoubtedly one of the reasons for his success. BIL's current chairman, Bruce Hancox, once said that, given the hours Brierley puts into his business, he would have to be 'bloody thick' not to have succeeded.

The new-found wealth brought some obvious advantages. He no longer had to take the half-price midnight 'Starlight' flights with Don McDonald to Australia, he drove a good car and he lived in a reasonable hotel in Sydney. Yet he had no interest in having possessions. Not for him the mansion, rural estate, yacht, holiday home or art collection. He deliberately shunned the champagne lifestyle and opted instead for a much simpler existence. Furthermore, his tastes have never changed: he has always worn crocodile shoes, driven either a Jaguar or a Mercedes, eaten steak and chips whenever possible, and drunk red wine — the rougher and richer the better. He keeps a set of clothes in Sydney and Wellington for convenience and often eats out, having never learned to cook.

He has never had a desire to settle down, and he left the Crest Hotel in Sydney after more than a decade for a house in Elizabeth Bay only because IEL executives made him. They bought the house for him, but initially he refused to move in. Months later the executives cancelled his room at the Crest, and when he went to collect his key he was told there was no longer a vacancy for him.

His homes tend to be decorated motel-style — modern, ordered and anonymous. In his Wellington home there are a few personal touches, and these have usually been added by someone else. There are small nineteenth-century landscapes by the likes of Douglas Perrett and C. D. Barraud, an Italian clock and Italian leather table. In Australia, pictures bought to adorn the walls lay face down on the floor for years.

That is not to say that Brierley does not enjoy the things money can buy. He does not have an ascetic's attitude towards comfort and ownership, but he simply cannot be bothered with the hassles.

Bob Jones sees this as a manifestation of his tidy nature. He recalls telling Brierley one day in 1982 in a fit of despair and pique that he was packing up and going to live in Australia.

'He is not an emotional man and with the slight exception of extreme anger never becomes excitable, but he did on this occasion,' Jones says.

'A look of absolute horror spread across his face and, with more emotion than I have ever witnessed in him, he virtually appealed to me to come to my senses. "You will never match this house, these grounds, this view, anywhere in the world. Don't be absurd," and much more in this vein.

'My comments were a flash-in-the-pan gesture, but I was astonished by Ron's reaction. Then I realised that he had seen the fourteen acres of the wilderness when I bought it in the mid-'60s, he had watched the house grow over the year of its construction and in numerous visits had seen it gradually evolve into a home with paintings and furnishings and all the trappings, and its grounds develop over fifteen years to the state they are today. And throughout he had never once made any comment of praise or criticism.'

Brierley has, however, allowed himself one major extra-curricular indulgence — cricket. His love of the game is as constant as his commitment to business, and in the early days he played whenever he could. From 1954 to 1964 he played regular cricket for the Midland Cricket Club (now called Midland St Pats). He joined the club as a teenager, disappointed with the lack of coaching he was receiving at school. He was a serious, if unspectacular, player and he accompanied the team on several tours in the districts surrounding Wellington. The club's records show his highest score was 97, while one year he took 45 wickets to win the Duthie Cup for the most improved bowler of the season.

Brierley was the club's treasurer from 1955 to 1958, but he was voted out for not putting enough time into the job. Typically, Ron Brierley did not accept this judgment lightly. He spoke at the annual meeting and brought proxies to support his vote. The chairman was quite taken aback — such behaviour was unheard of in the small cricket club. In any event Brierley lost the vote, although in 1984 he was elected president.

As Brierley's spare time dwindled and his fortune grew, his interest gradually shifted from playing the game to watching it, especially international games involving New Zealand. He rarely went on holiday, but when he did, as often as not the trip became a cricket-watching tour.

He started the practice in 1972 when he followed the New Zealand team to the West Indies, and it was on this tour his friendship with team members flourished; he was allowed into their dressing rooms and occasionally socialised with them. They were grateful for the support away from home, and there developed something of a symbiotic relationship between the businessman fan and the players. But wherever he was he kept working, usually rising at 4 a.m. to catch up on lost time. He told one of the players that, even as they slept or relaxed, he was working.

Unfortunately he missed the third, fourth and fifth tests. During that time the team was short of one player and was casting around for a stand-in. Had Brierley been there he might have had the chance to play for New Zealand, a missed opportunity he regrets with wry amusement. 'How could they pass me by?' he asks.

Brierley has, however, enjoyed helping with radio commentaries, although he takes a minimalist approach. Former New Zealand representative cricketer John Morrison remembers trying to draw Brierley out when the pair were commentating for television. 'There was recently a row between England and Pakistan over umpiring and I asked him while we were in the box about it. I said to him, "Ron, you've been all around the world and watched a lot of cricket. What do you think of this incident?" And he said, "Yes, John, I have been all around the world and seen a lot of international cricket. There are some good spots."'

Nevertheless, Morrison found that Brierley's sparse comments often summed up the game. 'Because he is analytical, a lot of his predictions are bloody sound. He has a gut feel for what might happen. He will say, "I get the feeling we'll win the toss and bat and lose four wickets before tea," and he is so often right. It's incredible.'

There is one aspect of cricket Brierley has thoroughly mastered.

Cricket statistics are his speciality and, should someone comment on a particular game, Brierley usually chips in with details about the weather and the players' performances.

As a cricketing purist, his passion is naturally five-day cricket. Test cricket has been likened to a gigantic game of chess, and it is no surprise that Brierley is also a keen chess player. He patiently savours the game as it unfolds day by day, analysing every element from the pitch and the weather to the players. His whole-hearted fascination with the strategies and tactics of cricket astonishes even cricket players.

Morrison, for instance, recalls getting a lift from Brierley in his flash red Mercedes. Morrison began looking for music to play and he spied a batch of cassettes. He could hardly believe his eyes. 'Hell, Ron,' he exclaimed, 'here I am looking for some music and all you've got is cassettes of cricket commentaries!'

The 1972 tour was the first of many cricket-watching holidays, and by the 1980s he was following the team wherever it played. These days an itinerary of the team's schedule and hotels it will stay in is sent to Brierley well before the tour begins.

Since the West Indies tour Brierley has become New Zealand cricket's most ardent fan and generous supporter. His financial backing of cricket began in the 1970s when the New Zealand Cricket Foundation was formed to develop cricket with a special emphasis on youth cricket.

In 1974 Brierley donated 4,400 BIL shares, worth $10,000, to the foundation. Those shares have provided the foundation with much of its income over the years. During the boom years of 1984 and 1985 it made $100,000 a year from the sale of BIL shares, and fortunately sold out before the crash of 1987. In addition, John Morrison worked for the foundation from 1975 to 1977 from the BIL office in Wellington, and Brierley is currently chairman of the foundation.

Brierley also personally assists players and at times has set up incentive schemes to reward them. He has even singled out a few cricketers for special assistance, such as John Wright, John Morrison and Martin Crowe. The arrangement is different for each player, but Martin Crowe receives fees for endorsing products by BIL subsidiaries. The subsidiaries are not forced to use Crowe, but he receives preferential treatment. The Ansett advertisements on television, when BIL owned a stake in the airline ('How come you've got a hot lunch?'), are an example of this patronage.

As the tentacles of his empire gradually extended overseas, Brierley developed an association with other cricket teams. He is now a trustee of the Sydney Cricket Ground in Australia, is well known at Lord's in London and was invited to the Lord's Bicentenary dinner in 1987. In 1988 he donated £100,000 to the Oval in London. Brierley is also a trustee of the new Bradman Museum in Sydney. So far, IEL has donated more than $400,000 to build the museum, and that contribution does not include the time and effort put in by IEL's executives. The name Ron Brierley is now well known and respected in cricketing circles all around the world.

Probably the only game he has continued to play regularly is chess. Although he was away often, the game could accommodate his absences. For example, he often played chess with IEL or BIL executives by telephone, dictating his next move during trans-Tasman business calls.

The introduction of computer chess added a whole new dimension to the game for someone with such short and fragmented periods of spare time. Brierley can now play chess whenever he feels like it, and he generally has a game set up at his home, often playing only one move a night.

Chess is not unlike business and cricket in the skills it demands. In all three pursuits it is the patience, plotting, order and intellectual rigour of the game that Brierley thrives on, though it has been said he is not an inspired player. Such criticism must be regarded with some caution, however, since the person who most often and most loudly derides Brierley's ability is his friend and rival Bob Jones.

Brierley and Jones first met at a party held by Colin Beyer in 1961. Jones says there was an immediate empathy between them and they retired to a corner exchanging anecdotes, 'confirming the realisation that we both felt anything was possible regardless of scale so long as it was logically based'.

Since then they have had a long love-hate relationship, and nothing brings out this polarity more than a game of chess. The Brierley-Jones chess matches are a comedy of opposites: Jones's blunderbuss approach, Brierley's pip-sqeak understatement; Jones's supercharged emotions pitched against Brierley's enigmatic indifference. It is a meeting of fire and ice, and those who have witnessed these games can never recall who was the better player. What they do remember is Brierley staring inscrutably at the board, a silent study in control, while Jones was busy trying to undermine him with a barrage of scorching remarks.

Brierley is probably one of the few people who are relatively immune to Jones's brand of sportsmanship; friends say this is because he doesn't care who wins. He will happily grant Jones points that don't matter to him and never publicly denies Jones's tales of one-upmanship, doubtless realising that if he did he would be inviting a slanging match that could last for years.

Despite Brierley's tact, however, Jones is responsible for a whole host of tales cataloguing Brierley's general incompetence. For instance, Jones's version of Brierley's chess ability begins by conceding that up until 1972 or 1973 Brierley used to win all their games. But that changed as Jones improved, and when, for the first time, it appeared that Brierley was going to lose, Jones summoned everyone in the vicinity and crowed about his achievement. At that moment Brierley got up, mumbling the excuse that he needed a handkerchief, and deliberately knocked over the table. From that day he never won another match, says Jones, who sums up Brierley's Achilles heel thus: 'For all his obsession with the game he is strangely lacking in guile on the chessboard.'

Bob Jones also claims that he is a better tennis player than Brierley. He recalls that after one tennis defeat he suggested Brierley play chess with his girlfriend, presumably on the premise that even he could beat a woman. But, alas, his girlfriend won the game.

Jones is a competitive animal and his memories often have the good story-teller's touch of unreality and wish-fulfilment, but with Brierley, Jones's will to win takes on a new fanatical dimension. This is probably because Brierley is his only real rival. The pair started in business at the same time, at a similar age, faced the same prejudices and they were both confident they could attain any goal they set themselves. They were part of a tiny cadre of true believers who were convinced they were going to be rich and successful.

So if there is anyone Jones can measure himself against it is Brierley. Moreover, he knows that even if he is the better tennis and chess player, the public will only remember the business prowess of each individual. On that scale his position as champion is less secure.

Perhaps to compensate, Jones is often at pains to establish his historical superiority over Brierley. According to Jones, he has helped Brierley in business, lent him money, is richer and has had more impact on the New Zealand economy with the New Zealand Party than Brierley's business activities over thirty years.

The truth is less simple. In the early days Brierley was responsible for funding many of Jones's property deals. In 1966 they formed a joint venture called Brierley-Jones Investments Ltd with the aim of using Jones's expertise and Brierley's money in the property arena. Both were to receive 50 per cent of the capital gain. Brierley-Jones owned commercial properties in Lower Hutt, Hamilton, New Plymouth and Masterton, many of which were developed into shopping arcades.

According to BIL's property manager, Brian Bennett, Jones is fond of saying that Brierley knows nothing about property, but he remembers Brierley as an uninterested but astute observer.

In 1972, for instance, the company was responsible for building a shopping centre in Masterton called Centrepoint, which featured a 1970s design including circular windows, odd turrets and misshapen rooms. Bennett recalls Brierley telling them that Centrepoint should be bulldozed and they should start again on that site. Bennett disagreed; razing the brand-new $300,000 building to the ground seemed an extreme option. But as it turned out, the structure required constant maintenance and later, having spent some thousands of dollars on it, Bennett had to concede that obliterating Centrepoint would have been the cheaper option.

However, nothing better illustrates Jones's rivalry with Brierley than the circumstances surrounding the construction of Robt Jones House. BIL predominantly funded the building, although no one was allowed to know that. Jones included a secrecy clause in the agreement stipulating that if anyone from BIL revealed who was responsible for putting up the capital for Robt Jones House, they would be liable for a $10,000 fine. The agreement had a ten-year time limit.

Jones now says that he regrets the egoism that motivated him to name the building after himself, for it caused a lot of unnecessary resentment and ill-feeling. Brierley used to tease Jones by threatening to put an advertisement in the newspaper advising of the sale of his half of the building. But the agreement turned out to be no joke when BIL did want to sell its share.

Brierley and Hancox discovered to their dismay that under the agreement they could sell only the shares and not their half-interest in a building. Each project within Brierley-Jones was set up as a separate company, so the construction of Robt Jones House was done by Robt Jones House Ltd. That company owned the building, and Brierley and Jones owned half the shares in the company.

But Jones's presence as the other half-shareholder, the secrecy clause and naming rights represented a major impediment when it came to an orthodox valuation of the building. There was even a pre-emptive clause stating that Jones had the first right of refusal. The negotiations were long and drawn-out.

Most of the money in the company had been borrowed and guaranteed by BIL. But by the time Brierley wanted to sell, BIL and Jones had received about $1 million each from the refinancing of the building, so the final sale price needed to reflect this. In the end Jones paid BIL $1 million for BIL's half with payment deferred for a year. By that time the building was worth more than $8 million.

Jones even ventured into Australia in 1970 in a joint venture with IEL. They bought properties in Sydney and its surrounds, but four years later both parties decided it was time to unravel the alliance. Jones says he was already wealthy and looking for other challenges — writing and boxing — while BIL thought the venture had served its purpose.

Even the dissolution of the joint venture was cause for argument. This time, Jones says, it was done amicably. They agreed on the values of each building and then he and Trevor Beyer tossed a coin to see who would start the selection. After they had chosen a few buildings, they would check that the values were comparable. However, some within the BIL camp, like Brian Bennett, believed that Jones took the better properties while they were dumped with the likes of Centrepoint.

In spite of Jones's rivalry and splenetic comments, he actually betrays more warmth for his friend than Brierley could ever muster in return. When asked to write on Brierley for a book, he produced an affectionate, perceptive and humorous article, with none of the competitive condescension that usually blurs his judgment. In it he recounts his first meeting with Brierley and the grateful discovery that both shared a similar vision.

However, the real discovery, he says, was an identical, rather weird sense of humour. It was a rare find for Jones, who reckons he could count the number of people on one hand who also share it. It is characteristically droll, dry and cynical in flavour, particularly where human relationships are concerned.

'Brierley takes great amusement in sending people and relationships up with an enormously clever but always understated humour. A stranger might not even know he was doing it,' says Jones.

Others might describe Brierley's sense of humour as callous. After the sharemarket crash of 1987 one of his acquaintances lost a fortune, and Brierley was part of a group of friends when the tale of this unfortunate was revealed. Everyone chortled when they heard the saga of mishaps he had suffered, but Brierley's laughter went on and on until those present felt uncomfortable.

The two friends also delight in sending one another up by playing practical jokes. For as long as they have known one another there has been a continuing contest to embarrass the other, says Jones. It might be Brierley ringing Jones and announcing, 'Wilson here; Fraud

Squad,' or 'You don't know me. I'm a life insurance executive but we've got a lot in common and must get together.'

'New secretaries are blooded by the other leaving odd messages intended to embarrass. Probably I lose that battle because he is totally devoid of ego and really doesn't give a damn what anyone thinks of him,' recounts Jones.

'He would not, as you and I certainly would, feel the need to explain to a new secretary that it's really only a joke when she conveyed the message that the Fraud Squad is on its way or that the Official Assignee is seeking an appointment or of a cancellation of his booking at a massage parlour. Ron would simply thank the girl and chuckle quietly to himself.'

Although Jones rarely offends Brierley, one episode caused a good deal of confusion and anger among Brierley's associates. In 1977 Jones was part of a group of people who decided to support New Zealand's most well-known transvestite, Carmen, as a candidate for mayor of Wellington. Jones claims Carmen was chosen to illustrate their frustration at what they saw was excessive political meddling and regulation. They wanted a mayor who would do nothing, and the vacuous Carmen was perfect. Barry Swift, station manager of Radio Windy, was also a member of Carmen's campaign group, which was trying to organise an election stunt every day of the last week before the election.

Brierley happened to be in New Zealand for Trevor Beyer's wedding a few days before election week. After the ceremony and later that evening, Jones decided to rope him into the campaign. Brierley was sitting down viewing the goings-on through half-lidded eyes when Jones came and asked him for a favour: he wanted Brierley to take part in a prank where his engagement to Carmen would be announced but she would reject him in favour of an unfortunate-looking professional wrestler.

'At first Ron said no and I said, "Don't be an arsehole. You'll be seen to be a sport." Ron then said, "What day is it planned for again?" I said Wednesday and he said, "What time will this radio station ring me?" Between nine and ten o'clock in the morning, I told him. All of a sudden he said, "All right then."'

Brierley had already worked out that he would be in Adelaide, not Sydney, on Wednesday morning and so he was happy to agree, knowing they would not be able to contact him on that day.

On Monday, 3 October 1977, a full-page advertisement headed 'Citizens for Carmen' appeared in the *Dominion* with the endorsement of a list of prominent citizens, often with their names slightly misspelt. For instance, R. A. Brierley became R. I. Brierley. Naturally some of those named were none too pleased and Tuesday's newspaper was full of retractions, which put an end to further advertisements for Carmen.

Her campaign committee then decided to bring forward the date of the engagement prank to Tuesday. On that day Brierley was in Sydney and, to his dismay, Radio Windy succeeded in contacting him. A resigned Brierley went along with the spoof.

Yes, Brierley told Barry Swift live on air, he was engaged to Carmen. He had bought her a ruby ring — which just showed his ignorance, says Jones; it should have been diamonds. Would Carmen go on the BIL board? Probably, and as for children, well, it was too early to say. He would be talking to Carmen about that.

The arrangement, according to Jones, was that they would play the taped interview at half-hour intervals for a couple of hours only. But when it went on air the response at BIL was more dramatic than anyone imagined. Bruce Judge, then general manager of BIL, was furious. Other BIL directors were also upset and there was talk of resignations.

Jones said Judge then verbally savaged Barry Swift on the telephone, and a BIL employee was sent to research the Radio Windy register in an attempt to unsettle them. He says Swift was subjected to so much abuse he retaliated by playing the tape every fifteen minutes and for much longer than originally agreed. Both Carmen and Jones remember that Swift actually became so overwrought by the events he had to be sent home.

Brierley meanwhile was hiding in Sydney, fending off calls from angry directors asking him what on earth made him agree to the interview. The only person really enjoying the fun was Carmen.

It's hard to believe the incident sparked such a reaction from BIL. It was plainly a joke, but the BIL executives were wary of the public's reaction. Ron Brierley was forty years old, wealthy, unmarried and rarely seen in public with women. Speculation about his sexuality was inevitable, and BIL people had often been at pains to deny the popular assumption that he was a homosexual. They feared their denials might sound a trifle hollow when the man himself publicly admitted he intended to marry a transvestite.

The Carmen fiasco has largely been erased from public memory, but Brierley seems to be the subject of persistent rumours. A recent one links him with a particular cricketer. Brierley dismisses this rumour, though he finds it rather humorous. In fact, Ron Brierley has had many young and attractive girlfriends. He generally treats them with a courtly, polite detachment, yet he has sustained long friendships with a number of these women.

The first and most important relationship he had was with a New Zealand woman, Sylvia Olamani, who lived with him informally in Sydney. He was then in his early thirties and she was more than ten years younger. It was definitely a case of opposites attracting each other. Sylvia is brassy and vivacious and is remembered fondly for a certain blunt audacity. She is said to have greeted a prominent figure of the community at a party with, 'So you're the guy who's been staring at my cleavage all night.'

Although she and Ron had little in common, they got on well and the relationship lasted for some four years. Sylvia found he could be generous if prodded and her nickname for him was LB or BB — Lord Bountiful or Bountiful Benefactor. Even after the relationship broke up, he continued to buy her gifts, such as new cars, and paid for overseas holidays.

Since then the women have come and gone, making little impact on his life, which is exactly as he would wish it.

Typically, Ron Brierley has deliberately avoided any emotional commitments and he is not envious of people who are married and have children. On the contrary, he is rather pleased with himself for having avoided these traps, and if he hears a friend is going through a bitter divorce battle with disputes over the ownership of assets, he is likely to find this amusing rather than sad. Paul Collins always remembers Brierley's words on being told he was to marry: 'Well, naturally congratulations are in order, Paul, but of course you'll never make a great businessman now.'

Brierley regards a wife and family in the same light he views possessions — as a nuisance. They demand time, effort and commitment and prevent him giving himself wholeheartedly to his work.

It would appear that Brierley is incapable of feeling any strong emotion, even for friends he has known since childhood. They are fond of Brierley but know that he is limited to a kindly but pragmatic response to them. Yet it would be unfair to describe him as a bloodless and cold. At parties his reserve is easily melted with the aid of a little alcohol and he can become sweet and affectionate.

In psychological terms, Brierley is a narcissist. In the Greek myth, Narcissus was the beautiful young man who fell in love with his reflection in a pool and pined away before becoming the flower that bears his name. Psychologists use it to describe someone who is totally self-absorbed and displays an unshakeable certainty in their own judgment.

Part of the psychological signature of the narcissist is an inability to relate to people equal to themselves on a close emotional level. Narcissistic men may be reluctant to have a relationship with a grown woman because they fear she will demand too much of them and will want to intrude into their lives. Young women are preferred: they are less threatening and less likely to require commitment.

Brierley's closest emotional relationship is with his mother. Although he is notorious for ignoring women partners at parties and functions, he is attentive to May Brierley. He brings her small gifts, rings two or three times a week, visits several times a year and worries about her when she is ill.

She confirms that Brierley was an affectionate child and had no difficulty saying he loved her. He has continued to be faithful to that relationship, which, after all, is the only emotional tie that has ever mattered to him and has superseded any need for a marital bond.

Unlike some other businessmen, Brierley has never exhibited a strong sexual drive and he often jokingly complains that the truth about his private life is deadly dull. He is doubtless too busy to expend much energy on this pursuit except when he is on holiday.

Brierley has travelled frequently to Asia, mostly to Thailand. He often goes there to avoid family occasions such as Christmas, and it provides a perfect contrast for him. Most Western social and moral conventions are meaningless in Asia and, like many Western men, Brierley revels in the luxury of freedom run loose.

He enjoys encounters with young women, often teenage prostitutes, in Thailand, probably because they do not threaten his primary relationship with his mother and they also leave him free to pursue his central objective which is business. These sexually immature young women are not as demanding, physically or emotionally, as an older woman, who might want to develop the relationship further.

Brierley seems completely comfortable with this aspect of his life and showed no signs of embarrassment when teased about his frequent visits to Thailand. 'You know how I like to visit the Buddhist temples,' he told me with a knowing smile.

Brierley enjoys travelling, though his holiday destinations and style of travel have improved considerably since his first sojourns in Tauranga and thereabouts in the early 1960s. Then he slept in empty garages and ate fish and chips or baked beans for dinner. These days he travels first class to Europe or Asia and stays in good hotels.

He makes an amiable, if helpless, travelling companion, for he usually abdicates control to the person he is with and they soon learn there are things Ron must be shielded from, especially discomfort.

'Ron gets upset very easily,' his friend Alan Perry says. 'Once when we were in the Nevada desert he kept getting sand in his eyes and became very distressed. The sand was getting under his contact lenses and he almost closed up as a result.

'Another time we went with Bob Seldon to Haiti on Bob Jones's recommendation. We stayed in the Grand Hotel there, which Ron always said was not very grand. It was pretty ramshackle. We went to our respective rooms and arranged to meet in the bar. When Ron came to the bar later, he was semi-naked, covered in soap and really upset. He told me, "The bloody water's gone off again, Perry." He couldn't handle that. To him it wasn't a joke. It was distressing.'

Brierley has also travelled extensively in Europe, usually by Eurail, stopping where and when he feels like it. He once owned twenty-seven hectares of a Spanish peasant farm with Bill Hallam-Eames and two others. Now he owns a holiday home with a friend in Mackeral Bay, twenty kilometres north of Sydney. He loves the privacy there, which is accentuated by the fact that his house can only be reached by boat.

But his friends all say that one of the most remarkable things about holidaying with Ron Brierley is his memory for detail. Perry says that in all their travels together Brierley can still recall what airline they flew on, the flight number and where they sat on the plane.

He recalls an exchange at a dinner recently: 'Ron said to me, "Perry boy, have you ever seen a play called *How to Make Money Without Really Trying?*" and I said no. He said, "Are you sure?" and since I couldn't think of it, I said no again. Then he said, "It was 22 November, the day President Kennedy was assassinated and we were in Melbourne that year, 1963. We went to see this play the night he was assassinated."'

TWELVE

The Judge Factor

STOCK EXCHANGE LISTING and the creation of AMOIL in 1970 marked the beginning of a new era at Brierley Investments Ltd. The company had finally been accepted in New Zealand and for the first time was able to raise large sums of money. Investing at home had never been easier and was long overdue, for, apart from the Auckland operation run by Don McDonald, in the late 1960s Brierley had largely abandoned New Zealand in favour of Australia.

At the beginning of the 1970s BIL was in a better position than it had ever been. For years the company had consisted of nothing more than Brierley and a few support personnel, but now it had actually taken on some semblance of organisation for the first time.

In 1970 BIL appointed Peter Vere O'Brien as general manager. O'Brien had worked for the DFC in Australia, and Brierley knew him slightly when he asked him to run the company's office in Wellington. O'Brien, later to become known as a contributor to *National Business Review*, lasted as general manager for only eighteen months, when personality differences prompted his departure.

BIL then advertised in the local papers for a general manager, and the advertisement caught the eye of a young superintendent of investments at the Royal Insurance Company in Christchurch. Bruce Raymond Judge was twenty-eight years old with a background in insurance and a Bachelor of Commerce degree when he joined BIL in New Zealand in 1971.

Judge was born into a shop-keeping family. His father was a general store owner in Timaru and later Christchurch, and Judge maintained that he first began to understand business while working behind the counter with his father. The young Bruce Judge turned out to be a handsome lad, blessed with considerable sporting prowess and a good mind. In 1964 and 1968 he was selected to represent New Zealand as a hockey player at the Olympic Games, and he was also a fine tennis player, with a number of provincial awards under his belt. It is not surprising, therefore, that he became a charming, confident, well-liked adult.

But beneath the charm and bonhomie lurked a furiously ambitious individual who would let nothing stand in his way. He was fiercely competitive, tackling every task with a gusto bordering on aggression, and his impact on BIL was immense. Judge's double-tempo pace quickly catapulted the company into the public eye. As time wore on, Judge took more and more of the initiative, although officially he answered to the managing director, Trevor Beyer.

Judge's takeover activities in BIL started with a small Hawke's Bay firm, Murtons Chemical Industries Ltd, which had produced arsenic-based weedkiller. Murtons was finally liquidated and Judge's BIL colleagues watched with admiration as he negotiated the redundancies. In what was to become regarded as a typical Judge operation, John Lawrey says he succeeded in making the employees feel happy to be laid off.

As a result of this move into Hawke's Bay, Selwyn Cushing, a chartered accountant, stockbroker and partner in the local firm Esam Cushing & Co., rang Judge with a proposal. Cushing's name was not new to the BIL organisation. They were already aware of his support for the unsecured deposit notes and knew he had been recommending BIL shares to his clients in Hawke's Bay. Cushing had great faith in the potential of BIL, so when he saw an opportunity to become more closely involved as well as to improve the performance of a company he was involved in, he was quick to take advantage of the situation.

Cushing was a 5 per cent shareholder in a private company called Asparagus Ltd, which did not grow asparagus but owned some 100 hectares of land growing fruit and vegetables between Havelock North and Hastings. The company had recorded a loss for two years and most shareholders were dissatisfied with the management.

Supported by Cushing, BIL took over Asparagus Ltd, and for his pains Cushing was rewarded with an external directorship. The following years saw him applying the BIL philosophy to more sleepy companies. In 1975 he became a director of BIL, and in 1986 an executive director.

Cushing is a slight man with narrow eyes and aquiline features set in a square face, and his voice is distinctively slow and precise, marked by a heavy New Zealand accent. His background was in management accounting, and by the time he came to BIL he had established a successful practice and his firm had country membership of the stock exchange. He had strong links to the Hawke's Bay region, playing representative cricket and performing as first violinist with the regional orchestra. In 1983 he became president of the Hastings-based Eastern Central Savings Bank.

The number of Hawke's Bay shareholders in BIL swelled following Cushing's involvement, for he introduced a number of his clients to the company and was also instrumental in expanding the company's involvement in the area. There followed the takeover of Furnware Industries Ltd in 1973 and the sixty-five-year-old Hastings draper and soft furnisher Westerman & Co. Ltd in 1975.

Cushing worked closely with Judge on takeovers of small to medium-sized businesses that today look insignificant. For example, Asparagus Ltd cost BIL about $220,000 and its assets were valued at $298,000 in their annual report. BIL then had issued capital of $646,000, shareholders' funds of $2 million and $20 million of assets.

Nevertheless, Brierley shareholders had nothing to complain about. Anyone who bought $1,000 worth of BIL shares in 1962 could have sold them ten years later for more than $24,000. The only share that came close to BIL for performance was Property Securities, yet even its growth rate was less than half that of BIL. Property Securities shares worth $1,000 in 1964, when the company first went public, were worth $9,870 in 1972.

Brierley's promise of rationalisation of industry in New Zealand was also being fulfilled. For example, because Furnware was seen to have a close affinity with steel and wire product manufacturer Cyclone Industries (NZ) Ltd, the trading assets of Cyclone were transferred to Furnware for a cash payment and shares, with Furnware retaining the properties.

Similarly, when BIL gained control of clothing firm Woolcraft-Klipper, it sold the Woolcraft operation, which became a success for its new owner, and ran Klipper as a subsidiary. The shell that remained of Woolcraft-Klipper then became the property firm City Realties Ltd.

In 1974 Brierley said in his annual report that this was a more difficult period than any other in the company's history. A year later he said the outlook for New Zealand had rarely been bleaker. The recorded profit of $1.3 million that year was satisfactory, but the company's growth rate had slowed considerably on previous years. That year's rate of 14.1 per cent did not compare favourably with 1974's at 49.6 per cent and 1973's at 24.8 per cent.

The major event of that year was the 47 per cent reverse takeover of Jas J. Niven and Co. Ltd, the Wellington-based engineering company. The reverse takeover was a relatively new strategy on the business scene. On this occasion Nivens bought all of the wholly owned BIL subsidiary Kidd Garrett Holdings Ltd, the Auckland-based engineers' merchant, through an issue of shares so that BIL's holding of 10 per cent of Nivens jumped to over 40 per cent. The reverse takeover was said to be done at a small loss to BIL, but since it had bought Kidd Garrett for $1.4 million and its stake in Nivens was worth $3 million, it hardly mattered.

BIL later added to its Nivens shareholding, using a similar strategy when it sold a 25 per cent stake in Wellington engineering company Richardson McCabe and Co. Ltd to Nivens.

Perhaps one of the more important acquisitions in the early 1970s was a 20 per cent stake in the Wellington Gas Company Ltd. Through Wellington Gas and further investments, BIL later emerged as a serious player in the gas industry in New Zealand. BIL used the cash flow of one gas company to take over the other. It was a politically sensitive strategy and had to be carefully executed. Many companies were bought for a third of their value. By 1987 Welgas, as the holding company was known, controlled Auckland Gas and East Coast gas interests. It had already closed down the Christchurch Gas Company at great profit to Welgas. Welgas was also active in oil and gas exploration.

Wellington Gas proved to harbour more than its fair share of undervalued assets. As well as the usual assortment of properties, plant and buildings, Wellington Gas introduced BIL to a bright trainee accountant called Paul Collins. Collins would later become the chief executive of BIL, but in the early 1970s he was in his late teens and just starting out.

It was at this time that BIL entered its most unpopular phase. It had always been loathed by some politicians, journalists, accountants and directors, but now it was being feared by ordinary citizens. As an agent of change often leading to company closure, BIL was viewed as a relentless juggernaut led by young, arrogant men looking for a fast buck.

Although it had taken on some form of organisational structure, BIL was still really just a collection of individuals, many of whom were still learning the ropes. They were opportunists, often inexperienced, and consequently mistakes were made. For example, Brian Bennett, a former pharmacist, was in charge of property, though he had no expertise in this field. He also helped run companies like Beath and Co., Medical Supplies and Mason Struthers, and he is the first to admit that he and others in BIL were mediocre managers.

BIL's reputation was particularly low in Christchurch, where the company's impact had been most strongly felt. In 1976 Bruce Judge set up a part-time office in his home town with Paul Collins and embarked on a programme of acquisition that left the Garden City feeling battered.

The antipathy toward BIL in Christchurch was understandable, for it seemed everything the company touched folded soon afterwards. Aulsebrooks, Cyclone, Beath and Co., Mason Struthers, E. E. Reece and the Christchurch Gas Company were all closed, and a feature in the local newspaper, the *Press*, titled 'Are Corporate Raiders Turning Chch Into "Brierley Ghost Town"?' summed up local concern. Although Judge was the BIL representative, everything that occurred in the BIL organisation was attributed to its founder, and so it was Brierley who was called the 'most hated man in Christchurch' by a former manager of a firm BIL rationalised. Another businessman called him a 'commercial pirate running rampant' in the city.

Brierley, however, was not so much running rampant as following a deliberate path he had mapped out some years earlier. He had come to Christchurch years before, looked around at the department stores in the central shopping area and decided that the block was over-shopped. He saw the same articles in Beaths, DIC, Mason Struthers and E. E. Reece, and he decided that Christchurch was not buoyant enough to carry such a concentration of retailing in exactly the same lines.

Retailers seemed to have come to the same conclusion themselves. Beaths had actually been casting around for an alliance with another retailer when Brierley acquired its stores in 1976. Brierley had also noticed that DIC was poorly accommodated and sat next door to two Beaths properties. The day his bid for Beaths was declared unconditional he had already sold Beaths stores to DIC and New Zealand Farmers' Co-operative Association of Canterbury Ltd. In return, BIL gained a foothold in DIC, since the store DIC obtained was run by an independent board serving under Bruce Judge.

It was a large bid for its time. BIL was capitalised at $6.69 million and it was putting in a $2.14 million bid for the retailer.

Could Brierley be blamed for the redundancies that followed the DIC acquisition? Most of the other companies that folded were on the skids anyway, and where he was responsible for laying people off, Brierley said his company's involvement led to a much happier conclusion than would otherwise have been the case. He challenged anyone to compare six companies closed down by BIL with six that failed on their own account. In every case, he argued, staff would be better off with BIL.

Muldoon took a dimmer view. In 1977 BIL beat off British

company Thos Borthwick and Sons (A'asia) Ltd in a bid for Gear Meat Co. Ltd. Some regarded BIL as the local hero riding to the rescue of the small defenceless meat works, but when Muldoon announced the Government had rejected Borthwicks' proposal, he said the Brierley involvement was an 'adverse factor', adding, 'I don't look upon Mr Brierley as a philanthropist.'

While Muldoon respected Brierley's ability, he had always been sceptical of his benefits to the wider community. He knew that Brierley's central objective was to maximise the return to his company, and in his mind it did not follow that Brierley's involvement in an industry would necessarily be beneficial to anyone but Brierley.

Today Muldoon says, 'I never regarded his influence as making industry more efficient. His executive force was too small. BIL does not have dynamic management. Its expertise is in the area of organising takeovers, asset stripping and mergers and generally putting value into things that were undervalued.'

Borthwicks' offer was very generous. At $1.80 a share, it was $825,000 more than the company's sharemarket capitalisation (the shares were selling at $1.50). Shareholders lived to regret listening to the board's rejection of that offer.

With Borthwicks beaten off, BIL soon found itself with 50 per cent of the capital in a company plagued with financial and plant problems such as old buildings and hygiene requirements. So half the shareholding was sold to the Hawke's Bay Farmers' Meat Company Ltd. But that year the company posted a substantial loss, totalling $323,363, plus a further $205,000 relating to costs and expenses.

At the annual meeting in March the next year, angry shareholders criticised the directors for their 'misleading' advice to refuse the Borthwicks offer of $1.80. Gear shares were now worth only $1.

Two years later things had hardly improved and Brierley termed Gear's $4 million loss 'catastrophic'. The embarrassing figures were eventually hidden inside Huttons NZ Ltd.

By 1975 Bruce Judge had been appointed to the board. A thunderbolt of energy and ideas, he became impatient with those who moved at a slower pace or had the temerity to demand explanations of his activities, and he scathingly referred to those people as the non-performers. This amused Brierley, even though Judge was talking about his friends John Lawrey and Trevor Beyer.

Judge reserved a special disdain for Beyer. A heavily set man of Danish extraction, Beyer is credited with having a sharp mind but a more easy-going attitude to the demands of work than others. Although Beyer is not noted for his innovation and energy, his contribution to BIL has been to establish contacts and smooth the waters. When he became an executive director of BIL in 1971, Beyer had already been a partner in a substantial accounting practice in Wellington and was a member of the Wellesley Club. He represented the Establishment, and McDonald was so heartened by his proposed involvement in the company he decided that he, too, would become a director the same year.

But Beyer and Judge were like chalk and cheese, and although Judge complained Beyer plotted against him, the overwhelming view of other staff is that Judge, as the more highly charged, ambitious character, was keen to show Beyer in the poorest light possible. Judge, however, had more opportunities to turn the tables. Their discord coincided with Beyer experiencing marital difficulties, and as a result his energy for work was at a low ebb.

These were unhappy years of internecine warfare in the BIL headquarters in Wellington. Judge had his own camp followers, as did Beyer, and a few sat miserably on the fence. Both sides complained to Brierley, who acted as the father confessor. He listened, he nodded, but he did nothing. Later, people began to suspect that it suited him to have two warring factions keeping one another in check and at the same time keeping him well informed.

It was not until BIL became involved with AB Consolidated Holdings Ltd in 1976 that Brierley witnessed Judge's free-wheeling *modus operandi* first-hand.

AB Cons was well known for its biscuit and confectionery products, which included Aulsebrooks, Bycroft, Huntley and Palmers and Peek Frean biscuits, Rowntree Mackintosh chocolates and confectionery, Smiths potato crisps and Kelloggs cereals and flour. Its major trading activity was Aulsebrooks, with factories in Christchurch, Otahuhu and Makikihi (South Canterbury).

The company was formed the same year as BIL, in 1961, with the merger of Aulsebrook and Co. and Bycroft. But the benefits of the merger had never been realised, and in 1976 AB Cons shares were selling at about 33 cents when their net asset backing was $1.11. Profits had fallen from $368,000 in 1973 to $195,000 in 1975. In the first half of 1976 the company was facing a $240,000 loss.

Through BIL's involvement in Christchurch, Bruce Judge had got to know several of the directors on the AB Cons board. So when the Wellington-based flour milling and bakery group A. S. Paterson began bidding for AB Cons in April 1976, the board ran to BIL for assistance. The board feared that if Paterson acquired the company it might result in the break-up of AB Cons, with the biscuit-making activity going to the Australian biscuit giant Arnotts Ltd.

The first-come, first-served bid for 49 per cent of AB Cons at 50 cents a share by Paterson began in April, but by June BIL had 42 per cent of AB Cons, which it achieved by selling Asparagus Ltd for two million 50-cent shares in AB Cons. This left AB Cons directors with 8 per cent, UK-based Associated Biscuit Manufacturers with 7 per cent, Paterson with 26 per cent, Atlas Majestic with 2 per cent and the rest held by the public.

The BIL team spent the following weeks sweating, wondering whether Paterson would challenge their share allotment via Asparagus, and they could not believe their luck when this didn't happen. Paterson was locked in.

In the middle of all this drama Alex Paterson was the victim of a coup by executives Pat and Peter Goodman and Bob Gunn. This rarely happened in New Zealand, especially when the chairman was also the descendant of one of the founding families. Subsequently, the Goodmans bought enough shares to ensure control of the company, which they renamed the Goodman Group.

But the combined skills of Paterson and BIL could not save AB Cons, and although its profit in 1977 was $314,395, it was scarcely a satisfactory return on assets of over $21 million. It had not been idle that year, however. AB Cons had taken over NZ Coffee and Spice Co. Ltd, established a joint venture with George Weston Foods Ltd to own and operate a flourmill in Auckland, developed Big Apple Products Ltd at Havelock North and merged their South Island milling interests with Zealandia Milling Co. Ltd.

It became clear something had to be done about the unstable shareholding. No one was happy with the knowledge that either Paterson or BIL could rock the boat by selling their interests on the open market. So in 1977 Paterson and Brierley transferred their AB Cons shares to a new company called Food Holdings Ltd. BIL held 50.1 per cent of the capital of Food Holdings and A. S. Paterson had 49.9 per cent. Capitalisation of the new company was $2.5 million. A year later things were no better, with AB Cons showing a $1.79 million loss. The Aulsebrooks factory in Christchurch had also closed.

Brierley came to the conclusion that AB Cons' problems were tied up with the unresolved shareholding of the company, and so he entered into negotiations to buy Paterson's holding in the company.

One afternoon during those negotiations Brierley remembers delivering a particularly compelling speech on the merits of their proposal to both Bruce Judge and Paterson's representative, George

Shirtcliffe. He left convinced that his stunning oratory had won the day. To his 'horror and disbelief', the following morning he discovered that BIL was no longer buying Paterson's stake in AB Cons; instead, it was selling AB Cons shares to Paterson. The agreed plan was forgotten, his powerful words dismissed.

It appeared that overnight Bruce Judge had turned the tables, and it was not long before Brierley was also persuaded this was for the best. After all, Paterson was the food industry specialist and BIL stood to make several million dollars on the sale of their shares. Brierley's surprise switched quickly to admiration.

'It was an illustration of the eccentricities of the Bruce Judge era and shows the way Judge can be totally flexible in achieving the desired end,' he says. 'I still don't know whether the initial negotiations were a clever ploy aimed at selling our shares or whether he genuinely changed his mind between the evening and the next morning.'

Nevertheless, Brierley was relieved to be rid of AB Cons, for it had proved to be a costly investment and BIL now had more pressing problems. The company was currently embroiled in an even more expensive, uncertain investment — the battle for Kempthorne Prosser.

THIRTEEN

A Fertile Imagination

PETER FELS had no reason to be well disposed towards Ron Brierley. In 1960, as chairman of Hallensteins Ltd, Fels had endured his tart criticisms, both in print and in person, when Brierley and his company secretary, Alistair Hutchison, tried to get a seat on the Hallensteins board. In almost every sense of the word, Fels was an old-fashioned businessman. Conservative in approach and valuing the unspoken conventions of courtesy, he did not take too kindly to Brierley's tactics then.

But more than a decade after the Hallensteins debacle he found himself working with the Brierley team on the DIC board, where he was deputy chairman. Later he was involved in the BIL-owned City Realties and National Insurance joint venture. Fels was a director of National Insurance and subsequently became a director of City Realties.

As a result of these experiences his opinion of Brierley must have changed, for in 1977 he asked BIL to assist him in a takeover. Fels was then chairman of Kempthorne Prosser Ltd, a large fertiliser-manufacturing company with factories in Canterbury and Wanganui and bulk-storage facilities in Dunedin and Nelson. Kempthorne Prosser was also the country's biggest manufacturer of pills and other pharmaceuticals.

In addition, it held some 20 per cent of its only other major competitor in the South Island, Dominion Fertiliser Co. Ltd, and also had a seat on the board. Dominion was a highly profitable enterprise and, unlike KP, it had the strong support of farmers. What Fels was asking BIL to do was to assist KP in a takeover bid for Dominion Fertiliser.

From the outset, Brierley knew it would be a controversial bid, since farmers had strong views on the fertiliser industry. Attempts to establish a farmers' co-operative on two other occasions had failed because of a lack of funding and support, but the enthusiasm for the concept was still there. In addition, farmers had been unhappy with KP's service in recent years and felt its board, peopled as it was with city gents, had little understanding of or sympathy for their plight.

But when Fels asked Bruce Judge if BIL would hold shares for them and work with KP to take over Dominion Fertiliser, Brierley was delighted. He valued an association with such a huge, established and well-known organisation as KP. Neither would it hurt his reputation to develop a friendship with Peter Fels, whose links with the Dunedin aristocracy went back several generations. Fels' grandfather had founded Hallensteins and his great-grandfather had been on the board of KP almost a hundred years earlier.

The bid also fitted Brierley's criterion of an undervalued asset, since the bidding price was $3 and the net asset backing was closer to $4.75 per share. So BIL willingly took the shares on the understanding KP would buy them back at a certain date, and KP announced its takeover bid for Dominion Fertiliser on 25 July 1977.

Joining them was a third player in the market. The Auckland-based manufacturer New Zealand Farmers Fertiliser thought KP's bid for Dominion was a mistake and warned KP that farmer opposition could be destabilising for the industry. But KP ignored their pleas, so NZFF decided it ought to buy Dominion shares simply to strengthen its own position.

As expected, farmers were immediately galvanised into action, and just three weeks after KP had trumpeted its bid, three Federated Farmers branch presidents set up Ravensdown Fertiliser Co-operative, ostensibly intended to take over Dominion. They knew, however, that this bid was bound to fail given KP's shareholding in Dominion, and from the beginning they had something bigger in mind — taking over KP itself. But in the meantime they continued vigorously buying Dominion shares.

No one could have guessed then that BIL would soon be assisting the farmers to do exactly as NZFF had predicted. Exactly when Bruce Judge changed sides is unclear, though it is recorded that, only two days after KP announced its bid, Judge visited the Meat Board offices to discuss Federated Farmers' plans. With him was Peter Elworthy, a Federated Farmers representative and soon to be chairman of Ravensdown.

Initially Elworthy had been swayed by KP's argument that greater efficiencies would result from a South Island monopoly, but at a later meeting, when the KP representative failed to produce information Elworthy had requested, he realised KP's first commitment was to the company, not farmers.

Elworthy's support for Ravensdown surprised some in his circle who insinuated he was betraying his heritage, since the young farmer hailed from a well-known South Canterbury farming family. Elworthy had already shown himself to be an able farmer in his own right. He pioneered deer farming in New Zealand, converting a harsh South Canterbury landscape into a huge, lush deer farm and was awarded a scholarship to Britain for his efforts. He was also well connected to the National Party through his younger brother Jonathon, MP for Waitaki, and he had already won the enthusiastic support of the Minister of Agriculture, Duncan MacIntyre.

So far the biggest stumbling block he had encountered with Ravensdown was finance. The sort of support the co-operative needed could only come from the corporate sector, from a group like BIL in fact. After being turned down by other corporate giants, Elworthy and his colleague, Federated Farmers president Alan Wright, decided they had nothing to lose by talking to BIL, so they contacted Bruce Judge. To their surprise, Judge proved to be a receptive, alert listener. He was quick to grasp the merits of the argument that the fertiliser industry should be farmer-controlled because farmers were the sole users of the product, and he liked the idea of helping them to take over KP.

Judge's conversion was whole-hearted. By the time BIL's Dominion shares were to be sold back to KP, Judge was backing Ravensdown. Selwyn Cushing well remembers the pressure Judge put on BIL staff to keep the Dominion shares intended for KP. Cushing shakes his head in wonder when he recalls those days. 'Judge turned turtle on Fels. Of that there is no doubt.'

Naturally Fels was extremely distressed by Judge's betrayal. He was a patrician. He thought good manners and capitalism need not be mutually exclusive, and in his experience the behaviour of the corporate sector generally confirmed this opinion. So he was unprepared for someone as insincere as Bruce Judge and was deeply hurt by the turn of events. After Judge's about-face, he refused to deal with him and also resigned from the board of City Realties.

Brierley was also upset by Judge's change of heart. He listened doubtfully to Judge's fervent endorsement of the farmers' co-operative. In his experience co-operatives had inherent drawbacks. He believed they were often pressured by their members to make emotional rather than business-like decisions. Besides, he had hoped to establish a cordial relationship with KP, so he was horrified to discover BIL had switched allegiance.

Meanwhile the market for Dominion shares was running hot. NZFF had launched a bid of $3.60, sixty cents higher than KP's price, and in retaliation, on 22 August, Ravensdown announced its intention to take over Dominion at a high $4.25 per share.

The market watched the spiralling prices closely, and *National Business Review* called the battle one of the highlights of the decade. Ravensdown got to 50 per cent of Dominion by late August, but then KP came in with a cash-and-share offer: $3 in cash for each Dominion share and one ordinary KP share, equalling $4.60.

Ravensdown was beaten. It had failed to marshal the necessary 60 per cent shareholding in Dominion in order for the company to be classified as a co-operative and qualify for taxation benefits and it bailed out — but not before it had won a concession that would eventually become KP's Achilles heel. KP had agreed to introduce a fertiliser rebate scheme for farmer shareholders and, swayed by Ravensdown's arguments that farmers' eagerness to become shareholders would drive the price beyond reach, it let Ravensdown buy a large parcel of KP shares to distribute to farmers as rebate-earning shares. This would give the farmers 17.87 per cent of KP.

Ravensdown knew even as it was putting this into place that it intended to bid for KP, with BIL's help of course. Together they had come up with a plan to finance the bid which was audacious, risky and, should it ever become public, political dynamite. The scheme centred on funds held by the Meat Board. Officially the money could not be released without the Minister of Finance's approval. But unofficially the Meat Board had deposited $1.5 million from its various reserve accounts with the ANZ bank, which then lent $1.5 million to Ravensdown, guaranteed by BIL, who also paid the interest.

This arrangement was crucial because a credit squeeze at that time meant BIL would have had extreme difficulty raising money elsewhere. It was also 'pretty radical stuff', as Brierley was quick to admit. The arrangement was little more than a legal — though questionable — way of laundering semi-public money to eliminate an historic commercial enterprise and, had it been exposed for what it was, it would have brought the house down in Parliament. Even without knowing this, the takeover became, as one Cabinet minister put it, 'a hell of a dilemma' for the Government.

In 1977 the National Party was in power and looking forward to its traditional votes from both the farming and business sectors for the 1978 election. But support goes both ways, and when the farmers' co-operative bid for a commercial enterprise that year, both parties expected the National Government to rally behind them.

Fels, as divisional chairman of the Otago-Southland branch of the party and former vice-president of the National Party for three years, had every reason to expect the Government's loyalty. In addition he and his board represented the spirit of free enterprise, something the National Party was generally keen to be associated with. Fels let them know that, to satisfy KP, all the Government had to do was refuse the use of producer board funds and urge certain key ministers to make life difficult for the co-operative.

But the Ravensdown directors also believed they deserved the sympathetic ear of the Government. After all, it was said often enough that it was the farmers who put National in power. On top of that, they had their own political contacts through Jonathon Elworthy.

Even Bruce Judge was convinced he had the Government on his side. In a letter to the ANZ bank he stated that Duncan MacIntyre had assured him of Cabinet's approval. In fact the Cabinet had never discussed the matter, as it was not yet a matter requiring Cabinet approval.

Ravensdown's first-come, first-served bid of $2 for KP on 14 October got off to a promising start. A flood of shares was offered to Ravensdown, which was able to snap up 1.6 million shares in 48 hours. That, with BIL's holding of 200,000 shares, acquired after accepting KP's cash and share offer for Dominion, took Ravensdown to 42 per cent of KP. But KP's ally, NZFF, also held a large slice of the total holding of six million shares and the co-operative needed 60 per cent to succeed.

Meanwhile the young accountant Paul Collins was working closely with Judge on the takeover. If Bruce Judge was the sorcerer, spinning off ideas and persuasive incantations, Paul Collins was the sorcerer's apprentice. He wielded the broom, swept up the lost details and tidied the loose ends.

He worked tirelessly on Ravensdown and estimates he put together fifty-five different proposals during the entire KP drama. Whenever Brierley appeared from Australia to discuss the issue, he would always ask in a voice bristling with cynicism, 'What version is this — number 943?'

Throughout November, Collins and Ravensdown hammered out an agreement to put to KP at the end of that month. The agreement involved BIL buying Ravensdown's KP shares and then selling KP's fertiliser division back to Ravensdown. Ravensdown would convert this into a farmer co-operative, using producer board funds to repay BIL. This way KP would retain its identity and remain Dunedin-based, for, other than BIL board representation, there would be no other changes.

However, a letter written by Bruce Judge to Peter Fels, dated 8 November, painted a far grander picture. Now recognised as a classic example of Judge's stream-of-consciousness technique, the letter was later released to the news media. In his defence, Judge claims that Fels asked him to write the letter and then conned him by making it public.

Judge's letter began promisingly enough with suggestions to restructure KP to capture the tax benefits of a co-operative. This entailed Dominion becoming a co-operative and owning KP's South Island fertiliser interests, though the head office would stay with KP. All assets and earnings would also stay with KP, while Dominion could pay for future capital expenditure out of pre-tax profits. This could mean a greatly increased capital investment for KP at the expense only of the Inland Revenue Department, wrote Judge. He even offered personnel to assist the company in a rationalisation of the pharmaceutical industry.

But then Judge's thoughts spilled over into an elaborate master plan. He offered control of not one but two companies to KP — Printing and Packaging Corporation Ltd and Allied Press Ltd. He said BIL had a key holding in Printing and Packaging (20 per cent in fact). Once that was acquired, he suggested, KP could sell its surplus property assets and franchise key retail operations to pay for the investment. A similar technique was suggested to acquire Allied Press, which owned the *Otago Daily Times*. Sale of its surplus assets could leave KP with the Dunedin papers and enough money in the kitty to snare the rest of Printpac. Judge even provided KP with a draft press release outlining these proposals.

In hindsight, Judge's plan was probably feasible and might have ensured KP's existence. As it turned out, both Printpac and Allied Press were later taken over; BIL got Printpac and took a cut from another company's takeover of Allied Press.

But KP was incensed by the letter, and when Allied Press and Printpac read about Judge's plans in the news media they were deeply affronted. Not surprisingly, the letter damaged BIL's relations with both companies for some time and made life difficult for Elworthy, who was already having trouble justifying BIL's involvement to farmers. Now they were asking him, 'What do you want to get involved with people like this for?'

Elworthy's faith in his business colleagues, however, was unwavering, although at no time in Ravensdown's association with BIL was anything put on paper. He took the company entirely on trust, and his own credibility and reputation depended on its support. He often had occasion to think of Bruce Judge's words of comfort at their first meeting. At that time BIL was reviled by the business community and it was only natural that Alan Wright should have asked Judge hesitantly, 'You'll play this with a straight bat, won't you?' Judge had laughed. 'Yes, of course. BIL always plays with a straight bat,' he said.

Even after the publication of Judge's letter, Elworthy was confident BIL would not let him down. 'I wasn't as concerned as you might think by things like this because I saw Ron Brierley with his steadfastness and conservatism and Judge with his mercurial tongue and personality and action and Collins doing the homework. They seemed to balance one another. I can remember saying I thought those three were a good combination.'

But the steadfast Brierley did not feel particularly in control and soon found himself making yet another reluctant decision. On 29 November, through a sharebroker acting for KP, Brierley learned KP was about to put a defensive arrangement in place with NZFF that afternoon.

So although Brierley believed it was 'grossly premature', that same day BIL announced its intention to bid for the balance of the capital already held — some $13 million. By then BIL had some three million shares and it was bidding for the 3.5 million outstanding shares.

Brierley read the *Dominion* billboard's headline 'Takeover Wizard Waves $13m Wand' with a sickening sense of not being completely in control. It was as if he was on a roller-coaster ride with someone else's hands on the wheel. He realised how ridiculous his desire had been to keep things low-key. Bruce Judge, the farmers' clout, private enterprise pride and possible political embarrassment were a potent brew and unlikely to simmer on the back burner for long.

The $13 million takeover was the biggest cash takeover offer in New Zealand's history. By today's standards $13 million is not a large sum, but Brierley estimates that it would be the equivalent of over a billion dollars in 1990. The risk was enormous and, as always in a high-risk play, the potential gains were huge, as were the potential losses.

All this took place the same week as BIL's 1977 annual general meeting, so the company came under further scrutiny. The profit of $2.3 million was 33 per cent higher than the previous year's but below expectations, and Brierley would later admit that the KP takeover had been a major reason for that. Furthermore, with the AB Cons problems in the background, the KP affair also meant the company was unable to take on any other opportunities that year.

Financial commentators were also concerned. They knew raising a loan in New Zealand at that time was extraordinarily difficult and wanted to know where the money for the takeover was coming from. Brierley's reply was typically veiled and wry. 'You'd be surprised where the money is coming from,' he said.

As expected, on the same day KP issued new shares to NZFF and negated BIL's offer. In what amounted to a share swap, KP and NZFF had acquired 2.2 million shares in each other, which effectively watered down KP's issued capital. Ravensdown's share diminished from 40 per cent to just 30 per cent, a long way from the magic 60 per cent.

But the takeover offer had legal benefits for BIL, who could now argue the swap was done to prevent a takeover and so legal proceedings were initiated immediately. Both BIL and Ravensdown placed interim injunctions on KP and NZFF restricting their activities (though the courts also placed similar restrictions on the applicants), but the most disturbing development was that the directors of NZFF and KP suddenly found themselves facing a writ for $1 million each, issued by BIL, accusing them of damaging shareholders' interests.

All the while Government officials were keeping a close eye on events and meeting frequently with producer boards and farmers' representatives. They had doubts about the benefits of a co-operative and thought Ravensdown had no clear plan of what to do with the company if it was successful. They also believed that producer board funds were not being distributed strictly in accordance with their statutory requirements.

Finally the Prime Minister's agricultural adviser, Jack McFaull, told his boss what he had learned. McFaull said Muldoon fixed a stern eye on him, jutted his jaw and barked, 'Get them in here.'

So by early December the Cabinet was aware that producer board funds were going to BIL via the ANZ. Cabinet minutes note that the Meat, Wool and Dairy Boards had each placed $1.5 million on deposit, with a later top-up of $500,000 each, making a total of $6 million.

Rumours about this arrangement had even reached the KP directors, who wrote to Muldoon, objecting to this practice. In Muldoon, at least, they had an ally. At the December Cabinet meeting he is reported to have said he believed Ron Brierley was a wheeler-dealer and therefore a dangerous element in the proceedings.

On 13 December, Muldoon told a delegation from the three producer boards and Federated Farmers he would have to refuse their proposal at that stage. It was clear from his comments that he was particularly uneasy about Brierley's involvement in the farming sector.

But Judge was ever-optimistic and never short of ideas on how to solve the mess. He seemed to be talking to anyone who would listen, and even KP director Tony Anderson had to admit some of his ideas had value: 'Judge was definitely playing both sides at the same time. Fels left all the talking to me because he wouldn't deal with Judge. Myself and Sid Smith had one session in the boardroom in which he offered to sell the fertiliser works to the farmers at a highly inflated price and convert KP into an investment company and swing all the money out of the deal from the farmers into KP. KP would be funded by other ventures that he had sorted out.

'I could see those ideas had some merit and I put this proposition to the board and got nowhere at all.'

Dryden Spring, from the NZFF board, also remembers Judge's capacity for capturing an audience: 'He talked the whole time. He was always trying out ideas on you to see what registered. I could see he was really an opportunist, not a clear strategic thinker. In the end it was Collins who put it all together for BIL and Ravensdown, and I was impressed by him.'

Although Fels refused to meet Judge, he was still on good terms with Brierley and received him warmly when Brierley flew to Dunedin for the first time in almost twenty years to put his case. But he was no more receptive to Brierley's plans than he had ever been. Despite the efforts of Brierley and others, KP was intransigent: it would never give up its fertiliser division to any co-operative nor shed its pharmaceutical division to BIL.

So on 30 March 1978 Peter Elworthy announced that Ravensdown would make a $20 million cash bid for KP on 10 April. What became known as the 'gumboot takeover' had begun in earnest.

Ravensdown already had 2,600 farmer shareholders, but the co-operative needed the financial support of at least 8,000 farmers. The only way to get them in quickly was to go out and canvas virtually door to door. So, armed with briefing sheets, NZFF officials talked to farmers at woolshed meetings, branch meetings, country clubs and over the fence with neighbours. By avoiding brokers, Ravensdown could pay the equivalent brokerage to the federation as a contribution.

The South Island was sympathetic, but in the North their hopes came close to being dashed. Many farmers were sceptical about co-operatives, and bad publicity had dampened any enthusiasm. The proportion of shareholders in the Wanganui-Rangitikei and Manawatu districts was only 3.5 per cent.

To bolster support, Collins and other BIL staff spent two weeks there on an intensive speaking campaign which brought the figure up to 7.5 per cent. Collins, then only twenty-five years old, remembers that at 8 a.m. he would be in a woolshed talking to up to thirty cynical farmers. They knew full well there had to be something in it for BIL and they wondered whether they would benefit from it at all after the company took its cut. The farmers were not easily persuaded and Collins was exhausted after each day's interrogation.

The exercise also alerted the Justice Department, which began investigating allegations that Collins had been share-hawking, but nothing came of this.

KP came under farmer scrutiny as well. In April farmers stacked the meeting planned to approve the share swap with NZFF. Busloads of farmers attended; some of those who climbed on board had been waiting at their farm gate as early as 4 a.m. So many turned up, KP had to move the meeting to bigger premises. The share swap was duly approved, but farmer dissatisfaction with their current KP rebate scheme, compared with Ravensdown's projections, was obvious.

Meanwhile, through the discovery process in the legal proceedings, KP had got hold of Judge's letter to the ANZ. The letter was quickly dispatched to Parliament, where it caused alarm and an abrupt cooling of support for Ravensdown.

Muldoon was furious. He knew that if the matter went to court several ministers would have to report their involvement under oath. In an election year these revelations could have sent seismic convulsions throughout the country. As soon as Muldoon read the letter he rang Brierley.

'Muldoon was rather agitated and he gave me chapter and verse as to this letter. He had checked his diary and the recollection of his colleagues and found Judge's claims were not supported by the facts. He told me he was very dissatisfied with the whole affair,' says Brierley.

Brierley, still cast in the role of the worried uncle, accepted Muldoon's criticisms and agreed the letter was a disaster.

'If he did give his blessing, it was stupid of Judge to make any claim in writing, and if there was no substance to it, then it was unthinkable to write the letter. It was vintage Bruce Judge — unnecessary overkill and exaggerated claims,' he says.

Brierley flew to London that day and on the flight he mulled over what he could do to minimise the damage. By the time he arrived he had made up his mind. He telexed Muldoon immediately and told him that if it became a public issue he would take full responsibility and deny any suggestion that Muldoon or any other Government minister had any involvement whatsoever. Later, McDonald arranged a dinner between the two men so Brierley could apologise to the Prime Minister for what had happened.

Shortly after the release of Judge's letter, Brierley and Peter Elworthy visited Muldoon to request the release of the producer board money. Instead, Muldoon told Elworthy that his prospectus was outside the law, though he would not reveal how, and warned him the penalty could be imprisonment or a heavy fine.

While both Elworthy and Brierley regarded his technical objection as a stalling tactic, Brierley was utterly disheartened. For him it was the lowest point in the whole Ravensdown battle. He told Elworthy he felt sure they would never get the money.

'There was no upside for Muldoon to bless anything and it would only confirm the outrageous claim that Bruce Judge had made earlier. I was very depressed about the whole thing.'

But Elworthy's political antennae were sending him more heartening signals. When Brierley had finished his gloomy outpouring, Elworthy said, 'Don't worry, Ron, all is not lost. I know more about politics than you do and I think farmers are bringing enormous pressure to bear.'

So they were. National Party canvassers in the provinces were told in no uncertain terms there would be no farmer money to fund the election campaign until the Government approved funds for Ravensdown. MPs also heard how their chances of re-election looked shaky if Ravensdown failed, and Mid-Canterbury farmers even told the party canvassing would not start until the issue had been resolved.

Meanwhile Ravensdown continued to mop up KP shares, and on 20 August the co-operative triumphantly declared the offer unconditional since it had more than 50 per cent of the shares.

The negotiations that followed were described by those present as 'torrid'. Collins, acting for Ravensdown, proved to be a tough, aggressive negotiator, a quality that won both admiration and alarm. KP's negotiating strength was negligible now that it was virtually owned by NZFF and Ravensdown, so it relied on its old friend NZFF to secure whatever it could on KP's behalf.

After days of heated discussion it was agreed that Ravensdown and BIL would sell their KP shares to NZFF. KP would then become a wholly owned subsidiary of NZFF. KP's fertiliser division was to become a co-operative with 60 per cent ownership by Ravensdown and the remainder by NZFF, who would also contribute financial expertise and management. NZFF was left with the pharmaceutical side of the business, including the former BIL company Medical Supplies Ltd. The entire acquisition would cost about $20 million.

Finally, by law, the remaining stake in NZFF, formerly owned by KP, had to be sold on the market. NZFF saw to it that those shares went to Auckland and Taranaki farmers, which helped foster its relationship with that community.

NZFF was pleased with the outcome. As former managing director of NZFF Peter Riddell puts it, it was better to have 40 per cent of a co-operative than 50 per cent of an ordinary company. 'It's just possible that might have been in the back of our minds all along,' he said.

The farmers were obviously happy. For less than $8 million they had control of fertiliser manufacturing plants at Dunedin, Hornby, Wanganui and Seadown, plus mixing stores at Nelson, Burnside, McNab and bulk depots at Taihape, Rakaia, Tinwald, Millers Flat, Invertiel and Clinton.

However, no one was probably more pleased than the Prime Minister, Robert Muldoon, who finally signed the agreement at the end of August.

For its part, BIL was at last reaping some of the benefits of the high-risk, troubled takeover. Despite their initial misgivings, farmers realised that BIL had been the most exposed party in the whole proceedings. It was no risk to the producer boards to arrange a back-to-back loan with the ANZ, and the bank had BIL's KP shares as security. BIL bore the greatest risk, and the longer the drama took, the more expensive it became. But in the end it won the company credibility and a cash profit of almost $2 million.

Only KP directors felt they had little to crow about. It was clear that in the early days they had vastly underestimated the political implications of their actions, and now their unwillingness to compromise meant their company had been dismembered.

Fels did not see it that way, however. At a meeting with NZFF's chairman, Charles Crookes, Fels was said to have told a story concerning a boat that left harbour and got into trouble. A rescue boat came out to save it but instead knocked it on the head and gathered it in as a trophy.

Today, farmers own all of Ravensdown, which is now called Agfert and is a highly efficient, profitable operation. NZFF became a subsidiary of Fernz, and BIL's holding in that company was sold in October 1987 for just over $2 a share. Brierley was said to be bitterly disappointed by the decision to sell. Perhaps he knew the share price was going to soar to $7 just over a year later.

Brierley at an annual meeting in the late 1970s
Fourth Estate

Rodney Price

Russell Goward

Paul Collins

Bruce Hancox

Bill Loewenthal (left) with Brierley at IEL's offices

IEL staff sharing a joke. Seated behind the desk is Alan Rector, in front of him is Peter Pedley and standing from left are Graeme Cureton, Kevin Mooney, Dr Gary Weiss and Sandra Bayliss

Holidaying in Fiji but still keeping in touch with the news

BIL directors in 1984. Standing at the back from left are Bruce Judge, Paul Collins, Trevor Beyer, Ray Robinson (secretary). Seated from left are Don McDonald, Ron Brierley, Bruce Hancox. Seated by the window are Selwyn Cushing and David Chalmers

FOURTEEN

The Last Straw

THE FORCES WITHIN BIL were by now marshalling against Bruce Judge. Those who had been uncertain, and even those who considered themselves his good friends, began to realise that his incandescent brilliance went hand in hand with a dangerous unpredictability.

Some, like Brian Bennett, BIL's property manager, learned first-hand what it was like to be on the losing end of a Judge deal. Bennett was a shareholder in a company called City and Provincial Properties Ltd that owned about a dozen properties throughout the country. It was an extra-curricular activity, but Bennett was led to believe it would be absorbed into the BIL empire. Instead, the company drifted and none of the shareholders knew what was happening. The shareholders contained some well-known names such as Ian Athfield, who says they all lost money — all except Bruce Judge, that is.

But this did not diminish his standing in Brierley's eyes. Judge seemed to cast a spell on Brierley. He was entranced by the man and he would always side with him, even if it meant snubbing his loyal lieutenants. For instance, some BIL staff remember how Judge's repeated criticisms of Trevor Beyer caused Brierley to stop communicating with Beyer for some time, such was the power of Judge in Brierley's imagination.

Bruce Judge was, after all, the antithesis of Ron Brierley. He was handsome, sporting and popular. He gave away large sums of money to charity and was apparently a devout Christian and respectable family man. He appeared to be the sort of hero seldom seen outside the pages of the *Reader's Digest*.

Brierley marvelled at his ability to keep everyone happy during the various stages of a deal, even though Judge frequently altered the terms. He remembered with wonder how Judge would say to the sceptics, 'I know it doesn't look good now, but wait until tomorrow,' and, more often than not, he was right. Unless you were Peter Fels, the Kempthorne Prosser-Ravensdown deal accommodated a variety of different interests.

Most of all, Brierley could not fail to admire Judge's fearlessness and creative energy. He embodied everything he had been fighting for all his life, and everyone who opposed Judge embodied every collectivist clod, bureaucrat or pessimist of microscopic vision that Brierley had ever kicked against. Judge was a can-do zealot in a world of be-careful bores.

With Judge there was a sense of limitless possibility. There was no problem that could not be solved, no opponent that could not be won over. Ideas flowed through him with all the charge and speed of electricity. The fact that he needed someone to tidy up the details and pin him down on commitments was conveniently overlooked.

Above all, Bruce Judge was the arch-persuader. According to his colleagues, Bruce Judge could sell condoms in a convent. He fairly glowed with pure intentions, personality and persuasive charm.

However, Bruce Judge also had less attractive qualities. His intense ambition caused a great deal of ill-feeling in BIL. He relentlessly attacked John Lawrey and Trevor Beyer, and it must have rankled with him that until about 1976 he was responsible to Beyer. After that they were put on an equal footing. The only advantage of such ugly jealousy was that Judge and Beyer kept a watchful eye on one another, and some people wondered if this secretly suited Brierley.

But while he made some enemies, Judge was also able to command a fierce loyalty from most of those who worked for him. Yet what was viewed at first as an astonishing mental agility came to be seen as unreliability. Colleagues also wondered how he could square his Christianity with some of his other activities. He was one of the berserk-after-work set and, if the stories are to be believed, his sexual exploits were as remarkable as his business achievements. During the KP drama, he fled with his mistress and Paul Collins to Fiji for a holiday. When the battle was over he rewarded himself with a repeat of the treat while his wife and four children stayed at home, yet Judge seemed to be genuinely unaware of his contradictory behaviour.

The entire Brierley team was mightily relieved when the KP deal was settled. While Brierley hailed it publicly as the anatomy of a takeover, the lingering memory for most was just how perilously close Judge had brought BIL to the brink of financial disaster. He had seriously overextended the company, offending Ron's own principle of the need for a minimum cash level.

As Cushing bluntly put it, KP pushed BIL as close as a gnat's what-not to collapse. What would have happened if they hadn't got the producer board money? 'Don't even think about it,' he says. Even

Brierley had to admit that it was not a question of if Bruce Judge would send them broke, but when.

Other incidents also contributed to the dwindling support for Judge. His boundless energy and capacity to have twenty irons in the fire at once meant that even during the KP fiasco he was off exploring new possibilities.

In 1977 he met merchant banker Frank Renouf in Singapore, where they attempted to arrange a meeting with the powerful Tan Sri Tan Chin Tuan. Tan Sri Tan was the chairman of Malayan Breweries and, more importantly, head of the Oversea-Chinese Banking Corporation in Singapore, which had assets of $1.56 billion. Malayan Breweries had begun to acquire shares in Lion Breweries Ltd (then called New Zealand Breweries) and it held shares with Lion in Leopard Breweries.

Judge was interested in Lion and had committed a rash of his ideas for the company to paper and sent them to Malayan Breweries chief executive Des Neill. He suggested Lion Breweries sell its share in Leopard to the public and sell a few of its breweries to Leopard.

Lion's hotels would also be sold and its aerated-water division hived off somewhere within the BIL empire. He talked of support from substantial European banks and a syndicate of New Zealand companies that controlled several million Lion shares. The result would be an influx of capital to Lion and board representation for BIL, which might go on to buy more than 50 per cent of the company.

Judge promised BIL's support would remain confidential for the time being and assured Malayan Breweries that discussions with senior Trade and Industry people had been most encouraging.

Judge and Renouf did not succeed in meeting Tan but spoke to his deputy, who was not enthusiastic. Once again Judge miscalculated his audience's response. Malayan Breweries was aware that as a foreign investor it was unwelcome in Lion anyway, and it did not want to be seen to be contributing to any instability. Although it had been buying shares heavily in recent months, it had no plans other than to regard Lion as an investment.

But it was Renouf who let the cat out of the bag when he told the Lion board that BIL was interested in becoming involved. The board, headed by Sir Clifford Plimmer, was a bastion of conservatism. In January 1978 Lion decided to form an anti-takeover vehicle called Androcles Corporation Ltd. Androcles was simply a paper company that held 50 million shares in Lion. Half these shares were held by Lion and the other half by Plimmer and another Lion director. The proposed issue of Lion shares to Androcles would give Androcles 27 per cent of the voting rights on the increased capital and would water down the interests of the Singapore group.

Selwyn Cushing, who had shares in Lion, took legal action for BIL in June 1978, challenging the validity of Lion's actions. BIL had no shares in Lion at the time, but, although it was interested in the company, BIL was more concerned about the use of paper companies to thwart hostile takeovers. If allowed to continue, this practice would seriously hinder BIL's activities. The business community was also outraged by Lion's defence strategy, and Androcles was eventually dismantled.

Some years after the incident, Ron Brierley visited Singapore and requested an audience with Tan Sri Tan. He was probably motivated by a mixture of awe and curiosity, for Brierley loves meeting the rich, famous or powerful. Tan had misgivings about the activities of BIL. After the unfortunate experience with Slater Walker in Singapore, asset strippers were poorly regarded, and Judge's letter ensured Brierley fell into that category.

But Tan agreed to meet Brierley and afterwards commented that he was not such a bad guy after all. Brierley was pleased with the meeting: 'I have met the great man at last,' he said contentedly.

But though this was an example of Judge's feverish intellect and ill-thought-through action, it did not herald the end of the Judge era. It was, in fact, a deal that never went ahead that would seal his fate.

In 1979 BIL had 20 per cent of Tappenden Industries Ltd, which owned an engineering business plus a series of General Motors franchises in Auckland. Bruce Judge devised a plan to sell the Tappenden shares to Ceramco, which was then making a takeover for the company. With that money he intended to buy back all the motor vehicle side, known as Tappenden Motors Ltd, at 60 per cent of the book asset backing.

Brierley was doubtful about the merits of the deal. It was another large plan involving some $13 million worth of assets with a property portfolio of $5 million, even though BIL was capitalised then at $38.9 million. He argued that BIL's strength lay in selling components of a company, not buying them. Besides, after the oil shocks of the 1970s, the motor vehicle industry was under great pressure.

Looking back, Brierley says he was probably shell-shocked after the AB Cons and Kempthorne Prosser dramas. He has come to the conclusion that Judge's plan could have worked, since General Motors was sitting on some extremely valuable sites. But at that time Brierley was spending most of his time in Australia and was out of touch with events back home.

In a rare show of authority, Brierley used his power of veto and blocked the deal. Judge was incensed, particularly as he had already committed BIL to the plan. Retreat was humiliating for him and he lost a great deal of credibility in Auckland. He understandably felt Brierley's opposition displayed a lack of confidence in his ability.

Although there was a written contract committing BIL to buying Tappenden Motors, Ceramco directors decided there would be little point in pursuing a claim. As it turned out, they had no cause to be displeased with the outcome. Alan Gibbs, who was then an advisor to Ceramco, together with Charles Bidwill, Warren Paine and John Fernyhough, put together a syndicate and carried out Judge's plan, making their first million dollars on the way.

What happened next still provokes heated debate within BIL, and it concerns Judge's departure. Though the AB Cons and KP deals had been successful, they were not enough to dispel the growing doubts about Judge at BIL. Judge had accumulated a great deal of ill-will within the company, and rumours about his failings had also begun to filter through to the business community.

The by-now-irascible Don McDonald had long ago lost faith in Bruce Judge. He no longer trusted him and believed Judge's judgment to be uneven and unreliable. McDonald had persistently badgered Brierley with his misgivings about Judge and, as his notoriety increased, McDonald decided that something had to be done quickly.

Brierley gave him the opening he needed. He, too, had become aware of Judge's tarnished reputation among the business fraternity, and he wrote to McDonald questioning how long the company could afford the luxury of employing Bruce Judge and suggested they discuss the matter later.

The letter was a significant departure for Brierley. Usually he studiously avoided confrontation, and people eventually divined he was unhappy because he would simply refuse to talk to them. If it was suggested a senior member of staff should be sacked, Brierley would ask, 'How much does he cost us with his car and all things included?' and on hearing the figure, would reply, 'Well, if I work a few extra hours on Saturday that should cover him.'

McDonald wrote back to Brierley immediately and then spoke to him by telephone on the day Judge was due to visit him in Auckland. He told Brierley that he was reluctant to talk to Judge, knowing he might not be around for long, and he is adamant that Brierley's response was, 'Well, talk about it with him then.'

So when Judge came to see him, McDonald announced that his relationship with the company was terminated. Judge was outraged and, according to McDonald, hissed, 'If you think Bob Blackburn was a problem, you wait till I get into action.'

Neither Judge nor Brierley will accept this account. Brierley denies it but refuses to be drawn into discussion on the issue, while Judge claims he left BIL of his own accord, sickened by the infighting. He says McDonald was jealous of his relationship with Brierley. As Judge tells it, he was able to get straight through to Brierley, while McDonald, the deputy chairman, was constantly fobbed off.

Selwyn Cushing was in Hastings the day Judge telephoned him from Auckland airport in the afternoon, clearly upset by what had happened. He told Cushing he felt punchdrunk. After all his hard work, he thought he deserved better.

There followed a round of phone calls which began with Cushing calling Paul Collins to say, 'The bugger is in a state of nervous trauma. Can you pick him up at the airport and drive him back to Wellington? Then ring me when you're back at BIL.'

Cushing then rang McDonald to confirm what had happened. McDonald told him Brierley had asked him to do it, but when Cushing rang Brierley, he flatly denied McDonald's claims. Cushing was confused but, like others at BIL, was inclined to favour McDonald's version, though he was unhappy with the decision. He was saddened to see this happen to his friend and colleague whose abilities he respected, and for a while he hoped the company could find a way of marrying Judge's individuality with the need for corporate discipline.

Cushing actually won a brief reprieve for Judge, but during that time Judge began laying the groundwork for new employment. Two months after his conversation with McDonald, Judge left BIL with a flourish, having secured a promising future for himself. Brierley looked on in open-mouthed admiration when he saw who was backing him financially.

Cyril Smith was the principal shareholder in the joinery and timber company of H. W. Smith Ltd. He was known to be wealthy but conservative, and Brierley had tried for some time to establish a fruitful relationship with him, but to no avail. In the end, Brierley concluded Smith was all cash but no action.

But where Brierley's powers of persuasion had failed, Judge had amply succeeded. Smith's ingrained caution had dissolved before Judge's winning ways. He was now in partnership with the Christchurch businessman and had full operational control of a well-respected company with a solid capital base, together with the prospect of working his way into equity. He had also gathered some talented people to work with him, two BIL staff in fact. In May 1979 BIL's principal investigating accountant, Paul Collins, and the South Island manager, Graeme McKenzie, left the company to join Judge and Smith.

McDonald was deeply disappointed, believing he had an undertaking from Judge not to steal BIL staff. Judge, however, denies there was such an undertaking. He claims Brierley knew McKenzie and Collins were so keen to join him that he had blessed their departure on the condition he could use them both as consultants.

In truth, Brierley was extremely sorry to see them go, but what could he do? It was their decision in the end. The only person he was relieved to have at arm's length was Bruce Judge. Brierley now had the perfect relationship. No longer responsible for Judge's decisions, he was freer than ever to work with him.

FIFTEEN

Bye Bye Baby Buntings

THE DEPARTURE of Bruce Judge, Paul Collins and Graeme McKenzie in 1979 had decimated the small team at BIL, and Brierley could see replacements were urgently required. Not only was the company suffering from the loss of their collective abilities, but morale in the office was brittle and depressed after years of divisive leadership under Judge. The company desperately needed a new general manager to pull it together. Although there were several contenders for the position, McDonald and Cushing were adamant that one man stood head and shoulders above the rest. They had seen Bruce Alan Hancox at work in AB Consolidated in Christchurch and were impressed.

Hancox's background was in management, not investment, and his early experience was gleaned at the textile manufacturing firm Lane Walker Rudkin Ltd in 1968. Armed with a Bachelor of Commerce degree from Canterbury University, the nineteen-year-old was given a job in production planning in the dyeworks. But it was not long before he moved to head office, where he became involved in management projects, accounting and administration.

From there he was headhunted by AB Consolidated Ltd and elevated to the position of financial assistant to the new general manager, Bob Binning. For years the company's profits had been crumbling because of trading difficulties. Hancox was instrumental in the savage restructuring that subsequently took place. The Christchurch confectionery operation was reduced to two lines and the biscuit operation was transferred to Auckland. Nearly 300 workers were laid off before the company began to thrive again.

Brierley first met Hancox on a visit to the factory. Hancox charmed Brierley with his unselfconscious patter. He is a natural story-teller, with an entertaining bluntness, and as he was wearing a white coat, Brierley assumed he was involved in production. He was surprised to find Hancox was the general manager.

Bruce Hancox was not the sort of person to alter his personality to suit his position. With his sharp blue eyes, dark moustache and rolling swagger, he looked like a Mexican bandit, and he made no attempt to be anything other than he was — a self-made, working-class man. He was confident, if a little unsophisticated, in his approach, aggressive and showed a commonsense approach to problems.

Although Brierley warmed to him, he appeared to have doubts about his suitability for the job, and when it came to voting he was the only person who did not support hiring Hancox. Cushing and McDonald voted for his appointment, Brierley against. Today the memory of his obduracy gives Brierley great pleasure, but he was probably confident Cushing and McDonald would outnumber him.

Any misgivings he may have had seemed to be entirely justified when Bruce Hancox arrived at BIL and Brierley discovered, to his horror, that the new general manger of his investment company knew nothing about investment.

Hancox reckons he didn't even know what a share was, but he set about learning as fast as he could. For the first weeks at BIL he read all the files, clippings and anything that might help familiarise himself with his new workplace. When he wasn't poring over documents he was on the telephone trying to make an appointment to see his new boss. But that would prove even more difficult than teaching himself the intricacies of the market.

Six weeks passed and Hancox began to wonder what on earth he was doing there. It had not escaped his notice that nothing had been prepared for his arrival. There was no desk in his office and no one to talk to. His frustration grew until, after nearly a year in the job, he finally went to see McDonald. He told him he couldn't do his job because Brierley was not making himself available for discussion. He said he felt just about ready to leave.

McDonald needed no convincing. He knew just how obtuse and evasive Brierley could be, and he was probably the only person in the company who could tell him that in no uncertain terms. His message to Brierley was firm: if he continued to ignore Bruce Hancox, not only would he leave, but Don McDonald would be following him.

The next day the telephone rang in Hancox's office and an unfamiliar voice asked him, 'Well, how are things going?'

To Brierley's relief, Hancox learned quickly and was not slow to act, though his inexperience was obvious. In his early days at BIL he made a partial takeover bid for his old employer, Lane Walker Rudkin, but this simply resulted in a major capital reconstruction and capital repayment.

Hancox's first task was to put his management skills to work.

Brierley tended to ignore investments once he had acquired them, and it showed. Most of BIL's subsidiaries were operating at a loss, and Hancox decided to tidy up those investments, by either selling or fixing them. Kanieri Gold Dredging was one of the first targets of this policy. It had had a number of indifferent years before Hancox sold it in 1980 to an American firm. That year the Petone works of the troubled Gear Meat Co. Ltd were also sold, to the Hawke's Bay Farmers Co-operative, though Gear still posted a loss of $4 million. A year later Gear's retail shops changed hands and its farms were on the market. Later the Dannevirke abbattoir was sold. The unprofitable divisions of engineer merchants Nivens Industries Ltd were also disposed of and the only survivor of the Nivens structure, Kidd Garrett, underwent savage rationalisation and reorganisation.

Mergers absorbed many familiar names. City Realties was merged with Property Securities. Gear Meat bought J. C. Huttons (NZ) Ltd and became a subsidiary under its new name, Huttons NZ Ltd. Kidd Garrett took over the South Island engineers merchant R. B. Denniston and Co. Ltd. Cyclone Industries (NZ) Ltd merged with Consolidated Metal Industries Ltd in 1982, and Welgas Holdings merged with Christchurch Gas Coal and Coke. Rationalisation between the well-known stationer Whitcoulls and stationer and paper distributor Williamson Jeffrey Ltd also continued.

As time passed, Hancox's relationship with Brierley gradually improved, although he saw less and less of him. Australia was Brierley's home now and Hancox could see that he was not really interested in the New Zealand market. Hancox suspected that Brierley eventually planned to have the local operation become a subsidiary of IEL.

The BIL portfolio reflected this approach. It was a rats-and-mice collection of holdings in small to medium-sized companies, and it was not until Hancox decided to shift the company onto a different playing field that BIL's explosive growth began. Hancox was responsible for expanding the company with bigger market plays. BIL's $10 million, 20 per cent stake in Dominion Breweries in 1981 was the first move in that direction. This led to investments in other liquor interests, starting with wholesale and retail merchants Quill Humphries and winemaker Cooks NZ Wine Co. Ltd. Eventually they came under the umbrella of Magnum (formerly Rothmans), which also incorporated Liquorland, Allied Liquor and Robbie Burns.

Hancox's expansionist programme received another boost on 9 February 1982, when BIL launched a huge share-buying programme in New Zealand News Ltd, Williamson Jeffrey Ltd and Printing and

Packaging Corporation Ltd (the parent company of Whitcoulls). It quickly gained 25 per cent of NZ News and Williamson Jeffrey and 43 per cent of Printpac — a total investment of $16 million. By 1983 BIL controlled all of Whitcoulls.

The rewards were immediate. Brierley hailed the 1980/81 year as the most successful ever, thanks to the improvement in the New Zealand result. While IEL's performance languished in the early 1980s, BIL was spurred on to produce bigger profits year by year. In 1979 its net profit was $2 million. Four years later it had increased five times to $25.4 million.

At the same time the company's needs were also growing. While Bruce Hancox had successfully stepped into Bruce Judge's shoes, no one had come forward to replace Paul Collins. BIL desperately needed a financial expert and really, Hancox had to admit, after considering all the alternatives, there was only one person he knew who was up to the task — Paul Collins himself.

'There's no training ground where you can hire people like Collins. His bent was finance. He was doing good work. He had BIL experience and he knew the takeover legislation. He was definitely an asset,' said Hancox.

At that time Collins was still with Bruce Judge, and their venture with Cyril Smith had worked well. After disposing of the joinery and lumber business of H. W. Smith Ltd, the company was restructured to become an investment company, H. W. Smith Holdings, with the capital jointly owned by Smith and Judge.

One of their first targets was Bunting and Company, the Christchurch manufacturer of paint and brushware. In 1979 Buntings had lost $123,000 on shareholders' funds of $3 million. Judge took control of the company and rationalised it, leaving it with no staff whatsoever. H. W. Smith was then contracted to manage Buntings on a performance basis. It was agreed that H. W. Smith would receive 10 per cent of the profits in excess of a million dollars. The company would not wait long to collect, for the following year Buntings was in the black and by 1984 its profit was $3 million on shareholders' funds of $20 million.

Through H. W. Smith, Buntings or both, the former BIL trio used the skills and experience they had gained while at BIL to trade in a wide variety of companies involved in activities as diverse as horticulture, motorcar accessories, hotels, property and department stores.

Hancox had plenty of opportunities to see how Collins worked. Buntings was competing with BIL for investment opportunities in a small market, and it was inevitable the two would be rivals at times. For example, in 1982 they were both angling for board representation on Neil Holdings Ltd, but this association ended when BIL bought Buntings' stake from them a year later.

At one stage Judge was even making overtures to Hancox, who admits he considered joining the Buntings team. But after thinking it through he decided his future lay with BIL. Instead, he concentrated on acquiring Collins. He knew Collins would be reluctant to leave Judge, for he had just signed a generous management contract and was now an integral part of the company. After considering all the possibilities, Hancox decided his only option was to take over Buntings.

He knew it would not be an easy takeover. This time the opposition would not only come from the target company but also from the raider itself. Hancox had no doubts about that, for he had seen something of the in-house antipathy towards Bruce Judge when Brierley started acting in concert with him in the early 1980s.

Having established what he called the perfect working relationship with Bruce Judge, Brierley had been keen to continue dealing with his former general manager. Judge felt the same way, although at times he had acted in opposition to Brierley. For example, not long after H. W. Smith had been revamped as an investment house and consultancy, Judge was approached by New Zealand Insurance Corporation to devise a defence against a takeover bid from BIL. In 1980 BIL had built up a small stake in NZI, buying through nominee companies, and might have gone further if it had not been for Muldoon invoking a regulation forcing the real owners to reveal their identity upon registering their shares.

NZI was alarmed by BIL's interest and looked to Judge for assistance. By then he had close links with the big insurance company, which had backed him in numerous enterprises, lending him money, often becoming a substantial shareholder and sometimes buying companies it had helped Judge acquire in the first place.

Judge's defence for NZI consisted of the company putting money into H. W. Smith, which then bought 10 per cent of NZI. Judge was even invited on to the NZI board. Collins and Judge were asked to prepare a report on the possibility of NZI taking over BIL, which they did, but NZI eventually decided to abandon this option because it was too ambitious and not financially viable.

Judge then turned his attention to Brierley. He managed to convince Brierley that he was in danger of losing the strategic value of his shares because a hostile NZI was likely to encourage other parties to buy large stakes in the company. Brierley's astonished colleagues then learned that Judge had persuaded Brierley to sell his NZI holding to a company formed to protect NZI. That company was called Ariadne Investments Ltd.

Judge also had other information that had a bearing on his argument. He knew NZI was considering a merger with South British Insurance and that BIL's involvement in NZI posed a threat to the merger. Once Brierley was removed from NZI, the merger was announced in early 1981 and the share price took off, easily outstripping the price Brierley received for his shares.

It looked as if Brierley had been duped by Judge, and certainly that was the feeling in BIL. McDonald was fuming. He believed that anything with Judge's signature on it had to be a 'dog', and he was determined to stop Brierley dealing with Judge again. So he organised a meeting with Brierley and Trevor Beyer at the Logan Park Motel in Auckland to thrash out the issue. McDonald's strong feelings on the subject were underlined when he threatened to leave once again if this liaising with Judge continued. But Brierley reassured him this would not be necessary; he would not be working with Judge again.

Bruce Hancox, therefore, was under no illusions. He knew nothing would be more inflammatory to the old guard than a plan to bring back Bruce Judge, even if Paul Collins was included in the package. Collins might well be an asset but Judge was a gigantic liability. Nevertheless this was his plan.

Initial negotiations with Buntings early in 1984 went well and a one-for-one exchange was approved. The deal was to be finalised on a Sunday evening at Paul Collins's home, where he had been laid up for weeks with a viral illness. Over that weekend both Hancox's and Brierley's enthusiasm wavered. Brierley was still mulling over the proposal on the final day and it was all he, Hancox and his partner, Judi Lenart, talked about on the way back from the beach that Sunday. Finally Brierley said, 'You know, I think Judge wants the deal more than we do. Let's try for a nine-for-ten deal.'

He was right. Although BIL had to raise the sum paid for the management contract binding Judge, Collins and McKenzie by an extra $1 million, it did get a discount for the shares. It was so easy that Brierley has always wondered since then whether he could have wrung an eight-for-ten deal out of Judge.

BIL's offer valued Buntings at $116 million and boosted its own capitalisation to $811.8 million, or number three in the market. In return BIL acquired Buntings' holdings in Winstones, Odlins, DIC, Ariadne, Trans Tours plus its $16 million property portfolio.

But the three men who had left Brierley five years ago were the first to reap the benefits of the merger. In this short time they had become millionaires in their own right. They had built up a company using the leverage of a small base and numerous share issues at a low price and letting the market price provide the wealth, just as Brierley had done for years. As a result of the merger, Judge was now the second-largest non-institutional shareholder in BIL after Brierley himself, who had 6.2 per cent of the shares. Bruce Ross, author of *The Ariadne Story*, calculated that Judge's initial $100,000 investment in H. W. Smith was valued by BIL less than five years later at $7 million.

As expected, the news of the deal was greeted by a storm of protest within BIL, although the takeover was a *fait accompli* by the time the directors were informed. Brierley broke the news to them at the end of a directors' meeting in Hastings in February 1984. Just as they were gathering up their papers and readying themselves to leave the room, he dropped the bombshell: 'By the way, we've decided to take over Buntings.'

'You should have seen Trevor's and Don's faces,' says Hancox. 'I remember walking out and the two of them running after us saying, "You can't possibly do this. Ron, you don't mean it?" I reckon that was the best part for Ron.'

Despite their fears, Bruce Judge's subsequent involvement in BIL was minimal. As a non-executive director he had no particular role in the company, he rarely attended meetings, and it was understood that he was free to pursue his interests in Ariadne in Australia. Hancox hoped his Australian activities might generate spin-offs for BIL, but little of any significance eventuated.

The only impact Judge was to have on the Brierley group was to create new enemies, this time in Australia. The young chief executive of IEL, Russell Goward, took a dislike to Judge and complained to Brierley that although he could understand the man, he couldn't understand his figures. In 1985 Goward was actually responsible for selling IEL's small stake in Ariadne.

Those who knew both Goward and Judge were mildly surprised at the hostility between the two men, for they were remarkably similar. They worked hard, coveted the limelight and shared a natural overabundance of energy, which spilled over into their personal lives.

It soon became apparent to all concerned that there was little point in Judge remaining at BIL, so, after eighteen months with his old company, he left for the second time.

In hindsight, the merits of the Buntings deal are debatable, and even Brierley has to admit it was riddled with drawbacks. BIL gained a mixed bag of investments including the troubled tourist company Trans Tours, the Wellington department store DIC, which was crippled by cost escalations, and the poorly performing Odlins. But, unlike Don McDonald, Brierley and Hancox never regretted the takeover.

Brierley says that while the advantages of the deal were probably pretty marginal financially, there were other benefits. Many of BIL's most able people today, such as group accountant Vicky Lawson, date back to the Buntings merger. But overriding all doubts about the worth of the Buntings portfolio was the invaluable gain of Paul Collins, for in Collins lay the future of BIL.

SIXTEEN

Tilting at Windmills

OVER THE YEARS Brierley's constant jousting with the law has frustrated his executives as much as the authorities. They contend that he would be more gainfully employed building up the company. Moreover, they have come to the conclusion that many of the corporate battles have been utterly futile. In their experience, the authorities have rarely changed their stance to accommodate Brierley and, more often than not, he has inspired them to tighten the rules even further.

It was his intervention, for example, that prompted the West Australian Government to protect the West Australian Trustee Co. Ltd in 1979, and a year later, thanks to Ron Brierley, the South Australian Government legislated to limit shareholders in the South Australian Gas Co. Ltd. In 1981 special legislation was passed to thwart Brierley's entry into the Executor Trustee and Agency Co. Ltd. Brierley's holding in that company was actually confiscated by the South Australian Corporate Affairs Commission and eventually sold to the ANZ bank in 1984, albeit at a handsome profit for IEL.

Meanwhile the commission was still occupied examining the Marra Developments Ltd debacle, in which Brierley played a major role. Brierley entered the saga after the planned takeover of the Scottish Australian Company by another corporate raider, Peter Yunghanns, met strong opposition from shareholders. In 1974 the company merged with Marra Developments to avert the bid, and when the company's performance slipped, Yunghanns was keen to implement a controlled winding-up of the company. But once again his plans met heated objections and in the end he decided to sell out to Brierley in 1979.

Both thought that, with Yunghanns' removal, the furore would die down. Instead it went from bad to worse and Brierley was even accused of raping the assets of his takeover targets by NSW Attorney-General Frank Walker, who ordered the state's Corporate Affairs Commission to investigate his involvement in Marra.

Brierley became incensed by the length and cost of the investigation and entered into a volley of correspondence in what has become known among his colleagues as 'classic R.A.B. style'.

There is nothing haphazard about Brierley's use of the English language. He labours over the selection of the words he employs and demonstrates a great deal of pride in the end product. The letters on Marra are a fine example of Brierley's sarcasm. For example, in June 1979 he wrote to the special investigator, J. H. Tuckfield:

> In my opinion (which I believe is shared by many others) it is long overdue that some semblance of sanity was introduced into this matter and the whole unfunny farce brought to a conclusion as quickly as possible. In saying this, I am not necessarily critical of yourself in a personal sense (you being merely the organ grinder's monkey, so to speak). In fact, as a businessman you are to be congratulated on obtaining yet another extension of the most magnificent sinecure ever handed to a private individual by a benevolent State Government in Australia. Furthermore, at the present rate of progress this bonanza at the expense of the public of NSW shows distinct promise for almost unlimited exploitation in the future.

Brierley calculated that Tuckfield was receiving a salary of $208,000 per annum, making him one of the most highly paid executives in Australia, 'if not the world'. He went on:

> If this is not the case, can you please tell us how much longer and how much more money you will require before Mr Walker and his band of intrepid sleuths can stir themselves into action over events now five years old, instead of turning to harass those who have been solely responsible for recovering anything at all from this mess. Surely, this is not an unreasonable request (for a mere $457,000 and still going strong!).

IEL was eventually forced to compromise and buy the whole company, but despite Brierley's protests, the investigation continued until 1987.

However, the takeover that really looms large in the minds of IEL's executives as particularly provocative and pointless was the bid for the meat company Huttons Ltd in 1981.

At the time Brierley had been publicly fulminating against the revamped National Corporate and Securities Commission (NCSC) in Melbourne and the new Companies Act. He damned the legislation as oppressive and discriminatory and, in a burst of hyperbole, he wrote in his 1980 annual report:

> A 'new' Federal Companies Bill seems to be based on only the most grudging concession that to be a director or a shareholder of a company is not an offence in itself. At State Government level, shareholders are

> being increasingly assailed with measures verging on expropriation in order to protect the entrenched Board on politically favoured corporations. And possibly worst of all, critical comments such as appear in this report will become essentially illegal in themselves under the censorship functions of the new National Companies Commission.

Not content with verbally battering the authorities, Brierley then challenged them to a stand-up fight. By increasing IEL's holding in Huttons to 27.6 per cent in 1980, he was breaching the proposed regulations that require a company to make a full takeover once the 20 per cent limit has been reached. IEL's notice of acquisition was made on 30 June, the eve of the NCSC code coming into operation. Brierley knew the timing of IEL's notice meant he was under no legal obligation to bow to their constraints, and he did not.

There was no doubt in anyone's mind, least of all the commission's, that Brierley was pushing the system for the last time. His flagrant breaching of the new listing requirements was an act of bravado, clever and boastful and irritating, and Brierley loved it. As always, it was also his personal protest against all forms of regulation.

This time, however, Brierley had made a colossal mistake. Little did he know that Huttons was actually a financial disaster, but later it was obvious to all concerned that the smart move would have been to sit on the 19.9 per cent limit and wait to find out what the company's prospects were.

Instead he provoked the NCSC's first clash with the corporate sector, and as a result IEL's shares were suspended from trading. Not long after that Brierley must have decided he had made his point, for he backed down and announced a takeover offer for Huttons.

The board soon learned the true state of Huttons' financial affairs: total borrowings for the group were more than $19 million and the projected loss for the year was $1.3 million. (It was, in fact, $1.7 million.) Brierley knew then that if he had stayed at the 19.9 per cent limit he could have bought the Huttons shares at bargain prices once these losses were revealed. But he was now required to offer the highest price he had paid for Huttons shares to the shareholders. So, rather than buying an ailing company at overinflated prices, Brierley decided to stick to his original plan. They would not be making a takeover after all.

The authorities pounced. Once again Huttons and IEL were delisted, the Victorian Corporate Affairs Commission began an enquiry and the NCSC took IEL to the Equity Court to force it to pursue the offer. Although Huttons was relisted in October for the benefit of its shareholders, IEL stayed off the board. Meanwhile, in what Brierley and Loewenthal viewed as a vendetta by the commission, IEL found itself in court for failing to supply books for inspection.

Although the company won the court battle with the NCSC in December 1981, there were no real winners in this fiasco. Brierley eventually agreed to reduce his holding to 20 per cent and, after five months off the exchange, IEL was finally relisted in February 1982.

But Huttons' troubles continued to make a dent in the balance sheet, and in 1982 the meat company wiped $2.5 million off IEL's profits, not to mention the $800,000 loss on the sale of its shares earlier in the year. In 1983 IEL finally severed its links with Huttons when the principal operating subsidiary was sold after another bad year.

It had been a harrowing six months for IEL executives, but McDonald, not for the first time worried about what Brierley was doing, recalls a conversation he had with Brierley at the time: 'He said to me "I don't want to talk about Huttons but when we first got together you and I made a pact that we would not go broke. That's what I'm doing now. We are not going to go broke."'

The executives noted, however, that the suffering had not been evenly distributed. While they had experienced feelings of extreme frustration and annoyance, Brierley seemed to be gaining strength from the battle, as if all the resistance provided a tonic for tired Brierley blood.

Brierley knew only too well how irritating he could be to others. 'It would be fair to say that I underestimated the degree of reaction the purchasing provoked. My colleagues were tearing their hair out wishing they had never heard of Huttons, while I was getting more enjoyment out of it than one would have thought I deserved.'

Despite their best efforts, the executives could never persuade Brierley to abandon his intellectual jousting. For him, it was the essence of the way he operated, and he believes people made the mistake of perceiving his strengths as his weakness, when in fact they are one and the same thing.

'As the record shows there have been a lot of unique achievements which would not have been done without the Don Quixote element. They said it was hopeless buying Southern Farmers Co-operative shares, but I knew it was a company. When I stood for Hallenstein Brothers in 1961, was I tilting at windmills? It's all the same thing. You can't separate the good from the bad.

'It's true that the wrangle in itself is not productive, but it is part of the overall picture. There are downsides and upsides.

'You might say,' he says with obvious pride, 'that I'm someone who goes to the absolute brink and has a fair degree of nerve and determination and doesn't go under when the crunch goes on.'

Fortunately for IEL, Brierley's sparring with the authorities did not halt the growth of his company. Throughout the early 1980s, IEL continued to make inroads into the pastoral sector, adding other food manufacturers to the Southern Farmers banner. After a decade of determined opposition, Brierley also won control of the highly respected Winchcombe Carson group of companies. In 1982 IEL's investments in the textile industry resulted in the merger of three companies, thus forming the largest woollen and worsted milling group in Australia, Macquarie Worsteds Ltd.

IEL even had some investments in the more speculative energy sector that year, notably in gas supply utilities, oil drilling and exploration, and during this period Brierley also began to invest in the insurance sector.

Perhaps the only advantage of the 1974 recession had been the opportunity to buy good shares cheaply. Despite IEL's straitened circumstances at the time, the company did make a few new investments, some of which were finally coming to fruition in the early 1980s. The most important of these early purchases was probably the MLC Ltd. The MLC Ltd was one of the new publicly listed insurance holding companies in Australia. In 1982 this prestigious institution controlled one of the nation's top five insurance companies, Mutual Life and Citizen's Company, and ranked as the third-largest insurance company in the country. Its reputation was well known to Brierley.

'Many years before, when I suggested to a broker that I wanted to attack the MLC, he said, "If you oppose them, you'll find you won't get your milk delivered in the morning." Such was their standing in Australia.'

For years the company had been regarded as invulnerable, with the two largest shareholders, Sun Alliance and Land Lease Investments Pty Ltd, blocking the entry of any newcomer. But Brierley kept on buying shares and finally accumulated the same shareholding as the two dominant parties.

He was never going to let something as valuable as the MLC slip through his hands. At the time, MLC Ltd was valued by the sharemarket at between $13 million and $20 million, yet the company controlled assets of over $2 billion. It was a grossly undervalued asset, and it became the motto in the IEL camp never to sell MLC shares.

But for a long time it was not clear how Brierley intended to release that value. How could he unlock wealth for shareholders in this publicly listed company rather than for policy holders in the unlisted insurance company?

In 1983 the key was turned when, under a new surplus sharing agreement, the percentage of the surplus earned by the life company and made available to the holding company was lifted from 2.5 per cent to 10 per cent under certain conditions. The MLC proved to be an outstanding success for Brierley, and in 1985 his original $10 million investment was sold for $70 million to Land Lease.

With a market capitalisation of $83.2 million in July 1982, IEL was now one of the corporate heavyweights in Australia and it was also expanding overseas. Holdings in the British market had been increased, encouraged by a favourable sterling exchange rate and a period of industry restructuring. Investment in the United States had also begun on a small scale, and in 1982 IEL gained 24 per cent of the Ohio-based department store chain Higbee Company.

As a sign of its growing stature, IEL was also one of the first companies to take advantage of changes in lending trends by accepting $US27.5 million in an unsecured negative pledge arrangement from a banking consortium. Under this pledge, a syndicate of borrowers had lent money to IEL, who agreed not to negate that security by pledging assets to people outside the syndicate. It really meant that IEL was secured by deed but not by specific items, so if things went under, it would stand in line with all the other unsecured lenders.

The pledge streamlined the fragmented borrowings of the past and saved stamp duty and other charges. It also gave IEL the ability to raise large amounts of money very quickly for a takeover. As one IEL member put it, 'There'll be no more of "Where will the money come from?"'

The 1982 loan was followed by loans for BIL and Southern Farmers, and in 1985 all IEL's group-funding requirements were converted to the unsecured negative pledge.

But despite these highlights, by 1982 IEL was under pressure. The previous four years had been particularly active in the takeover field, with the number of bids in Australia in 1978 reaching 107, a more than 30 per cent increase from 1977. The numbers peaked in 1980 when 132 takeover bids were made.

Brierley repeatedly warned the market was overheated and admitted that his caution during this time was responsible for a number of missed opportunities. But his warnings were finally realised in 1982/83. Worsening economic conditions and a downward turn in the sharemarket buffeted IEL at the time it was also grappling with losses sustained through the Huttons saga. In 1983 a prolonged rural drought placed the operations of Southern Farmers under further stress and the profit increase was only 6 per cent.

Brierley regarded the 1982 profit of $13.3 million as barely satisfactory in relation to the $280 million of funds employed, and he hinted the company had been spending too much time on long-term projects instead of exploiting more immediate possibilities.

The market, too, was rerating 'corporate raiders'. Although in 1983 Australian Ratings gave IEL an A minus compared with BB for Bond Corporation and B for Adelaide Steamship, it was pointed out that IEL lacked an identifiable and predictable cash flow.

This was right, but if the IEL executives had had their way in 1980 and 1981, that would not have been the case. In 1980 IEL had a 10 per cent stake in quality retail store David Jones, and by the end of the year it was buying shares in the NSW brewer Tooth and Co. The executives were keen to take over these two massive companies, but Brierley refused to act.

It would have meant a substantial commitment, though the companies were ripe for the picking. David Jones was sitting on plum assets of $301 million, yet showing disappointing profits of only $6.2 million. A full takeover of David Jones was estimated then to cost about $73 million. But Brierley said the company, once top in its field, was at the crossroads and he was doubtful about IEL's role in its future.

Of the two, Tooths would have been the bigger undertaking. IEL outlaid about $17 million for its 10 per cent share in the company, which was about 50 per cent of its shareholders' funds and 9 per cent of the total assets of the group.

But as investment manager Geoff Pickles remembers, Brierley's doubts about the two transactions held sway. 'I don't think he could comprehend us getting control of David Jones and Tooths. He didn't think we had the expertise to take on such enormous undertakings. They were bigger than anything we had done before and they were great situations in terms of the underlying assets, but he didn't appear willing to take risks. I think it was the size that daunted him. Then again, maybe it was because it wasn't his idea. It came from the analysts.'

Whatever the reason, it was one of the first signs of doubt Brierley had ever displayed and a signal that the company was getting beyond his grasp. Pickles was not the only IEL executive to notice in 1982 that Brierley seemed dispirited and unwilling to make decisions.

But John Spalvins, the Latvian-born Australian entrepreneur, did not share Brierley's doubts and, not long after, IEL's holdings in both companies were sold to him at a creditable profit. Ironically, the David Jones board allowed Spalvins' Adsteam to take control just to negate IEL's presence, yet the first thing Adsteam did on taking over the company was to sell $100 million worth of property and start rationalising the company. Brierley walked away with the second prize of about $800,000. In June 1981 IEL sold its 10 per cent of Tooths to Adsteam for $21 million — a $5 million profit, which was tax-free because Brierley sold a subsidiary company that held the shares to Spalvins.

Since then, of course, David Jones and Tooths have become the cornerstone of Spalvins' empire and a source of lingering regret to those at IEL who remembered how close they had come to acquiring David Jones.

IEL's unexceptional profit of $14.4 million in 1983 was once again a cause of some concern to Brierley, and he admitted in his annual report that the company's growth had been stifled by a 'creeping complacency'. IEL had failed to apply to itself the criteria it used for investments in other companies — the maximising of resources.

The truth was that the company had become lazy. Comforted by years of easy profits and lacking any firm leadership by Brierley himself, it had sunk gently into a complacent torpor. Although its staff worked hard, the company was run on a loose, free-wheeling basis that allowed for the occasional long lunch, eccentric characters, odd behaviour and a lack of discipline.

The stories are legion. One concerns operations manager Jim Patrick, who was said to have brought a small television into IEL and settled down with his feet on his desk to watch a sports match during the day. Apparently Brierley popped into Patrick's office to talk to him but saw at once that he was engrossed in what was happening on the television, and so Brierley quietly closed the door and left without saying a word. These were the days that staff at IEL would later recall as being a lot of fun.

In a sense this free-wheeling spirit was a reflection of Brierley's own personality. He allowed people to have a relatively long rein and a lot of responsibility, and for years this had worked well. Decisions were made quickly and the company did not develop an unwieldy bureaucracy. Since Brierley was a poor manager, this suited him well. He had made a virtue out of a vice.

But by 1983 the company had become too large to accommodate

such an informal structure and lackadaisical approach. It badly needed a shake-up, but Brierley's mood was as subdued as the company's profit margin. He was not likely to provide the impetus for change.

Bill Loewenthal saw the problem clearly. He also realised that he was past revving the corporate engine himself but knew somebody had to, both for the company's sake and because across the Tasman the energetic Bruce Hancox was beginning to ask a lot of questions. Loewenthal could see Hancox's patience with IEL's slack performance was wearing thin.

SEVENTEEN

The Goward Years

RUSSELL GOWARD burst onto the IEL scene with all the might of a Force 10 gale. 'He was almost an inevitability,' said an IEL executive. 'Goward was just one bundle of energy.'

His energy had propelled him from the Treasury in Canberra, where he worked for five years after leaving school, to the merchant bank Hill Samuel in Sydney, where he worked for another five years. Goward also had an economics degree to his name and had studied law.

While at Hill Samuel he decided that, rather than advising people to make money, he wanted to be making it himself, and as far as he could see, IEL was the best place in Australia to do it. So after pestering Bill Loewenthal repeatedly for a job, he was finally appointed to the property department of IEL in 1981.

Goward swept into IEL determined to learn everything about the company he could. In the evenings and weekends he scoured IEL's files, absorbing as much information as he was able. Under Goward, IEL's property department swelled enormously and its projects escalated from the $1 million range to the $100 million level.

Although Goward looked like a miracle of technology with his year-round tan and permed hair, his charm and enthusiasm were infectious. So in 1983, when it appeared the company desperately needed a boost in tempo, Russell Goward's name sprang immediately to mind.

Loewenthal was fed up with the easy-going, contented atmosphere permeating IEL and is said to have issued a terse memorandum calling for a meeting to discuss the company's performance. He also knew that, at Bruce Hancox's insistence, the historic divisions that had kept the interests of BIL and IEL apart were breaking down, and BIL was as anxious as he was to fire up its Australian counterpart.

Until Hancox's arrival, the two companies had been run by Brierley as separate entities with himself as the only informed link between the two. Brierley's explanation for this was that 'IEL was me really. I could tell them anything they wanted to know.' Privately, however, other directors suspected it was simply a way of cementing his power-base and resisting interference. But since a great proportion of BIL's assets were tied up in IEL, Bruce Hancox wanted more control over this arm of the operation. In fact he told the assembled throng at IEL that if they didn't do better BIL would have to consider selling them. Brierley looked on quietly amused, saying little.

What Loewenthal, Hancox and also Don McDonald were demanding was a new spirit of zest and achievement. Anyone not interested in devoting themselves to the company was invited to leave, and anyone who accepted the challenge would be given their head. Geoff Pickles and, later, Jim Patrick bade their farewells and a young man stepped forward. Russell Goward said he was prepared to devote all his energy to IEL.

Goward was still only twenty-nine when he was earmarked for the top position in IEL. In July 1983 he was promoted to deputy general manager of IEL, and a year later he became chief executive. Bill Loewenthal, then general manager, was made a non-executive director, while Brierley continued as chairman in a non-executive role.

For a time, the elevation of one so young caused some disgruntlement within IEL's ranks, but the critics were silenced by Goward's impact on the company. Almost immediately he stepped up the pace at IEL and hounded the executives with demands.

'When he was heir-designate he gave IEL the kick-start it needed. You had no peace with Russell. You were unmercifully hammered for the things you said you would do,' recalls IEL special projects manager Ross Daniels.

For the first time in many years Brierley found himself being prodded into action. It was just what he needed and he responded with great vigour.

He had already started the year well with a bid for Australia's first merchant bank, the DFC. The DFC was founded by Sir John Marks, an able, venerated, and by now elderly, chairman of the company. IEL's bid was greeted with hostility, and by August that year the ANZ bank had stepped in with a counter-bid. IEL walked away with what was then a gigantic profit of over $6 million.

Looking back, the bid for the DFC was Brierley's warm-up for a three-year period of unprecedented activity in IEL. Goward made the team tidy up holdings that had been in the portfolio for months, if not years, and he estimates that in the first year the company was doing a deal a month. At the end of the 1984 financial year Brierley counted fourteen takeover offers, five of which had been successful and three still under way. The successful takeovers were for Acmex Holdings Ltd, Amalgamated Chemicals, Australian Oil & Gas Corporation Ltd, G. & R. Wills (Holdings) Ltd and The Cascade Brewery Company Ltd.

Of the five, Cascade was by far the most significant. It was a well-known, substantial company with a strong regional identity, and in the battle for control IEL had employed clever public relations and typically unorthodox tactics to good effect. The bid for Cascade was also the beginning of further involvement in the brewing industry for Brierley, and a substantial bid by IEL for Carlton & United Breweries (CUB) had immediate consequences for IEL's bid for Cascade.

Brierley had been accumulating shares in Cascade since 1976, and in response Cascade had put in place a number of defensive measures designed to thwart a takeover bid. They included bonus shares, industry diversification and a placement of almost 10 per cent of Cascade's capital to CUB. The placement also revealed that CUB already had 9.69 per cent of Cascade, acquired soon after IEL appeared on the Cascade register.

Any thoughts of IEL quitting once it realised someone else was interested were far too optimistic. Four years later the tenacious IEL was still clinging on to its stake and, moreover, the holding had grown. Brierley had singled out Cascade as the only remaining orphan in an industry he believed was in need of considerable rationalisation. Other takeover merchants had already been cutting a swath through the brewing industry, with Spalvins gaining control of Tooth and Co. and Swan Brewery falling to Alan Bond. Brierley believed the same trend would occur in New Zealand, where BIL held 20 per cent of Dominion Breweries.

So in September 1983 IEL made a partial offer for 48.21 per cent of Cascade. The fact that IEL's offer came as no surprise did not make it any more acceptable to Cascade. Cascade is the oldest brewer in Australia, dating back to 1824, and the company is an integral part of the Tasmanian community. It operates the only two breweries in the state, producing such well-known products as Cascade and Boags beer, Red, Blue and Green ale and stout. The company's identification with Tasmania meant there would be an enormous sensitivity to any move from the mainland to control a local company.

Brierley detected this sensitivity when he visited Tasmania, but the remote state cast a spell on him. 'I was so enchanted with Tasmania and Cascade's place in Tasmania's way of life that I had a conversion over the weekend. I decided we were going to own the brewery.'

This was easier said than done. At the end of three months IEL had 15 per cent of Cascade and was making little headway, when a startling development transformed circumstances of the bid. On 30 November 1983, Brierley and Russell Goward held a press conference at the grand Windsor Hotel in Melbourne. The news media was out in force, having been primed by Brierley's public relations firm, Network Communications, to expect a momentous declaration. Brierley appeared nervous and one Melbourne journalist noted how he 'perspired and fidgeted . . . obviously unaccustomed to the bright lights of a big television press conference', but Murray Williams from Network remembers how much Brierley enjoyed the media extravaganza.

At the conference Goward and Brierley announced that IEL was mounting a bid for 23.9 per cent of CUB, and in doing so, set in motion the biggest takeover attempt in Australian history.

The bid obviously had implications for Cascade, since CUB owned 25 per cent of that company, but that was the least of CUB's worries. CUB also held 49.4 per cent of Elders IXL, and for two years Elders' chief executive, John Elliott, had been concerned that any attempted takeover of the brewer could result in his having a new boss. IEL's bid was forcing Elliott to defend his fiefdom.

Until then CUB had been regarded as virtually impregnable, simply because of its size. Known as the 'colossus of Bouverie Street' (where its head office was), CUB was one of the biggest companies in the country, valued at $800 million. It was all the more astonishing that IEL, with a market capitalisation of $200 million, was planning to swallow the giant. A takeover of that magnitude had never been attempted in Australia before.

It was common knowledge in business circles that Elliott was worried about the company's long-term security, but few people knew that he had done a secret feasibility study on the possibility of Elders taking over CUB as a precaution.

Brierley probably suspected Elliott would make a substantial counter-bid, ensuring a huge profit for IEL. If he won CUB, he would have control of Elders as well, which to IEL was just as valuable. As one analyst put it, it was a 'heads I win, tails you lose' situation for Brierley. He could either win indirect control of the country's two most lucrative industries — brewing and pastoral — or he could make off with a hefty profit.

The CUB saga lasted almost two weeks. As expected, Elliott did retaliate with a $972 million cash-and-scrip counter-bid for CUB, and although CUB had to buy less than 1 per cent of Elders to take its holding above 50 per cent, it did nothing. For one thing, Elders warned them that the whole Elders management team would leave if that happened, and the brewers were well aware they were not capable of running it themselves, nor did they want to.

On Monday night, 6 December, Elliott rang Brierley to ask if he wanted to sell his CUB shares. He gave him twelve hours to consider his reply.

The market seemed to have anticipated the move and when Brierley rang at 10 a.m. on Tuesday morning to accept Elliott's offer of $83 million, CUB's share price was well down on the previous close. Brierley had made a profit of 50 cents a share on the deal and walked away with about $11 million. Elders now had 20 per cent of CUB and mopped up another 30 per cent of CUB by 12 December.

The CUB board was finally roused into action and that morning sold its 25 per cent stake in Cascade to an Adelaide duo, C-C Bottlers and B. Seppelt and Sons, which emerged with a joint bid for Cascade at $4.80, 30 cents above IEL's offer. Suddenly the battle was between IEL and the Adelaide pair.

But the experienced IEL team outmanoeuvred them and had control by 19 January. Their skills were ruefully acknowledged by C-C Bottlers managing director Peter Griffiths: 'IEL is unquestionably very professional in the takeover business . . . We are very professional in businesses which are important in terms of making money.'

IEL also mounted a massive public relations campaign to win shareholders' support, with advertisements in Tasmanian and Melbourne newspapers and on Tasmanian radio. Later in the bid for Cascade, IEL maintained a telephone campaign to ensure small shareholders were aware of the price differentials between the competing bids.

But the regulatory authorities were less impressed. From the outset IEL's tactics had exposed the apparent shortcomings of the takeover code. For example, Brierley and Goward would announce an offer price to focus attention on Cascade and then top it in the market themselves, thus generating share sales. They also did this with their offer for CUB.

The code also intended that if bidders pay more for their shares than their original bid offers, they have to top up the remaining shareholders to the value of the highest price paid. The intention is that no one is disadvantaged. But by using an associate company and exploiting a loophole in the code, IEL managed to circumvent this intention. Although the NCSC suspended IEL for this at one stage, IEL was allowed to keep its 2.7 per cent holding acquired by the associate, which meant, strategically, the operation was a success.

No one was blameless in this war. The sharebroking firm Potter Partners was accused by the commission of 'unacceptable conduct', and C-C Bottlers and Seppelts were scolded for failing to obtain the consent of the commission before announcing their intention to vary their offer.

Overall, the real winners were clearly Elliott and Brierley. Elliott now had control of Elders, the company that for the past two weeks had been only a whisker away from becoming a subsidiary of CUB, and Brierley had walked away with $11 million profit and control of the unique Tasmanian brewer.

Brierley was thrilled. Until that deal the biggest takeover IEL had made had been no more than $30 million. CUB was gigantic; it involved several hundred million dollars. One IEL analyst commented, 'It was far too big for IEL really, but it captured Ron's imagination and then anything was possible.'

To celebrate, Brierley brought out two bottles of Dom Perignon champagne he had kept in a private cellar. He had the wind in his sails and was delighted. Later he even had the two stories documented and produced in book form, just for the record.

The Cascade-CUB deal was also a fine example of Brierley's use of the news media. As far back as *New Zealand Stocks and Shares* days it is evident that Brierley displayed a keen instinct for the value of public relations, and in 1983 he decided to develop a close relationship with an agency in Australia. He hired Network Communications to assist him in his takeover campaign and worked side by side with consultant Murray Williams from then on. Later, when Williams left Network, Brierley continued his association with him.

Williams found Brierley an adventurous, innovative client who was prepared to try anything. 'We designed every campaign for that particular company and its shareholders. We looked for the best selling points and tarted up the offer and documents. We were the first to use telegrams and tapes to reach shareholders and the first to offer toll-free numbers in a takeover. We were also the first to use the logos and trademarks of the target company. We took words from the company itself and used them for our purposes.

'We went to court several times, but that didn't bother us, since we decided that by the time it was in court it would be a non-issue anyway, which was true. Ron gave me a tremendous flexibility to develop things.'

Williams remembers that, in 1983, business rarely featured on television and he spent a lot of time trying to generate enthusiasm for business news. The extensive media coverage of the CUB takeover announcement was something of a victory, and Williams believes Brierley must be given some credit for stimulating television's interest in business coverage.

Williams also learned a lot about Brierley's own media techniques. He saw how Brierley carefully controlled the interview to reveal only what he wanted to reveal. Murray Williams said Brierley would never agree to an interview if it did not serve his purpose and, even though Brierley often appears not to answer questions, he is always conveying a viewpoint.

But perhaps the most telling insight for Williams was Brierley's deliberate creation of an aura of mystery. 'Developing a mystique was a stated element of your *modus operandi*. He never fully explained anything to anyone. He believed this draws people to you, people with ideas and money, and in a takeover it affects people by putting them on guard.'

The 1984 annual report was a happy vindication of the company's new direction. It boasted a record profit of $26 million, 83 per cent higher than the previous year's. By the time the video celebrating twenty years of IEL was shown at the annual meeting, IEL was rated the twentieth-largest company in Australia. A mere eighteen months before, it had been 150th.

The 1985 result was even better. Profit soared to $51 million and a confident IEL sported an immodest silver hologram on the cover of its annual report. The image featured a slice of the globe, with Australia leaping out at the viewer on the left, and on the right the letters IEL swirled out from the Australian map in bold relief. It was the first time a hologram had appeared on a company report.

IEL's aim of industry rationalisation saw it enter the merchant banking field, the oil sector (which incurred losses of $50 million in 1985 in market value) and continuing investments in the pastoral industry.

Bennetts Farmers Ltd merged with two other operations to form a smaller pastoral house, while Southern Farmers continued to expand with new acquisitions including G. & R. Wills. By April 1985 it was the second-largest industry company in South Australia after Mitsubishi and its aggressive expansionist policy had resulted in its shares trading at a substantial premium on-market, although, to date, its earnings had been unremarkable.

In 1985 Brierley also precipitated major convulsions in the Australian food industry with his $110 million bid for 40 per cent of food products group Allied Mills Ltd. Within weeks the giant United States packaged-food manufacturer Pilsbury Co. emerged as a white knight for Allied and the two announced a joint venture in February. But the New Zealand food company Goodman Group was also biting into Allied and was revealed to have 12 per cent of the company.

Not to be left out, biscuit-maker Arnotts, which owned 14.9 per cent of Allied (while Allied owned 19.9 per cent of Arnotts), bid for the company at a higher price, prompting IEL to match the offer. The entry of Bond Corporation into the fray did little to clear the muddle and by the end of March it had launched a $404 million takeover bid for Arnotts. In April, IEL bowed out of the race, delivering its 14 million Allied shares to Arnotts, which took its share of the company to 36 per cent.

More and more players entered the fray after IEL left, including the NCSC, Campbell Soup Company, Fielder Gillespie, Entrad Corporation and Lipkies Brothers. The final result saw the Goodman Group as the winners of the prized Allied Mills.

The deft hand of Murray Williams and the public relations machine was also evident throughout the proceedings. Instead of sending shareholders the usual offer document printed on cheap buff-coloured paper, IEL had opted for a high-quality glossy booklet with a colour photograph on the cover. Accompanying the booklet was a tape cassette extolling the virtues of IEL's offer. The whole package looked like an annual report.

More than 8,000 tapes were sent to Allied shareholders on the premise that, since people tend to ignore takeover documents, they would be more inclined to listen to a tape. It was the first time tapes had been employed as a takeover tool, but the ploy failed. By the time shareholders received the tape, the facts had changed and as a result the tapes became the subject of litigation. Allied alleged that certain statements on the tape were in breach of the takeover code, and the courts agreed. Williams ruefully remembered that during the trial the prosecution lawyer referred to him as a 'snake-oil salesman'.

In late 1985 the much-revitalised Ron Brierley also led the charge on the Australian Gas Light Co. Ltd. AGL was the perfect Brierley target. It was old, undervalued, unwelcoming, and as solid as brass. AGL had been set up by a Royal Charter in 1837 and technically it was not a company but a statutory partnership governed by its own Act of Parliament. The company had bylaws, not articles of association, which set tough limits on the size of an individual's shareholdings. AGL had long been regarded as impenetrable, but Brierley and his legal Houdini Dr Gary Weiss detected that in its strength also lay its weakness.

First, new legislation limited holdings in AGL to 5 per cent except for existing shareholders. This was introduced just to accommodate an insurance company that held 8 per cent. Second, for the first time in its history, AGL was going to be covered by the Companies Act, starting in January 1986. Until then it operated outside this legal code, and Brierley reasoned therefore the disclosure rules would not apply to shareholdings bought before that time.

So, on the strategic date of New Year's Eve 1985, IEL announced it had outlayed $105 million to acquire 41.5 per cent of AGL. Using its old ploy of parcelling the shares in small lots among hundreds of shareholders, it was able to avoid recognition. The Government quickly withdrew the section in the legislation containing the loophole on maximum shareholding for redrafting.

AGL was slow to welcome IEL into the fold, but over the years Brierley has developed an enduring fondness for the company and has even bought a personal stake in it.

His level of involvement and interest remained high throughout this period. He would check all the analysts' work, often reading files two feet deep and picking up obscure but nevertheless significant oversights. They called him 'The Master' and looked forward to working with him. When Brierley was inspired, he was interesting, astute and demanding, and for some analysts he was the reason they had come to work at IEL. Goward said Brierley was the best analyst at IEL and they worked hard together.

Brierley's view of Goward was as heightened as the pitch at which they were working. He thought Goward was smarter, more energetic and more dynamic than most people he knew.

In hindsight Goward credits himself for having taken IEL out of its shell. He says that under his stewardship IEL's profile was lifted, making it easier to raise money, a trading base was put in place and he built up a good team of analysts. He says when he arrived he saw that IEL needed a strong personality to weld together the individual talents in the company. Until then IEL had been in danger of becoming a collection of outstanding players rather than an outstanding team, he says.

Certainly Goward revitalised a lacklustre IEL, pushing Brierley and his executives to perform, and the results were soon measurable. When he arrived the share price was $2.20, though the net asset backing was $4. Goward helped push up the share price and by late 1985 it had soared to $6.40. Goward is also remembered at IEL for his excellent communication skills and superb administrative ability.

However, at twenty-nine, he lacked the maturity of a more experienced executive. He became intoxicated with his own meteoric success, and his excesses, both private and public, have caused him to be compared with the hyperkinetic Bruce Judge. Although Goward's charm worked in his favour, the feeling grew at IEL that he was becoming consumed by his own ego.

As Goward's confidence swelled, outstripping his ability, he began to make investment decisions without referring them back to his chairman, Ron Brierley. He stopped accepting Brierley's authority and began to operate largely alone. It appeared increasingly obvious to others at IEL that Goward's ambitions stretched far beyond his current appointment. They believed that ultimately he wanted to run the company himself.

But Brierley stood in his way, and even Goward could see he would never give way. Goward's frustrations mounted and he also began to direct his criticisms at Paul Collins. As another youthful pretender to the throne, Collins was his immediate rival. Furthermore, he was richer than Goward.

Goward was heard to complain that Brierley was pedantic and too cautious, but the result of his own optimism was a string of dubious investments in the property and energy sector, the most famous of which was the North Broken Hill (NBH) takeover. North Broken Hill also became a media feast when IEL's devious tax-avoidance tactics were exposed.

In January 1986 IEL's 7 per cent stake in NBH was held through a loose chain of nominee companies stretching from Sydney to the Cook Islands, Channel Islands, Panama, Macau, Liberia and Holland. This guided tour of the world's tax havens came to a halt in a Swiss bank, where the confidentiality requirements protected the identity of the nominee company.

But Section 261 of the Companies Code in Australia gives companies the right to ask shareholders whether they hold the shares in their own right and, if not, who the beneficial owner is. When NBH's queries to find out the owner of the shares failed, the shares were frozen and vested with the NCSC.

Loewenthal publicly denied IEL was the owner of the shares, but Brierley later explained he had been misunderstood. When IEL made a $450 million partial bid for just over 20 per cent of the shares, IEL revealed it already had 17.7 per cent of NBH.

But the news that prompted the managing director of NBH, Mark Bethwaite, to cut short his windsurfing holiday was that IEL proposed what it called a 'demerger' if it won control. That meant IEL planned to voluntarily liquidate the company, since the mainstream businesses of zinc, lead, silver mining and forestry and paper had no affinity with each other — which had been proved when NBH announced a $279,000 pre-tax group loss in February.

The New South Wales Government was also alerted, for it had made extensive concessions in royalty and electricity charges in recent years in recognition of the company's importance to the local community.

NBH was quick to reject the offer and instituted legal proceedings to establish the beneficial ownership of the shares. The first round was decided in February 1986 when the Supreme Court ordered that 23 million NBH shares be vested in the NCSC and sold within six months. The judgment was applauded by many who felt that corporate law had fallen into disrepute in recent years as a result of clever lawyers and accountants subverting its intention.

But NBH's victory was short-lived. In June the Victorian Supreme Court overturned that decision on a technicality and IEL was able to sell the shares to Rada Corporation in New Zealand.

IEL never disclosed the profit on the deal, but the prevailing view within the company was that the final result barely justified the effort. The shares had been purchased at too high a price and the demerger was just a contrived plan to push up the value of the company. It was making a virtue out of a necessity.

The dissatisfaction within the company was not directed only towards Goward. Goward had his own complaints about working with Brierley. Brierley's disenchantment with him, although never brought out into the open, was making his working life impossible. Instead of calling Goward to task, Brierley's anger smouldered on silently. He would walk out of the room if Goward presented a proposal he objected to, and Goward found it difficult to gain an audience with The Master. In the end, he barely saw him at all.

Goward was isolated. Brierley had effectively banished him and there was nothing he could do about it. It was hard to believe this was the same man who had said of Goward in 1983: 'The ideal IEL person is someone with a mixture of entrepreneurial and administrative ability — I think Russell Goward is what I would call the IEL type.'

Goward decided Brierley's cold-war tactics stemmed from a clash of egos. They were two queen bees fighting for the same hive and he believed his judgment was confirmed when Brierley called him into his room one day. 'He said to me, "Russell, it worries me what you're saying to the press. I don't want you to talk to the press anymore," and I agreed. I had committed the cardinal sin of pinching his press.'

Bystanders in IEL and BIL agreed this was true up to a point, but that essentially the problem lay with Brierley's inability to deal with Goward's perceived flaws. Goward was seen to be taking unnecessary risks by not keeping the company informed and not always making the best investment decisions, but Brierley did not know how to control these excesses. Although Brierley told Robert Holmes à Court he would never sell Woodley Wines, when Goward disposed of the company in 1985 he could not stop him. But the sale upset Brierley and for some time afterwards he was carpy and bad-tempered.

Brierley was a reluctant manager at the best of times and disliked dealing with people. He did not know what to do with Goward and tried to divorce himself from the situation, withdrawing sourly into himself. But neither Goward nor the company could operate in a vacuum, and the management decided there was no longer a place in the company for him.

In February 1986 he left to take control of a Melbourne-listed cashed-up company, Westmex Ltd. His successor at IEL was to be the managing director of Southern Farmers, Rodney Price. Loewenthal remembers Goward's words of warning to Price as he departed. 'He looked at him and said, "You won't last six months here, a strong bugger like you."'

EIGHTEEN

Brierleymania

WITH THE REMOVAL of Buntings from the New Zealand share register in 1984, Brierley thought he had cleaned up the competition overnight. But even then the concept of investment companies was gaining new adherents and, by 1985, a myriad of fledgling Brierley imitators had emerged in the marketplace.

Equiticorp was formed in early 1984 and not long after it was floated on the stock exchange Renouf Corporation, an investment company founded by Sir Frank Renouf, and Rainbow Corporation were formed. Others, with names Brierley regarded as bizarre and inappropriate, followed in their wake and, like reproducing amoebae, split off various parts of their organism.

Encouraged by the runaway success of BIL in recent years and aided and abetted by the increasing availability of money internationally in the form of debt, investment companies had become the baby boom of the New Zealand stock market.

At first the development of these companies took place against a backdrop of restrictive financial regulations. Controls on interest rates had been in place since 1981 and the country was in the grip of a wage and price freeze, yet even the best efforts of Prime Minister Muldoon could not hermetically seal the country from the internationalisation of the global money market.

Chase Corporation was a prime example of a company that flourished only when overseas finance was injected into its lifeblood. Chase had been around since 1970, when it was just a small-time property company. Although it had added restaurants, a bakery and blueberry farms to its list of assets by the early 1980s, it was still relatively small. Its breakthrough did not come until 1982 when Chase bought Amalgamated Theatres with a $6 million loan from the Bank of Kuwait. By 1983 it was listed on the stock exchange, and by 1986 Chase's share price had soared to $8.45. In 1982 its issued capital was less than a million dollars and shareholders' funds were just under $2 million. In 1986 those figures had climbed to $18.5 million and $139 million respectively.

The move towards corporate rationalisation and 'bigness' in the economy did not surprise Brierley. As far back as 1980 he had picked the trend and he suggested that some major companies would reach a market capitalisation of $1 billion before 1990. BIL actually reached this size by 1985. Brierley expected the trend would continue until the middle of the decade, by which time fifty or sixty companies would dominate the business landscape.

But even Brierley could not have accounted for the fourth Labour Government. Although the process of reform had already begun by the time Labour was elected to power in 1984, it provided an unexpected impetus for this change. Almost immediately it began dismantling the old system of controls. Four days after the election in July, the new Minister of Finance, Roger Douglas, scrapped the controls on lending and deposit rates. On 30 August he ended controls on interest for term deposits, and as a result money poured into the country attracted by the high interest rates. On 21 November restrictions on lending to and by foreigners in New Zealand were axed. On 21 December New Zealanders were finally permitted to buy foreign exchange to invest overseas. Less than a year after the Labour Government was elected it floated the dollar, and on 1 April 1987 banking was deregulated.

These reforms were dubbed Rogernomics and they were welcomed greedily by a country that had been dominated by a divisive, regulatory administration for so long. In the early phase of these reforms, the country was swept along on a warm and healing tide of national pride and naive optimism. Young, self-important entrepreneurs were the new messiahs of this era, and people flocked to join their cause. As the New Zealand market continued its vertical ascent, success seemed assured and even normally staid investors were carried away by the excitement created by the turmoil.

The business establishment crumbled under the onslaught of these go-go capitalists. Farmers Trading Co. Ltd fell to Chase, the old family whiteware company Fisher and Paykel to Equiticorp, and the once-mighty Kerridge empire succumbed to small, unproven Pacer Pacific Corporation. An open share register sprinkled with many small, passive investors was not a source of anxiety as the country underwent the biggest corporate feeding frenzy in its history. Instead of concentrating on their business, companies became obsessed with shoring up their share register or fending off bids.

Even before the worst excesses began, Brierley was appalled by events and lashed out at the speculative nature of the new listings on the market, particularly mining and property companies. In 1983 he was moved to write that, although it had been a phenomenal year on the New Zealand sharemarket, 'price levels quite beyond belief suggest the stock exchange has replaced the totalisator as a symbol of financial escapism'.

Although Brierley was openly critical of these developments, the success of his investment company was used as a validation for many of the events that took place. Whenever the old guard resisted these young aggressors, it simply confirmed in the public's mind that they were conservative non-performers. It was just a case of history repeating itself. After all, wasn't the Brierley experience a gleaming testimony to this?

Ironically, in this unstable environment the grand-daddy of all the takeover experts, BIL, came to be seen as a blue-chip conservative and loyal ally. Bruce Hancox was known for ringing the chief executives of companies involved in a takeover with the message that if they needed any help to give BIL a call. For a substantial fee, BIL assisted Goodmans to buy shares in Watties to stave off a takeover by New Zealand Forest Products in 1983.

Corrupt practices were also rife during this period, but, lacking information, expertise and legal clout, there was precious little the regulatory bodies could do. Not even Brierley was immune to criticism. The company's practice of gaining a foothold in a target company and using the information gained at board level to decide whether the company had the potential to warrant a full takeover or whether BIL should sell its holdings came under scrutiny. The Securities Commission was unhappy with the procedure but was powerless to forbid this form of insider trading. In 1982 the commission instigated an enquiry into this tactic as used in the Bing Harris takeover by BIL, but the result was inconclusive. Finally, in 1989, the commission promised to introduce new laws to prohibit the practice.

Meanwhile, BIL continued to build up substantial stakes in major cash-flow companies. In 1984 its stake in New Zealand News Ltd had increased to 40 per cent, and BIL took over all of Williamson Jeffrey that year. It had also carved up a large share of the radio market with stakes in Radio Avon and Hauraki Enterprises, both of which had holdings in other radio stations.

All this activity propelled BIL to second place in terms of market capitalisation by September 1984. FCL was nudged into third place. Two months later BIL pushed NZFP out of the top slot and became the largest company in New Zealand. In Australia, IEL was the twentieth-largest company, although a mere eighteen months before it had ranked 150th.

Naturally, at a time when the market was generously rerating investment companies, Brierley's stature, as founder of the original investment company, soared. At home he experienced something akin to the prodigal son's return. After years of enduring open hostility or suspicion from successive governments in New Zealand and Australia, Brierley had finally found acceptance within the fourth Labour Government in his home country.

His first dealings with the new Government came in September 1984 when he was invited to speak at the Economic Summit, and in November he spoke to interested Labour Party members at the Wednesday Club at Bellamy's.

Roger Douglas admired Brierley's summit speech and afterwards made a point of talking to Treasury staff about him. His enquiries satisfied him that Brierley would make a fine director of the Bank of New Zealand. Douglas was looking for someone who could examine the role of the BNZ in the light of changes in the New Zealand economy and who also had an international perspective. He thought Brierley's detached analysis would enable him to develop a strategy for the bank.

So on 2 February 1985 a delighted Ron Brierley joined the élite on the twenty-fourth floor of the BNZ. To Brierley, who craved status more than power, this achievement was a shining symbol of success. The fact that he had spent most of his career bloodying the noses of the Establishment did not mean he wanted to be shut out forever. He gloried in his new-found acceptance and was proud of his important new friends. Sometimes he met Douglas socially. They might have dinner or watch cricket together, and Brierley even flew him to Australia in his private jet to a cricket match. But it was Paul Collins, not Brierley, who discussed 'issues of the day' with Douglas every six weeks.

It seemed inevitable that during this era, when the interests of business coincided happily with those of Government, BIL's lobbying for Brierley's knighthood would intensify. Everyone close to Brierley knew how much he yearned for the title.

Bob Jones boasted he was able to extract sponsorship of $250,000 for the New Zealand Ballet Company from Brierley in 1983 by telling him it would be a deposit on his knighthood. Occasionally BIL executives would tell Brierley about their efforts on his behalf, and they knew they were on the right track when he listened quietly and smiled.

A conversation between Russell Goward and Brierley on the topic stuck in Murray Williams's mind for years. He dates it back to the time of the CUB takeover bid in 1983. Goward was referring to the extensive publicity they had been receiving when he said to Brierley, 'It won't be long before you are widely recognised. Everyone will be addressing you in future as *Mr* Brierley.' Brierley's reply surprised Williams. 'No,' he said, '*Sir* Ron Brierley.'

At one stage they believed they had bagged the prestigious title for him during the Muldoon administration, but it had proved elusive. However, the executives had every reason to believe this Government would be more receptive. After all, Frank Renouf had been successful. Why not Brierley?

The nomination itself was a simple procedure. All nominations for knighthoods are considered by a parliamentary committee known as the Honours, Appointments, and Travel Committee, which comprises up to eight Cabinet ministers appointed by the Prime Minister. Once the nominations have been discussed, the committee draws up an unofficial list, which is then passed to the Governor-General for unofficial palace approval. Next, the Governor-General's office approaches those named on the list and asks them unofficially if they would be willing to accept this honour. Once this procedure is completed an official list is approved by the Government.

The more cynical members of BIL thought there was more than a little self-interest behind Brierley's lavish praise of the Labour Government in his 1985 chairman's report. The great skill and courage of the Government had inspired 'an infusion of vigour and variety in a climate of unprecedented entrepreneurial activity', he wrote, despite his misgivings about much of that activity. He concluded that overall the winner must be the economy.

Certainly the sharemarket was roaring ahead at full throttle. In January 1980 the Barclays index stood at 410. Four years later it had soared to 1,487, in 1985 it was 1,931, and by February 1986 it had passed 2,000, reaching 3,912 by November.

Out of the crucible of the sharemarket frenzy, a new word was coined — Brierleymania. Everybody knew someone who was raking in the spoils of having been a devoted Brierley shareholder, and it seemed foolish not to join them. Margin traders were even borrowing up to $40,000 at interest rates of 25 per cent or more to buy BIL shares. Like everyone else, they were banking on the share price continuing its upward ascent, but it had to be fast so the debt could be paid off in a couple of days.

The company was not the only beneficiary of this public goodwill, for in this hothouse atmosphere Brierley blossomed. Suddenly he was lionised as the prophet of people's capitalism. People fed hungrily on stories of the Brierley millionaires and heard how £500 worth of BIL shares in 1961 was worth $3 million in 1985, taking all cash and bonus issues into account.

BIL annual meetings had always been well attended, but the numbers were mushrooming year by year. While 1,300 came in 1984, there were 3,500 two years later. In 1987, there was a mass rally of 5,000 in Auckland. They were Ron's army and the backbone of the company — thousands of small, often elderly shareholders who had invested their savings with the man they trusted.

What they were waiting for was not the profit forecast or even the refreshments, though these were attacked with great gusto, but for many it was a once-in-a-lifetime chance to met Ron Brierley himself. His visits to New Zealand were fleeting and his public appearances and utterances even more uncommon. For many New Zealanders he had become the Greta Garbo of the business world, mysterious and rare and gifted.

Minutes after the formalities were over, his lunar-pale visage was lost in a cluster of grateful, hand-shaking shareholders, and he rewarded them with a display of patience and endurance seldom witnessed outside the Royal family. He would stand stock-still for hours, smiling and nodding and saying little of any consequence until Hancox and Collins decided he had had enough and whisked him away for another year.

Brierley loved the public adulation and, after years of solitary endeavour, he began to relax his rigid work routine to allow for a little socialising. His friend Frank Renouf credits himself for Brierley's coming-out and can pinpoint the turning-point exactly.

Though Brierley had made a poor impression on the stately banker in the early 1960s, Renouf's opinion of Brierley had improved enormously over the following decades, and by the mid-1980s he found himself defending his New Zealand friend at dinner parties and functions against suspicious Australians. Renouf saw that, though Brierley had been in the country for twenty years, he had not won the hearts and minds of the people. In fact few people knew him at all.

Then Frank Renouf's friend Lady Mary Fairfax, the well-known socialite and member of the Fairfax media family, expressed an interest in meeting Brierley, so Renouf arranged an introduction. Renouf recalls that Lady Mary asked Brierley if he could give her son, Warwick, a job. Brierley brushed the request aside and instead gave Lady Mary a job by appointing her to the board of IEL in 1985. And that introduction, apparently, was the first of many encounters with the doyennes of the Sydney social set. Renouf recalls: 'He then appeared at all her cocktail and dinner parties and was meeting a new range of people who would never run into him in the normal course of business. All of a sudden he was being seen with all the right people in all the right places. That started making an enormous difference to his own feeling of how well known he was becoming. It precipitated a major social flowering.'

His friends and colleagues watched Brierley's 'flowering' with amazement, and privately some wondered if he were not becoming a swizzle-stick for the smart set. The shy workaholic was even making headlines in gossip columns, where he was reported to have been seen cavorting on the dance floor with famous divorcee Susan Rossiter Peacock Sangster at a $60-a-head fund-raising party for the Opera Foundation. The *Daily Telegraph* columnist noted that they danced energetically to 'In the Mood' and 'Do You Know the Way to San Jose?' but sat it out during 'The Twist'.

The story told within BIL and IEL is that Brierley, although flattered, was also alarmed by the attentions of Susan Sangster, and so on a party on the IEL boat, *Lionheart*, he deliberately steered her in the direction of the six-foot-five, newly knighted, sixty-nine-year-old Sir Frank Renouf. The rest is history.

Brierley was also beginning to enjoy some of the fruits of his wealth. Although he was never frugal, his needs had generally been simple and he was genuinely not interested in accumulating money or possessions for himself. He had never tried to beef up his personal holding in BIL or IEL and, despite being the largest shareholder, his 5 per cent or less was all the personal wealth he had. He did not take a salary at BIL, but the company paid his expenses. Hancox said that ensured Brierley was the cheapest executive in the company. Certainly, measured against his imitators, he was by no means the king of consumerism or capital.

What he did have was shares in a Spanish peasant farm, which he later sold, and he also enjoyed the use of IEL's holiday home in Kilcare in New South Wales. In 1987 he bought his own holiday home on Mackeral Beach on the Hawkesbury River.

But at home and abroad this was a time when executives' personal wealth and company opulence was at its zenith. Houses worth millions were bought and sold in New Zealand and Australia, fortunes were paid for art, cars, clothes and food, and companies as new and unproven as Energycorp owned a fleet of jets and conducted their business from designer-styled offices.

BIL had never been that sort of company. Brierley's personal minimalism had permeated the ethos of BIL and wanton expenditure was frowned upon. But in 1986 the company moved itself upmarket with the purchase of its first company jet, a Cessna Citation 111. Later another jet was acquired for IEL. In Wellington BIL shifted into plush offices in the CML building, and in Australia IEL was well situated in the MLC Centre in Sydney's Martin Place.

BIL made these purchases at the height of its activity, for 1985 and 1986 had been the two most buoyant years in the company's history. With Hancox at the helm the company had undergone something of a metamorphosis from an investor-asset trader to an entrepreneurial company funded by a growing operational base. The 1985/86 year saw the addition of nine new listed subsidiaries in New Zealand, including Dominion Breweries Ltd, Winstones Ltd and NZ News Ltd. Substantial holdings were acquired in NZI Corporation, Cable Price Downer Ltd, Skellerup Industries Ltd and Lane Walker Rudkin Industries Ltd. A joint venture was established with the merger of the production division of Whitcoulls and AHI Industries. Quill Humphries was merged with Hughes and Cossar Ltd, and DIC Stores Ltd with Apparel Holdings Ltd.

In March 1985, BIL became the first New Zealand company to reach a market capitalisation of $1 billion. The company by then accounted for 12 per cent of the New Zealand sharemarket and, psychologically and literally, it dominated the business landscape as no other company had ever done. *National Business Review*'s column 'Without a Word of a Lie' captured this feeling when it jokingly suggested Dominion Breweries change its name to BONZA — Brierley Owns New Zealand and Australia.

Much of the dynamism of the company has to be attributed to Bruce Hancox. He brought zest and vigour to the group, skilfully exercising his management abilities without creating a bureaucracy in BIL. He (and therefore BIL) was known for the speed and flexibility with which he responded to problems. Hancox could reply to a suggestion within half an hour, while other general managers often had to get board approval before they could proceed, said one broker.

Although the public rewarded the company with ever-increasing numbers on its share register, Hancox realised there was a limit to their generosity. The company's growth was dependent on their contribution through various rights and bonus issues, and though BIL had managed to raise $400 million in two such issues in 1986, New Zealand had, after all, only the population of Sydney. The future of the company lay elsewhere.

Brierley had been investing overseas for twenty years, but it was not until the mid-1980s that BIL began to stoke its international base. In 1985 it raised more than $650 million in European and United States markets, and a year later established a $US250 million note issuance facility and a $50 million Euro Sterling issue. The equity base was widened by the placement of twenty million shares in Australia and London and a $100 million Swiss Franc convertible bond issue.

BIL listed in Australia in 1985 and on the London exchange in 1986, but Brierley confused the City by not turning up for the event.

IEP listed on the New Zealand Stock Exchange in February 1986 and the shares were immediately snapped up by eager local investors who previously had to buy IEP stock through the Hong Kong exchange.

BIL was also making investments and establishing an office in the United States. The forerunner to investment in that country was its acquisition of an Ohio-based retail chain, the Higbee Company Ltd, for $NZ150 million, and Russell Goward announced then that IEP had undisclosed holdings in forty-two United Kingdom companies and twenty-four United States companies. As a result the share price leapt from $HK3 at the beginning of that year to $HK99 in early 1985. IEP still maintained a registered office in Hong Kong for tax purposes, and the jump in the share price prompted the Commissioner of Securities to suggest IEP establish a physical presence in the country.

In June 1985, IEP made its biggest investment to date when it bought a contro ing interest in British motor and property group Tozer Kemsley & Millbourn (Holdings) Plc, and that same year it bid for one of Britain's biggest motor dealers and van hire companies, Kenning Motor Group.

Acceptance in Britain was an uphill battle, since both antipodean and investment companies were regarded with distaste. Slater Walker had seen to it that investment companies had never really made a comeback in the United Kingdom, so when Brierley bought stakes in companies such as 30 per cent of Ocean Transport & Trading Plc, and was content to sit and wait, it was taken as a loss. But in 1989 he sold his stake in OT & T, with a gross profit of £32 million.

Through IEP, Brierley had built up an idiosyncratic collection of assets including banks, hotels, building material companies, an insurance company, a stake in a ranch in Hawaii and even a share of the Playboy empire.

Brierley was not the only New Zealand investment company to be taking a closer interest in the United Kingdom. Some of the younger high flyers had also taken the leap, and both Rainbow and Chase had an office in London.

It was galling to someone like Brierley that in the space of a few years these youngsters had achieved a level of stature, investment and recognition BIL had fought twenty-five years to attain. Brierley continued to express his doubts about the merits and abilities of these companies and the inevitability of a shakeout, but to Bruce Hancox the irritations were closer to home. Every day such companies were competing with BIL for opportunities and investors, making it difficult for BIL to maintain its growth path and historical performance levels.

One of the most successful of the new breed of entrepreneurs was Craig Heatley, the managing director of Rainbow Corporation Ltd. In 1977 he was a twenty-one-year-old product manager with a commerce degree, working for Fletcher Steel. But on holiday one year with a friend, he became embued with enthusiasm for the vast commercial potential of mini-golf. The pair quit their jobs, opened a mini-golf complex in Taupo and then became involved in building another complex on Auckland's Tamaki Drive, to which they added boats and a hydroslide. Their biggest venture was the lurid Rainbow's End leisure park in Manukau City.

A year later Rainbow Corporation was listed with a market capitalisation of $6 million. Heatley and his team then diversified Rainbow into property and industrial developments, and as a result of a succession of new issues, spin-offs in new companies and easy credit, Rainbow quickly had an amusement park, property and resort interests, a supermarket, an underwater world and a 20 per cent stake in Australian Woolworths Ltd. In 1986 Heatley, then only thirty years old, was reputedly worth some $120 million, and in July of the same year his company's market capitalisation had rocketed to $350 million. It was large enough to begin crowding Brierley.

Rainbow had tried to buy Rothmans when BIL was cobbling together the Magnum deal, but it sold out profitably a few weeks later. Rainbow also spent $100 million in the United Kingdom and got in the way of BIL when it was building up stakes in British oil company Ultramar, Masport and Woolworths in Australia.

As a result of these encounters Hancox had a chance to see Craig Heatley and executive director Gary Lane at work and decided that they were two very talented men who could well have a place in BIL. BIL also had its eye on three of Rainbow's major investments — Woolworths, Progressive Enterprises and Kern Corporation. Although it suspected that the value of the rest of Rainbow's corporate assets were as ephemeral as its name, these three assets, plus Heatley and Lane, were considered worthy BIL takeover targets.

Brierley's role in New Zealand was minimal by now. He simply raised questions and gave wise counsel. But when he voiced his apprehensions about the Rainbow portfolio, he said he was comforted with hearty assurances that they knew what he meant but not to worry. Everything would be okay.

So in March 1987, when Rainbow announced it planned to merge with Progressive Enterprises by way of a share swap to form a new holding company, Astral Pacific, BIL went on the offensive. The first salvos it fired were verbal. Collins announced BIL was buying Progressive shares because they were worth twice as much as Rainbow shares. Since a crucial factor in the merger was the price parity between Rainbow and Progressive, these comments from a corporate heavyweight like BIL were devastating.

Rainbow's value had already dropped following a mini-crash in the New Zealand market in January, and from a high of $10.80 in late 1986, their share price wilted to $4 after Collins spoke out. Suddenly rumours began to percolate through the market about Rainbow's precarious finances and Collins continued to criticise aspects of its accounting and earnings forecast and questioned how Astral Pacific would be managed.

The BIL campaign forced the share price down to $2.10, all but scuttling Heatley's original share swap. Heatley retaliated and issued a $10 million defamation writ against Paul Collins and BIL. 'It was out-and-out warfare,' says Heatley. In the end the legal action was discontinued, since BIL bought 30 per cent of Rainbow's discounted scrip in May, while Rainbow took BIL's holding in Progressive Enterprises.

Three months later, in a move echoing the Buntings merger, BIL took full control of Rainbow, confirming its grip on Woolworths. It was hoped that Heatley as an executive director would provide a conceptual, intellectual thrust to the company and Lane would have a management role.

Rainbow vanished from the sharemarket and it looked as if BIL was once again victorious. But the benefits were not as enormous as BIL had imagined. The three jewels BIL executives had identified were valuable, but the downside of Rainbow's property portfolio exceeded even their worst imaginings. Two months after BIL swept Rainbow into oblivion, the biggest sharemarket crash ever to hit New Zealand occurred, wiping millions off the over-valued Rainbow assets. With hindsight, BIL would decide that the Rainbow deal had not been financially worthwhile.

In the meantime the National Corporate and Securities Commission in Australia had also begun legal proceedings against BIL following its acquisition of 20 per cent of Woolworths via Rainbow. This stake, plus its own 20 per cent holding, put IEL in breach of the Australian takeover code, which requires companies to make a full bid after passing the 20 per cent ownership threshold. BIL was found guilty of breaching the code, but no action was taken because in May 1989 IEL completed a full takeover of Woolworths.

Heatley and Lane were also rerated along with their former assets, and the judgment was harsh. 'They weren't and aren't talented,' Brierley says. They did not meet the standards set by BIL, and neither had anything to offer the company.

Although Heatley was never given an executive function, he took an interest in the investment side of the operation and travelled twice with Hancox to the IEP office in the United States. Nothing was put to him officially, but he guessed that Hancox was hoping he would get involved in IEP, thus sparing Hancox continual travel to the American office.

Heatley turned out to be what is known as a 'big picture' man. BIL did encourage people to think big, but Heatley's ideas were larger than life. When he began lobbying the company to take over the $30 billion General Motors company in the United States, it was obvious he was not BIL material. BIL analysts had investigated the possibility of taking over GM with a consortium and then selling off various parts of the gigantic organisation, but they had concluded that it was a moderate- to high-risk operation. It soon became clear to BIL executives that Heatley was prepared to take bigger risks than they were used to. 'That mentality was out of our ballpark,' said Collins.

After the crash Heatley promoted the idea of a management buyout of BIL, but the directors rejected this because it would have disadvantaged their shareholders.

Heatley was at BIL only a year when he left to pursue his own interests in Sky Television, another proposal BIL regarded as too risky. Heatley said he left because he had no real role in the company and conflicts with Collins were starting to develop. 'I think Paul Collins didn't want an involvement from me and Gary because it would have threatened his position. I didn't get on well with him, but I don't think many people do,' Heatley says.

As he made his farewells, it may have crossed Heatley's mind that, far from stopping him in his tracks, BIL had probably rescued him from an even worse fate. At any rate, that's how some people at BIL were ruefully reviewing the Rainbow takeover.

NINETEEN

Blue Lagoon

AFTER SEVEN YEARS at BIL, Bruce Hancox had won Brierley's goodwill and respect. It was official; Brierley publicly announced at an IEL annual meeting in 1986 that Hancox was one of the best chief executives in the world. This was a rare burst of praise from Brierley, and it had been hard-won.

Although Don McDonald's representations broke the ice in 1979, it took years for Brierley to accept his New Zealand deputy. Hancox said that, for the first three years he was at BIL, Brierley barely spoke to him, but by the mid-1980s hardly a day went by without a telephone call.

In that time Hancox had learned a lot about working with Brierley and knew just how to handle him. In fact he felt he knew him so well he could almost predict the way Brierley would react to any situation and what he would say.

One of the first lessons Hancox learned about his boss was that he almost always backed away from any conflict, and hence his contribution to management was limited. He rarely disagreed with a proposal openly and would never argue his case. He might play devil's advocate, but when it came to conveying his distaste, he chose the powerful path of passive resistance. Without saying a word he would quietly walk out of the room.

Bruce Hancox recalls working hard to get the support of all the BIL directors to sell the company's 20 per cent stake in Dominion Breweries. By the time the board meeting was held, Hancox was confident he had the numbers to push through the sale, but when it came to the crunch Brierley just got up and stalked out of the room. Since he had the power of veto, his departure effectively cancelled Hancox's plan.

Gradually Hancox and Collins realised that the obstacle was always the same — selling assets. Brierley was essentially a hoarder, squirrelling away assets as an end in itself. While not averse to pocketing a profit from the sale of a strategic stake in a company, Brierley took a different view of subsidiary companies. They were 'part of the family', and to sell a member of the family was a tragedy he viewed as avoidable.

He once told Hancox he would like to work out how much better off the company would be if it had never sold anything. Hancox, of course, pointed out if it had never sold anything, it would not have had the wherewithal to buy new assets; to which Brierley replied, 'That's what you say, Bruce.'

Hancox thought he understood Brierley's motivation. 'Ron doesn't assert his power and he never tells you not to do something. That way he doesn't have to take responsibility for things. Ron's never wrong because he never makes a decision.'

Hancox had watched him over the years putting off confrontations, engagements and decisions by using his inimitable technique of courteous avoidance. Brierley has stock phrases for such occasions, which he uses to fine, if sometimes mischievous, effect. I once complained to him that whenever he responded to my requests with, 'Leave it with me, Yvonne,' my heart sank, and he readily agreed.

'I have three standard phrases,' he told me. '"Leave it with me" or "I'll get in touch with you" usually work. Finally, absolutely failsafe, and only to be used in exceptional circumstances,' he said, wagging his finger and grinning, '"I won't let you down."'

Nevertheless, Hancox's perception of Brierley's foibles was tempered with a deep appreciation of his ability. For all his deficiencies, Brierley was invaluable in the role of devil's advocate. He was the team conscience, and he was not called The Master for nothing. As the company expanded over the decade, BIL executives found it became impossible to acquaint Brierley with every plan of action. But even when Hancox and Collins made a decision without Brierley's approval, his presence was ubiquitous.

'You know he's going to be there and he's going to go through it thoroughly, and you can always feel when you've let him down, though he never says a word,' says Hancox.

'Ron's there in your subconscious checking things. It's annoying, really. Sometimes you go to him, you've done a deal or something and you think you've checked everything, but he'll always find something you've overlooked. You come away from one of those sessions with Ron saying, "The bugger — he's still the master."'

By the mid-1980s a relationship had developed between the two men that was comic in its differences. Bruce Hancox had a paternalistic, affectionate regard for Brierley. He appreciated the humour of his pedantic habits and old-mannish behaviour, and just occasionally he enjoyed a quiet joke at Brierley's expense.

'He has such funny ways and sometimes I do things just to piss him off. He always has his pens arranged in front of him, one on the left, the other on the right. The other day I gave him a paper I wanted him to read and I was talking to him about it. I pushed his pens aside and put the paper in front of him. He just pushed the paper away and picked up the pens and put them back in place. He didn't listen to anything I was saying.'

But generally Hancox displays a kind, parental patience with Brierley, and even tolerates repetitive, circumlocutory conversations designed to off-load responsibility and seek approval. Hancox calls them a stupid charade and they usually begin with a telephone call from Brierley.

'I've stopped buying X stock,' Brierley opens.

'What for? How much have we got?' asks Hancox.

'Not much.'

'Well, what do you want to do that for? Why don't you buy some more?'

'What do you think, Bruce?'

'I haven't got a clue, but I say, "Go ahead, Ron, buy more of that stock then,"' Hancox says, knowing that if it wasn't any good Brierley wouldn't be buying it anyway.

'If you say so, Bruce,' is the familiar rejoinder. 'How would you go about it?'

When Hancox tells him his voice drops. 'Oh, I wouldn't do that, Bruce.'

'Well, what do you think then?'

'Well, I would . . .' and so on it goes.

Younger staff who worked with Brierley tired of these rituals and few could be bothered indulging him. In IEL, Bill Loewenthal had been through these routines dozens of times and had probably survived over fifteen years as Brierley's right-hand man at IEL because he behaved the same way as Hancox. Like Hancox, he was a peacemaker who never threatened Brierley's position as number one, although he was capable of being mischievous.

He knew, for instance, that when Brierley came into his office and said, 'Bill, there's something I'd like to discuss with you. What would you say to putting Lady Mary Fairfax on the board?' that he had already told her she would have a seat at the IEL table. Loewenthal was not above extracting maximum mileage out of Brierley's need for approval, and so he might respond with a scornful, 'Oh Ron, what the hell would we want to do that for? It doesn't make sense. That would be ridiculous.'

As the years went by, Brierley took to spending Christmas at Motueka with Bruce Hancox and his partner, Judi Lenart, whom he has known for many years. In other years he had always made sure he was overseas. Although Hancox declares spending time with Ron is 'boring as hell', he and Judi enjoy him hugely.

For Brierley it is hardly a holiday. He is up at six thirty, working at a desk underneath a tree, which Hancox calls his outside office. He might stop at midday and relax with Bruce and Judi, but he will put in a few more hours later on. By the end of the day, without any undue huffing or puffing, he would have put in a full eight hours' work. His pace is sure and steady and, like the tortoise in the fable, he usually wins the race.

His traditional New Year gesture is to haul out a fresh diary and plan the year ahead, marking in dates of significance. Bruce and Judi would often see him staring into the distance for hours, his pen hovering over the page. Then suddenly the hand would fall and he would scribble something in the book. Intrigued by what the result of such ponderings could be, Judi once peeked over his shoulder to see what he had written. It was 'October — London', but, not wanting to make too firm a commitment, he had added '?'

Clearly, Brierley felt comfortable with Bruce Hancox, and in 1986 McDonald stood down willingly as deputy chairman in favour of Hancox. Although Brierley had never been captivated by him in the same way he had been with Russell Goward or Bruce Judge, Hancox had earned his respect over a long period. Moreover, Hancox understood Brierley and knew that, whatever happened, Brierley wanted to retain his position, at least publicly, as undisputed head of the BIL empire. Fortunately, Hancox was not interested in this role. He preferred being the number two, for he calculated that way he had the twin luxuries of obscurity and power.

But the truth was that Ron Brierley was increasingly drifting away from the nuts and bolts of the company's business. Although he was still chairman of BIL, IEL and IEP, most of the day-to-day running of the company was done by his chief executives in New Zealand and Australia.

He was not as consumed by the company as he had been in the past, and for once he was enjoying a status and social respectability he had never experienced before. Instead of being condemned as a corporate raider, he was hailed as an entrepreneur, and in 1986 he was even named one of Australia's top five managers, with IEL ranked second-equal and BIL fifth-equal in a survey of companies carried out by the *Business Review Weekly* magazine. That year *The*

Australian newspaper named him one of the top ten businessmen in Australia.

IEL had a box at the Sydney Cricket Ground, Brierley travelled frequently, following cricket tours, and was seen more often at society functions. He was even photographed accompanying young, attractive women — such as Robyn Alexander at a Haley's Comet black-tie party at the Sydney Power House Museum.

His appointment as chairman of the BNZ and his coveted knighthood in 1987 just served to cement Brierley's position as corporate elder statesman.

In 1987 he also became a member of a very select group of international business people to be invited to the White House as part of the International Council. Brierley, Sir Ron Trotter from Fletcher Challenge, Mike Robson (Independent Newspapers Ltd), and Michael Horton (Wilson and Horton) were the four who represented New Zealand at the three-day meeting. The guest roll at the council showed a heavy bias towards influential people in the news media. There, with United States Secretary of State George Shultz, Secretary of the Treasury James Baker and Vice-President George Bush, they were invited to contribute to solutions to problems facing the United States. They listened to briefings and took part in discussion.

At the 1988 council Brierley was the appointed leader of a discussion group and, after they had thrashed out the issue at hand, he had to report back to the assembled throng. The council considered such weighty matters as, 'Why is America losing the image war?' and 'What should the USA be doing to combat the evils of drugs?' Brierley calls it pure American farce and jokes that his suggestions have since been adopted as United States foreign policy.

The meeting ended with a luncheon at the White House with President Ronald Reagan. A photograph of Brierley shaking the President's hand is proudly displayed in his office and Wellington home. He has attended every council gathering since 1987 and looks upon the invitation as a great honour. It thrills him to know that at the end of the session he is able to put a name and a face to the United States Government.

'By the middle of the afternoon of the third day, when you are just another face in the crowd, you look at the White House and say to yourself, "Did all that really happen?"'

While all these new titles and honours were being heaped on Brierley, he was more than happy to take on the role of roving ambassador for the company and was not at all sorry to hand over the management to his executives. After all, he had been in the business for twenty-six years by 1987 and, though every deal was different, there was a sense of *déjà vu* with each new proposal. He had done it all before and his cutting edge had been rubbed smooth with time and repetition.

IEL's top analyst, Peter Pedley, recalls asking him in desperation one day, 'God, Ron, aren't you bored? Here I am talking to you about a deal that's probably number 974 for you and it's only number 458 for me and I'm bored. What keeps you going?'

He says Brierley replied, 'I hate to see other people doing good deals.' At other times he would claim that getting better returns for shareholders motivated him, or working with such talented people, but the truth was his heart had gone out of the business and, in many ways, this was related to the size of the company. In recent years the BIL empire had grown beyond his grasp. It was investing internationally and its shareholder base had mushroomed. In 1986, BIL had 95,059 shareholders; a year later it had 159,245 with a market capitalisation of $4471.9 million. Its total assets of $11.8 billion in 1987 were scattered all over the world.

Special expertise was now required to run such an enormous company. For example, banking had become a complex exercise and vital to the company's operation, but it had never interested Brierley. In fact, Collins complained that Brierley was not interested in the liability side of the balance sheet at all, and Hancox could see he was unfamiliar with deals of the magnitude now being undertaken. It had all become too big for him and he appeared to have lost some of his old confidence.

'He never did big deals before and he used to do everything by himself. The whole battle plan, everything. Now deals need liaising with bankers and brokers, and he never talks to anyone about anything,' Hancox says.

Brierley was not the only person who thought the fun had gone out of the business. Pedley remembers wistfully the day Brierley proudly cracked open the two bottles of Dom Perignon champagne to celebrate the CUB deal in 1983, but three years later they were doing deals ten times as large without so much as a can of Coke being opened in celebration.

His unwillingness to sell assets was also a point of growing frustration within the group. He could not be persuaded that the Ohio-based department store Higbee should be sold, and when Collins and Hancox disposed of the company for a profit of more than $100 million, he was inconsolable. They joked about this dispute at the 1987 profit announcement.

'It's just as well Ron Brierley isn't here, because the Higbee results of August/September are great. Ron would just look at it and say, "I cannot understand why we are selling this." We have an enormous difference of opinion with Ron on that. But a group of us has looked at it and we can't bring value to that company any more. And so we made a decision to sell,' Hancox told *National Business Review* in October 1987.

Hancox's explanation was also a signal that Brierley had lost his ultimate power — the power of veto. He had retained this dominance until well into the 1980s. But as Hancox and Collins gained confidence, their dissatisfaction with Brierley's leadership and judgment began to be voiced. At this stage the dissent was not threatening, and publicly it was couched in jocular tones.

Hancox's and Collins' jokes about Brierley at the 1987 presentation caused *National Business Review*'s 'Shoeshine' columnist to wonder if he was not witnessing the development of a McPhail and Gadsby of the financial world. Take Hancox's statements on what Brierley thought was the best way for BIL to handle the soaring kiwi dollar: 'His idea was that we should have continued to pour funds out of New Zealand at a rapid rate and have enormous asset exposure offshore. If we had done that, I think we would have probably been down about $250 million on our accounting basis.'

Although Hancox and Collins did not say so at the time, they were also unhappy with a deal he was currently negotiating. In their view, the Equity & Law deal just didn't add up.

Equity & Law Life Assurance Society Plc was a 143-year-old insurance company formed initially to cater for the legal profession, though it now marketed itself to all sections of the community and ranked as the sixth-largest life insurance company in the United Kingdom. It had also branched out into the northern European market and sales from its Dutch and German offices accounted for 41 per cent of its profit.

Brierley's bid was the first hostile takeover bid for a British life company in twenty years, and he had chosen a formidable opponent. Equity & Law was governed by a board bristling with members of the British upper crust. Its chairman, Sir Douglas Wass, was for nine years Secretary to the Treasury and later joint head of the British civil service. The directors include Lord Rockley, managing director of Kleinwort Benson, and Sir Claus Mosel, former vice-chairman of N. M. Rothschild & Sons, a director of the Economist Newspaper Group and Octopus Publishing and chairman of the Royal Opera House at Covent Garden. Wass's non-executive colleagues included two wardens of Oxford colleges and the president of the Royal Horticultural Society.

The company was well protected against outsiders by a raft of rules and laws drawn up to prevent dishonest practices, but they also had the effect of maintaining the status quo.

The British insurance industry was equally cosy. Insurance companies had welded strong interlocking links by owning large blocks of each other's shares. So any predator mounting a takeover bid would have to win over the insurance industry at large to succeed. For example, Equity & Law had institutional shareholders such as Legal and General (2.5 per cent), Royal London Mutual Insurance (2.4 per cent) and the Prudential (1.8 per cent).

Brierley should have been aware of this trap, since institutional opposition had foiled their last two takeover bids in Britain — for Ocean Transport & Trading and Molins Plc.

But the biggest questionmark in the Equity & Law equation rested on how BIL could unlock its value. No one doubted the value was there. The MLC experience had taught them that because Equity & Law was a proprietary life assurance company, its balance sheet bore no relationship to the true worth of the acquisition. The real value of the company lay in the policyholders' funds. Equity & Law managed their funds and received a percentage of the profit.

But acquiring Equity & Law would cost BIL some £400 million, and the cost of funding this was calculated to be about £40 million a year. With an annual return of only £8 million and shareholders' funds of £2.8 million, the group executives wanted to know where the rest of the money would come from. It appeared to be impossible to unlock the policyholders' funds without returning the money to the policyholders.

Collins was not happy with the deal, and Bruce Hancox stated bluntly that he 'had the shits about it all'. He asked Brierley more than once, 'How do you make a profit out of it?' and he was none the wiser when Brierley replied, 'If you can't see that by now, perhaps you shouldn't be in this business.' Hancox recognised this as one of Brierley's familiar ploys of undermining his opponent.

Brierley was typically unperturbed by these discussions. 'It sounds arrogant but it simply indicated that those expressing the disagreement knew less about it than I did,' he says.

He decided there was no point in explaining what he was doing, since the concepts were difficult to grasp and the judged value of Equity & Law was open to interpretation. He thought the value was there and that was the main thing.

'If you own the value, the unlocking is secondary. Once you own something, if the value is there, you might have to rack your brains to find a solution, but it is better than finding there is no value to unlock. Just say the discontent was brushed aside.'

But his assistant in the Equity & Law deal, corporate general manager Paddy Marra, was hard at work trying to find ways to unlock the value. One possibility was accessing some of the profit through NZI. BIL then owned a third of NZI, and Paul Collins was the deputy chairman. Because NZI already had approval to take over UK Life, Equity & Law could have diverted some of their profit through product lines operating through UK life. This would be easier if UK Life and Equity & Law had common ownership so NZI could sell a share of UK Life to IEP.

Another longer-term prospect involved Equity & Law adding the sort of assets Brierley wanted to its portfolio, enabling him to bid for these assets at a discount later. In effect, he was using Equity & Law's money to buy the assets he wanted at a discount.

But all the time he knew there was a strong possibility another rival insurance company would be flushed out by his bid. Brierley had already snared about 30 per cent of Equity & Law by early 1987, and in the process he learned that there were other suitors for the company. Two representatives of a French insurance company approached Brierley about the possibility of doing a joint venture. The discussions came to nothing, but it was clear to Marra and Brierley that these gentlemen were keen to get Equity & Law and they started to take a closer look at the French company. Their research confirmed their initial impressions and they realised with delight that there was another factor in their favour. The odds were stacking up in what Marra called 'a huge game of poker'.

But little of this was known to the BIL team, for Brierley, perhaps cultivating that famous mystique, remained tightlipped. Hancox knew that without an adequate explanation and given the potential risk, no one could support the proposal. The board would be completely against him and he considered the implications. Perhaps the 'old bugger' deserved the benefit of the doubt. After all these years the company owed him something. A little respect at least. 'You say you'll do it and I'll put my hand up with you,' he told Brierley. 'And I'll make sure it gets through.'

So it was on. Bidding in Europe and Britain is a complicated matter because of the web of rules and regulations, and the whole procedure is handled by merchant banks. Brierley's representative was J. Henry Schroder Wagg and Co. Ltd (Schroders). Their code name for the deal was Blue Lagoon — Blue for Brierley and Lagoon for Equity & Law.

Bidding began in earnest in September 1987, but Brierley had laid the battle plans for over two years. He knew that under the Insurance Companies Act 1982 any person who controlled 15 per cent or more of an insurance company needed the approval of the Department of Trade and Industry (DTI). However, if a person controlled 15 per cent or more of the insurance company as at 12 January 1987, approval was not required until a limit of 33.3 per cent of the voting power had been reached.

On 12 January, BIL had 18 per cent of Equity & Law, so therefore it was allowed to go to the 33.3 per cent threshold. By mid-year BIL's share held by IEP Securities Ltd had increased to 29.6 per cent at a cost of more than £100 million, and Brierley was hoping to supplement this with a parcel held by the merchant bank Warburgs, which was understood to have between 11 and 14 per cent. Brierley and his solicitors were working hard trying to find a way of picking up the shares without alerting the authorities. They investigated blind trusts, nominee companies and other avenues, but nothing worked.

Their aversion to the DTI was based on the time it would take to gain approval. In their favour was Brierley's knighthood, and their holdings in NZI, EPI, and Central Pacific Corporation. But they calculated that the six weeks it would take the DTI to approve the proposal was actually a week shorter than the time allowed to complete a takeover.

The penalty for breaching the limit was that BIL would have to bid for the entire company at the highest price paid in the last six months. But since that price was a low 363p, that posed no problems.

However, Brierley's research revealed that Warburgs had only 5 per cent because it had sold the bulk of its shares to BIL anyway. He decided that breaching the limit for 2 per cent was not worth the offence it would cause.

Meanwhile, Brierley with his advisors was busy devising a structure that could take over Equity & Law and avoid stamp duty and taxes in the United Kingdom and New Zealand. The final result was a three-tiered structure stretching from New Zealand to the Cook Islands, with the bid company resident in Britain but managed and controlled in Monaco.

BIL's first bid, on 4 September 1987, of 365p cash per share was rejected by the Equity & Law board as unwelcome and undervalued.

Shortly after making the bid Brierley travelled to Bangkok on his way to Sydney. As he sat in the airport lounge idly reading the newspapers, he came upon an article that mentioned a bid for Equity & Law. Thinking it was BIL's bid, he read on and, to his surprise, found it was in fact referring to a higher bid of 400p per share from a leading French insurance company, Compagnie du Midi.

This was also rejected, but its revised offer later in the month of 435p cash or a mixture of Midi shares and cash, worth at worst 446p cash and stock valuing the company at £449 million, was accepted.

Compagnie du Midi was France's fifth-largest quoted company, worth almost £2,000 million on the French stock market. Midi had been wanting to buy into the British life assurance industry since 1982 but had been hampered by French exchange control laws. But Equity & Law, with its northern European offices and acknowledged British expertise in life assurance, was a perfect fit for the French company, which had strong southern European representation.

Brierley was asleep in Australia when Equity & Law approved the new bid by the French, but the financial pundits were predicting that as soon as he woke up to the news he would take the money and run.

The BIL team was expecting the same outcome. The gamble had paid off and they thought Brierley would be pleased with the result. So they were appalled when Brierley announced the company would be increasing its bid by a mere 4p to 450p per share on 29 September.

His latest offer valued the company at £453 million and put the board in the embarrassing position of having recommended an offer that was lower than the most current price. It could hardly refuse BIL now.

Before announcing the bid, Brierley had given Midi the chance to raise its bid to 450p. The issue was discussed by telephone since he was in Sydney at the time and he remembers he gave the company half an hour to decide. Brierley was, as ever, unfazed by the risk and confident at an almost subconscious level.

'I was getting very irritated by these telephone calls, which were interfering with the television. Thirty minutes was almost tongue in cheek, yet it was not completely frivolous. I had got to the point of complete frustration, and deep down I knew it was the right thing to do. It was a bold move, but something deep down was telling me it was right.'

Although Brierley's colleagues at BIL were supportive in that they arranged the finance for the deal, the level of anxiety was high. The new chief executive at IEL, Rodney Price, is said to have visibly blanched when he heard the news. The executives' early uneasiness with the proposal was now turning to a gut-wrenching fear. Price and the other executives were all sending the same message for Bruce Hancox to relay to Brierley: 'For Christ's sake, let's do the deal.' They could not see the point of Brierley's game of bluff. With 50 cents in his pocket, why was Brierley finessing for the small change?

For his part, Brierley remained enigmatically mute.

Pedley was convinced the market was due for a severe downturn, and he would often talk about that possibility with Brierley. He had sold all his personal holdings in IEP and most of his IEL shares by mid-1987, but when an analyst put forward a plan to sell assets Brierley shook his head. 'You are selling the lifeboats,' he said.

Instead of feeling chastened, Brierley was perversely heartened by the outcry. This was a role he was familiar with. Once again he was playing the valiant, misunderstood outcast, and once again he would show his critics that he was no play-it-safe Corporation Man, a bankable blank looking no higher than the bottom line. He took risks.

Yet more often than not the risks of his market plays were not as great as people imagined. Brierley's research was usually so thorough and his knowledge so extensive that he was able to see opportunities and outcomes not immediately obvious to others. This was true of Equity & Law.

Marra's research led him to believe that the managing director and finance director of Midi badly needed a successful takeover, because they had had a poor track record lately and their positions were in danger. He noticed the Midi executives were becoming increasingly restive.

So although BIL negotiators had been advised by Schroders to halt all initiatives until Brierley arrived in London to discuss the options, they decided to launch a new bid. We knew they were panicking, said Marra.

He calculated the odds of acquiring the company were 1 in 9, but these odds reduced to 1 in 4 with a chance phone call. Marra listened as their Schroders representative rang his Kleinworts counterpart. He wasn't there, neither was his secretary. A temp answered the phone and Marra heard her say, 'Mr Robertson is not here today. He's in Paris.' Marra was elated. He felt sure he knew what Robertson was doing in France.

Meetings with Kleinwort representatives and Equity & Law directors were fruitless, and in the middle of the negotiations Brierley flew to the United States for a meeting of international business leaders with President Ronald Reagan. He was in a jubilant mood when he left and he instructed Marra to ring him at the White House if necessary and 'ask for Ronnie'.

But on 6 October the deal was finalised. IEPS would sell 22.9 per cent of its holding in Equity & Law to Compagnie du Midi and its advisors at 450p per share. Midi would buy 7 per cent, since it already had 7 per cent and was not permitted to go beyond 15 per cent, and Kleinworts would take the rest. That just left IEPS's remaining 6.4 per cent. Midi agreed to pay 455p per share for this tranche of shares with a cash election of 450p or Midi shares worth 455p per share. Midi had to make sure its shares did not fall below 455p, because then it would be the same as the original offer of Brierley, who would have to go ahead with it. Midi's offer also extended to all the other shareholders.

At the end of the day, after all the bureaucratic hurdles had been straddled, BIL walked away from Blue Lagoon with a £42.9 million ($NZ106 million) profit. This, plus money raised to fund the bid, had boosted BIL's cash resources by £290 million.

Congratulations were in order. Brierley had finessed it. He had put the whole group at risk and had won. Pedley, who had left the company in August that year, privately denounced the outcome as pure luck and argued that you can't do that and get away with it all the time. But not even the astute Peter Pedley would have realised at that moment how lucky Brierley had been.

Five days after the settlement on Equity & Law was approved, the Dow Jones index fell 508 points, or 22.6 per cent, compared with the 12.82 per cent fall on 28 October 1929 at the start of the Great Depression. The panic in New York set off a catastrophic fall in share prices worldwide. No country escaped the misery. Australia's all-ordinaries index shed 515 points, or 25 per cent, and Hong Kong decided the risks were so great they suspended trading for the rest of the week.

At BIL, Paddy Marra could not believe what was happening. During the Equity & Law negotiations the DTI actuary asked him how a 25 per cent drop in world sharemarkets would affect the BIL group. Marra said confidently this would never happen; one or two markets might fall but New Zealand would not be among them because their market had already dropped in January that year and would not fall again.

The New Zealand market had taken a beating in early 1987, drifting down some 25 per cent, but by mid-September it had made up all the lost ground and climbed to new heights. So when it fell, it fell hard. The market suffered its biggest one-day loss ever, dropping 504 points, or 14.7 per cent, on the first day. BIL fell as low as $2.70 from its overnight close of $4.43 before buyers pushed the price back up. More than $1.6 billion was wiped off the value of the sharemarket on the day after Black Monday in New Zealand.

As the implications of the crash began to emerge, it gradually dawned on the BIL and IEL team that they had narrowly escaped disaster. By missing out on Equity & Law, they had avoided the problem of how to extract an adequate return from the company and they had also conserved at least $300 million in cash in a new era when cash was king. The optimists in the group thought they would probably have been able to scramble out of this trough, but others fervently believed that if they had owned Equity & Law, the company would be facing receivership today.

So, ironically, the highly successful raid on Equity & Law had done little to enhance Brierley's standing in his group. His decision to push for the extra 4p was seen as disproportionate to the sum involved. It was at best irresponsible, at worst stupid. The crash followed immediately afterwards, underlining the magnitude of Brierley's gamble and wiping some of the sheen from his victory. The potency of the Brierley mystique was fading.

But Equity & Law signified a major watershed in the history of the company: it was the last time Brierley was able to call the shots.

TWENTY

New Zealand Incorporated

THERE'S A SAYING at the Bank of New Zealand that when you become a director or executive of the bank you rise above any past misdemeanours.

Len Bayliss had heard that saying many times when he was employed as an economist at the bank. His tenure at the BNZ lasted from 1966 until 1982, when he resigned amid political controversy, having criticised the Muldoon administration's economic policies. He then went into private practice as an economic consultant, believing the ties with his old workplace were well and truly severed.

Three years after he left the bank, however, Bayliss had cause to remember that adage: he, together with Ron Brierley, had been asked to join the board of the BNZ, and he thought the saying applied to both of them in their different ways. Both had shunned the Establishment and now with this appointment both were being welcomed back officially into the fold.

Although Bayliss looked forward to the challenge, his appointment was never finalised. Instead, the Minister of Finance, Roger Douglas, rang with news of a change in plans. He said he was sorry but the Labour Party wanted to appoint trade union leader Rob Campbell along with Brierley.

The two new board members were politically and psychologically poles apart — the understated yet uncompromising capitalist and the outgoing, high-profile unionist — and symbolised contrasting strands of this very different Labour Government. One of the new appointees was alleged to have links with the Socialist Unity Party; the other had been frequently reviled for his role as corporate raider.

Douglas must also have been conscious of this pairing of opposites when he rang Brierley with the news. Brierley remembers that he said, '"I thought you'd be interested to know who the other appointment is. We've decided to appoint Rob Campbell."

'I had seen Campbell at the summit where he seemed to have spent most of the time glaring at people. He was a symbol of the radical left.

'I was startled, to be honest. It was clearly to balance my appointment, coming from opposite ends of the spectrum, and I said to Roger, "Perhaps we might convert him to the capitalist system." I suppose that's what a lot of people would say has happened.'

Brierley's friendship with Roger Douglas was relatively new at this stage. He had never gone out of his way to court politicians and thought they were largely irrelevant to his concerns. But he and other business leaders had been invited to speak at the Economic Summit in 1984, where Brierley's short and pithy offering was warmly received. He called upon New Zealand to set up marketing boards for its produce around the world or, he said, 'even more preferable, let me buy them for you'.

Afterward, Brierley said, Mike Moore approached him and announced, 'We've got to find a job for you,' and Brierley agreed. But when he was offered an involvement in organisations such as the Government's cost-cutting committee, he declined with the explanation that 'they weren't me really'.

Then the BNZ was mentioned and Brierley's response was immediate and enthusiastic. He found out when the board met, decided he could fit this into his timetable, and agreed. This was an eminently suitable appointment, better than the 'glorified accountant's positions' he had been offered to date, and he was excited by the prospect of making a contribution to an organisation other than BIL.

There was also one other sneaking satisfaction: 'I must admit I was not unattracted by the thought that my finishing up on the board of the BNZ was something that would have been as likely as taking over Khrushchev's job in the early 1960s.'

So in February 1985 the unlikely pair of Ron Brierley and Rob Campbell joined the chairman, Sir Lewis Ross, and former National Party chairman Sir George Chapman, Wool Board chairman Pat Morrison, former Labour MP Ted Keating, and South Island retailer and company director Alan McKechnie on the BNZ board. Over the next two years the National Party appointees were all replaced, with the exception of Pat Morrison, who survived until 1989.

In July 1986 Bayliss and funds manager and investment analyst Frank Pearson joined the board; Dr Susan Lojkine, an accountant and present head of the Commerce Commission, and Christchurch businessman Peter Leeming arrived in April 1987.

At first Brierley was both awed and astonished by the bank. He loved the formality of meetings where the directors observed all the proper niceties including wearing BNZ ties. Like all visitors to the black BNZ tower, he could not fail to be impressed by the bank's superb fine art collection and its grand office suites on the twenty-fourth floor.

But it was the monthly lunches that really epitomised the bank's self-importance. Management and directors would sit down together in the splendour of the mahogany-panelled dining room, where the menu was tucked into the board papers along with instructions on where to sit and the name of the guest speaker. This was usually a notable New Zealander and included at various times the Governor-General, Prime Minister and business leaders.

It was like no other board Brierley had ever served on. The agenda followed pre-written minutes, and time was generally occupied approving loans above a certain size known as the discretionary limit. That limit was unusually low for a major bank, which meant the board devoted most of its time to piles of approvals.

From 1986 about eighty loans were approved every month, and during the boom years many approvals had to be signed between board meetings. Two Wellington-based directors were called in every two days to approve applications, and sometimes loan files were sent to their homes. The board even approved loans that had already been made.

Director Len Bayliss remembers querying in a memo a loan proposal to a property company. The proposal was based on a property valuation and he asked a BNZ executive on what basis the property was valued. A senior executive then rang Bayliss and informed him the bank took a dim view of such criticism. Not surprisingly, many of the newer directors came to feel they were simply rubber-stamping decisions made elsewhere.

Brierley remembers his doubts about some of the loan applications, and in his discussions with Sir Lewis Ross he was surprised by the liberality of the bank's lending policies.

'When I joined the board the first real discovery is that you have joined a major organisation where all the proprieties and all the protocols are meticulously observed, but where traditionally the board had very little influence whatsoever, and the first thought of any reasonably perceptive individual was, "What am I doing here?"'

As one of the newest board members in 1985 and much of 1986, there was little he could do. But by April 1987 five new directors had been appointed and they were keen to change board procedure. They had all reached similar conclusions to Brierley's and hoped the appointment of Sir Ron (he was knighted early that year) as chairman would herald a new era for the board.

Brierley tried to fulfil that expectation. He began his reign by obtaining the first comprehensive list of the bank's liabilities and then initiating a major review of information supplied to the board. The board wanted to improve the quality of the information it received, especially data supporting loan applications. New reporting requirements were imposed on executives and financial management systems began to be more closely attuned to the needs of the bank. The board was relieved of much of the time-consuming loan approvals process by raising the discretionary limit.

The board met informally for an hour before the formal meeting with management was held, and the discussion gradually moved from routine procedure to policy issues, although not as decisively as some directors would have liked. Brierley took the view that the best way to effect change was to have the executives on your side, while other members of the board believed it was essential they should assert their authority quickly and firmly.

But even the limited changes were perceived as a power struggle between management and the board, and the board faced the difficult task of questioning methods that were making a lot of money for the bank. The BNZ was on a winning streak and at the time was rated as one of the more profitable banks in the world.

Profits in the 1970s and early '80s had been unspectacular and, in response to the inevitable freeing-up of the banking sector and new banks setting up in New Zealand, the BNZ had decided to snare as much corporate market share as possible. Its new aggressive tactics worked. In the space of a few years its share of the corporate banking market swelled from about 30 to 60–70 per cent.

Internally, the structure of the bank was also changing to cater for this demand. Traditional tier-by-tier management, each with its fixed limits of responsibility and control, disappeared. A corporate banking division was set up with various subdivisions that were more responsive to the corporate sector's needs. But the lines of responsibility and accountability had blurred to such an extent that on one occasion a loan proposal turned down by the BNZ head office in Wellington was approved in a slightly altered form by the Auckland office a few weeks later.

The bank was certainly changing fast, but in important ways it was not changing fast enough. For instance, it lacked the technical skills to analyse a company's accounts and ensure the money lent was used appropriately. Corporate accounting was of a very low standard during the boom years while conservative banking yardsticks were dangerously relaxed. Unsustainable asset values were overemphasised to the detriment of the security of cash flow. For example, the

BNZ lent $190 million to Judgecorp even though the company lacked a proper cash flow and quality earnings.

Its assessment of credit risk was below international standards and the necessary prudential controls were not put in place. The BNZ was overlending to high-risk investment and property companies and foolishly took shares, debentures and real estate as security.

Outside the confines of the BNZ the world was also going mad. Merger, takeover and acquisition fever raged and helping to fuel the boom was the BNZ. It was renowned for the speed and willingness with which it processed applications and approved deals.

At the time, board members were only dimly aware that this was happening under their auspices, although some were apprehensive about the increasingly speculative nature of the New Zealand economy and expressed their concern to management.

Len Bayliss remembers a conversation he had with chief executive Bob McCay in 1987. 'I was prophesying doom and gloom and I asked him whether we had too much money out to these entrepreneurial people. The exact words of McCay were, "We feel absolute confidence lending this money. We have no grounds at all for believing there is any problem of security and safety. These people are the new shakers and movers of New Zealand."

'This showed a great deal of misjudgment. They were not running a scuttlebutt outfit. They are the core of New Zealand's financial system.'

But the booming market was making a fool out of conservative people, and board member Peter Leeming was not alone when he asked himself in 1986 whether there was another ingredient in the recipe of success he could not recognise. Was he perhaps misinterpreting events and missing the point?

Sir Ron's public statements showed that he had no such doubts. Back in 1983 he jokingly suggested the stock market had replaced the totalisator as a symbol of financial escapism, and by 1986 he was predicting a shakeout of the New Zealand market, riddled as it was with what he called fringe finance and investment companies of 'doubtful substance and little apparent constructive purpose'. He concluded that a shakeout of the New Zealand market was inevitable and looming ever closer. When Bayliss asked him how many companies would survive, Brierley replied, 'One in ten.'

But his words were stronger than his actions. In part this was due to his lack of knowledge of banking, although everyone was in the same position. None of the board members were bankers and all were grappling with understanding the fundamentals of the industry.

'We all wanted to be part of an effective influence on the bank, but how to do it — that's easier said than done. One needs time and experience and knowledge,' says Brierley.

'I think there's an apprenticeship of some years in terms of someone joining the board of the bank as against a company. There's definitely an element of "Yes, Minister" and it takes time to learn your role. Many directors have been there for decades and never learned anything.'

Eventually Brierley would decide that it really was not all that different to running a business, but for a long time this perception eluded him because he was overwhelmed by the organisation, tradition and mystique of banking.

'If it was my own business I would have handled it differently. I think it's just a matter of confidence. I would have abbreviated the gap between learning and acting rather than reacting.'

Sir Ron had been chairman of the bank for six months when the event precipitating the shakeout he predicted occurred on 19 October 1987. Wall Street's Dow Jones index dropped a record 507.99 points, prompting a huge worldwide sell-off. In New Zealand more than $4 billion was wiped off the value of the sharemarket before lunch the following day. The severity of the crash shocked the financial community, but the real impact of this crash would take over two years to work its way through the system.

One of the first indications the public had that all was not well with the BNZ was in January 1988 when Australian Ratings dropped their credit rating from AAA to AA plus.

Then in February the bank announced that its known potential losses in New Zealand and overseas were $186 million. Nevertheless, that year the bank posted a $181 million profit, 22.3 per cent higher than the previous year, but the provision for doubtful debt had climbed to $206 million.

Brierley announced these results the day after his investiture and said the bank believed it could improve further on this result. But the past continued to haunt the black monolith and in July the BNZ revealed it had lent $15.5 million to Energycorp and some of that had been paid out to the company after it stopped generating any cash. The bank was also being sued for over $30 million lost in foreign exchange deals.

The board did not all share Sir Ron's sanguine view of the bank. From heading a runaway success, it now looked like they might be responsible for a crashing failure.

Sir Ron's appointment as chairman on 1 April 1987 had coincided with the day banking was deregulated and eight new banks joined the big four as trading banks. As a result, bank lending shot up.

With the BNZ's 70 per cent share of the corporate market, it seems fair to conclude that much of the BNZ's money that went down the drain was lent in just six and a half months in 1987. The signatures of all the directors appear on some embarrassing loans.

Frank Pearson was the first to point out they would be criticised for having financed the boom and fuelled the crash. Early in the piece he identified these problems and the need to take action, and his criticisms were quickly picked up by Dr Susan Lojkine and then Peter Leeming.

Leeming had been a long-time admirer of Sir Ron, and one of the reasons he accepted the BNZ appointment was that it provided an opportunity to work with him. So when Frank Pearson voiced his concerns, Leeming looked to the chairman for direction. Brierley's response surprised him.

'He would sit there and appear to hear your view but frequently never expressed a comment. When you heard a query from a sharemarket commentator like Frank Pearson and there was no response from a commercial operator of the status of Sir Ron, well, that was a powerful silence indeed. I took it to mean that, really, Sir Ron was not a full-time chairman.'

In fact this was exactly what BIL executives had warned Brierley would happen. When Sir Ron's appointment as chairman was first discussed, BIL executives and Brierley's friends pointed out to him that the time he could devote to the bank would be fragmented and limited, given his responsibility as chairman of the Brierley empire. They knew that neither the bank nor BIL would receive the attention it deserved, and to them his acceptance was a telling indication of his commitment to the company. They also queried how someone living in Sydney could be an effective chairman of New Zealand's premier bank based in Wellington. Recently retired BIL director Don McDonald advised Brierley that it would be nothing more than a conceit on his part to take the position.

Although the BIL team may not have said so, they knew that if the board expected a dynamic chairman to lead the way ahead they had the wrong person. They knew from experience that his input at board level had always been economical. But his reputation as an aggressive corporate raider belied the reality, and board members who had expected a fierce, forceful presence often commented on how quiet and passive Brierley was.

Brierley himself once said, when asked by the *Australian Financial Review* how a man with as many board posts as he had could make an effective contribution: 'What say if I make very little contribution — is anybody worse off? It's not as if we're accepting full responsibility.'

Now the initial misgivings of the BIL crew were being shared by many of the BNZ directors. Leeming was one of a group on the board who felt Sir Ron was still reeling from the effects of the crash on his own company. He appeared stunned. 'Punch-drunk' was the word one director used.

Even when Brierley did focus on the board's problems, the majority of the board felt he was reluctant to act to stem the internal haemorrhaging. Board members were keen that he inform the bank's executives that the board was dissatisfied with their performance. Reluctantly Sir Ron did their bidding, but it was clear he was not leading the charge for change.

A Government announcement in July propelled the fate of the BNZ into the BIL arena. In that year's budget the Government announced it intended to sell its 84 per cent stake in the bank. It was not a popular decision with the Labour Party and just days after the budget the MP for Sydenham, party rebel Jim Anderton, refused to vote for part of a Bill relating to the sale, saying it went against traditional Labour principles.

In the meantime contenders for the bank were happily lining up; it was rumoured that Fletcher Challenge Ltd was interested, together with National Mutual, Elders Finance, the ANZ Banking Group, National Australia Bank and BIL.

As chairman of the bank and chairman of the company interested in buying the bank, Sir Ron was immediately accused of having a conflict of interest by the former BNZ chairman Sir Lewis Ross, who echoed the thoughts of Peter Leeming, Dr Susan Lojkine, Frank Pearson and Len Bayliss. Even his greatest ally on the board, Rob Campbell, believed it would be wiser if Brierley stood down simply to appease the public's concern.

But that was not the way Sir Ron saw things. When the subject was raised at a meeting in August, he refused point-blank to leave. He argued the conflict was more technical than real, and in one sense he was right: his knowledge of the bank was already extensive as a result of his privileged position as a director. But what concerned the other directors was that he would be in receipt of sensitive information about the other bidders if he remained on the board.

After that meeting Leeming, Lojkine and Pearson talked about Sir Ron's response. A picture of the man was beginning to emerge, and one of his overriding characteristics appeared to be an unwillingness to act to his own detriment unless forced to. He respected no authority other than that of the marketplace, and they realised this man would never stand down unless maximum pressure was applied.

They decided to call a meeting for a week hence where they intended to put a resolution to the board recording the fact that the chairman should stand down. As a director of Government Life, which had a shareholding in the National Australia Bank, Len Bayliss was also deemed to be in this position, but he had already agreed to heed the board's wishes.

The decision would have been embarrassing for Brierley, but the resolution was never put to the test. In what appeared like a fortunate coincidence, a day before the meeting was to be held Roger Douglas wrote to all the SOE heads advising them they were required to stand down if they had an interest in purchasing the SOE they were serving on. As a result Brierley reluctantly stood down in August 1988.

In his place the deputy chairman, Rob Campbell, was appointed acting chairman. It seemed as though Brierley's intentions to convert Campbell to capitalism had succeeded. Campbell said that when he first spied Sir Ron at the economic summit he had a typical unionist's view of corporate raiders, but his views shifted as a result of his involvement on the BNZ board and in the commercial world.

In late 1987 Campbell left the trade union movement to work for former National MP Derek Quigley's company, Strategos Consulting Ltd, much to the dismay of his union colleagues. They felt they were owed more loyalty from Campbell, given that he was on the BNZ board only because he had been appointed as their representative. By joining Strategos, he waved away the top job in the union movement, for Campbell had been earmarked to head the new Council of Trade Unions.

Campbell was one of the first academics to come through the union movement. He was the son of a banker and held a masters degree in philosophy and economics. Even his detractors agreed he was bright, able and ambitious. But they also saw in Campbell an insecurity and compensating egotism, which they believed formed the base of an unpredictable, potent cocktail.

But the Rob Campbell Brierley saw was a warm, outgoing man, possessing an interesting background and keen intelligence. The two formed a strong alliance and spent many hours together talking about the bank.

Campbell also appreciated Brierley's mind and delighted in his wit. He remembers inviting Brierley and prominent trade union leader Ken Douglas for a drink on his wife's birthday to a gay bar in Wellington. Both Campbell and Brierley saw the humour of the situation. On Campbell's birthday Brierley bought him the first issue of the *Southern Cross* newspaper, a Labour Party publication of the 1940s.

During the stand-down period Rob Campbell was Brierley's link with the board. Brierley could not have had a better ally, for Campbell's view of the bank mirrored his exactly. They believed the bank's troubles had been overstated. Although every snippet of information coming out about the bank was embarrassing and gloomy, they were resolutely optimistic.

In October the country learned that the BNZ had poured $230 million into the doomed Rada Corporation Ltd. There appeared to be no documentation supporting the loan and the bank was not even sure whether the loan was secured or not.

A month later Elders IXL, now the owner of Rada Corporation, announced it was suing the BNZ for $230 million, and at the same time let it be known that Elders was no longer interested in bidding for the BNZ.

The BNZ then grimly announced that total provision for losses arising from the crash was almost $400 million. Campbell, however, said cheerily the bank was in a very strong position. The market thought otherwise. The spiralling fortunes of the BNZ continued to gnaw away at market confidence in the bank. The board knew the problem had to be tackled somehow, but they could not agree on how.

The trio who wanted action were Leeming, Lojkine and Pearson, and by late 1988 they were pushing for management changes. The head of investment and corporate banking, Peter Travers, was seen as the architect of the expansion that cost the bank so dearly, although his perceived excesses should have been curbed by the chief executive, Bob McCay. Travers bore a remarkable similarity to the confident, free-wheeling entrepreneurs he was dealing with and he was very popular among the corporations, including BIL. Not surprisingly Travers and McCay were the first two in the firing line.

But Rob Campbell vociferously resisted any move to depose executives. He was supported by Pat Morrison, and the board was persuaded by his arguments to delay the decision. He said the bank needed to strengthen its retail network, and Peter Travers was the best person to do this. He was said to be a friend of Travers and he believed Travers had worn more of the blame than was appropriate.

Campbell also made the point that a serious reshuffle was not required while the bank was being sold, because the new owner would probably want to make their own appointments. By the end of that year it looked as if the new owner could be BIL.

During November some of the major contenders pulled out of the running: first Fletcher Challenge, then Elders Finance. By December, analysts were strongly tipping BIL to close the deal. The only other serious contender was the National Australia Bank.

Both were preparing offers for the bank. BIL put together a definite offer of just over $1 billion for the bank, while the NAB's tentative offer was understood to be similar but contingent upon further investigation of the bank's finances. The Government was likely to consider a bid from NAB more favourably than one from BIL, since a bid from another bank was more acceptable than one from the country's largest investment company.

But according to the Treasury, BIL had planned a structure that would safeguard the interests of the bank, and this plan had won the approval of the Reserve Bank. BIL, IEL, IEP and the BNZ would be separate arms of a mammoth holding company, often referred to as BNZ Incorporated. BIL would have been removed from the share register, and shareholders would now have scrip in BNZ Incorporated. So grandiose was the ultimate outcome that it was occasionally referred to mockingly as New Zealand Incorporated.

Three of the prospective directors of the BIL-owned BNZ were familiar — Dr Susan Lojkine, Frank Pearson and Rob Campbell — though Lojkine and Pearson never formally accepted the directorships offered by BIL.

The most interesting appointment was Rob Campbell's. Dr Lojkine was surprised to learn from Paul Collins that Campbell had secured the top job in the bank. He would become chairman of a BIL-owned BNZ, and Collins now concedes he might have even become a full-time executive chairman.

Campbell denies this vehemently, saying it was 'a piece of filth put out by the other directors'. However, Derek Quigley acknowledges that Campbell told him if BIL acquired the BNZ he would be leaving Strategos, and not only would he become the chairman of the BNZ, but he would secure one of the top positions in BIL. He would be their deputy chairman.

It was a dazzling rise for the man who had been in business for little more than a year, but Lojkine said she was reassured by Collins that the two BIL directors would lend a guiding hand initially.

Whatever the exact nature of his position, it was clear there was a lot at stake for Rob Campbell personally, and it was undeniably in his interests to facilitate the sale of the BNZ to BIL. Certainly some of the directors on the BNZ board had come to that conclusion.

'He always sat on the fence, equivocating, and then he could claim to be on the right side whatever it was. He was a real political animal. But there's no doubt in my mind that he supported the BIL purchase because of what it held for him,' said Dr Lojkine.

At first the political undercurrents and complexities of the situation were lost on some of the directors, since most were more familiar with the comparatively straightforward profit and loss dynamics of business. Campbell's responses bewildered people like Peter Leeming.

'He is a very clever, intelligent, extremely fluent person. But as far as his business judgment goes, I have never worked on a board with anyone whose opinions were so often at variance with my own. They were invariably diametrically opposed to my instincts. All of a sudden it dawned on me that Rob Campbell was politically driven.

'One couldn't help feeling that it would be very strange indeed if somebody who got on with someone of the power and business significance of Sir Ron couldn't benefit from it.'

The Treasury was also concerned about Campbell's role in the sale process. A director in the Treasury's industries branch, Richard Shallcrass, was in charge of the BNZ sale and he worried that any direct contact between the BNZ and BIL could undercut the Government's negotiating position.

Campbell was like a spider in the middle of a very complicated web. He had close links with the Labour Party, the Government, the trade union movement, the country's top investment company and its top bank.

To Shallcrass this was nerve-racking stuff. The Treasury was particularly worried the situation had the potential to become a serious conflict of interest. Because the BNZ itself controlled the information given to bidders, it would be possible for the bank to play favourites and even, in the worst case, to control the outcome of the sale. This would be very likely to reduce the price the Government received for its BNZ shares.

The Treasury was also concerned about the effect any favouritism towards BIL would have on international perceptions of New Zealand's privatisation programme. There were billions of dollars' worth of Government assets still to be sold, and it was important to protect the integrity of the process. Ministers responsible for the sale were informed of this danger, while BIL was told firmly of the importance of political neutrality.

Despite the potential for problems, none materialised and

Treasury was confident BIL would be the successful bidder. They led BIL — and the BNZ — to believe the BNZ was virtually theirs and both organisations were on stand-by to announce the proposal on 21 December. All the documentation had been done and a press release had been prepared.

Dr Lojkine remembers talking to Paul Collins on the Wednesday morning about the conditions she required if she was to become a director of this holding company. Not all of these could be met.

'As I left his office and walked over to the bank, I thought I would tell him "thanks but no thanks". I went into the bank and was greeted with the news that the bank was not going to be sold.'

The first explanation given for the change of heart was the price. Postbank had just been sold to the ANZ for $665 million with a potential increase, and BIL's offer seemed shabby in comparison.

But later it appeared that the political implications of the sale had been the overriding factor behind the postponement. Although the Reserve Bank had approved a structure designed to create 'Chinese walls' between BIL and the bank, the Prime Minister, David Lange, was frankly sceptical. The fact remained that the country's premier corporate raider would effectively own the country's premier bank. His advisers told him it was unacceptable internationally, and he couldn't think why it should be allowed in New Zealand. The potential for abuse was enormous. 'Would you put a cat in charge of a goldfish bowl?' asked Lange later, only half in jest.

Any doubts Lange might have had about the protection Chinese walls offered were amply illustrated by Rob Campbell's subsequent behaviour. Just days before the sale the well-tuned and sensitively wired Wellington political grapevine had been buzzing with speculation that BIL was likely to be the successful bidder and, curiously, Rob Campbell's name kept cropping up in that context.

As the level of activity intensified throughout December, it became clear to Lange that Campbell must be acting as a runner for BIL. The famed Chinese walls were already beginning to look a little thin.

In caucus that morning Lange successfully argued for the sale of two state assets, Postbank and Air New Zealand, and the postponement of the sale of the BNZ. Since Air New Zealand went to the BIL group, he said it could hardly be argued that he was anti-Brierley.

Naturally Brierley was deeply disappointed by the decision. Peter Leeming said he remembers walking with him after lunch one day in January. Brierley appeared to be somewhat stunned and quieter than usual. He then explained to Leeming the vision he had of the BNZ and NZ Incorporated. In his imagination BNZ Incorporated Ltd would become a conglomerate company representing all the best elements of New Zealand business, right through to manufacturing, banking and so on.

On hearing this, Leeming said he finally understood Brierley's inaction in early 1988. 'I then saw the long-term nature of his vision. It was such a broad vision that aberrations in the short term were just details. Brierley never explained this, but when suddenly one realised the breadth of the ambition, one could see it was a key part of a big vision that had foundered.'

The only consolation was that with the sales process out of the way, Brierley was free to return as chairman, but the BIL executives had other ideas. They knew the bank was in serious trouble, with potential losses they estimated of up to $300 million. Their advice to Sir Ron was, 'stay away'. The bad news still to come would do nothing for his reputation.

But Brierley was ever-optimistic about the bank. The problems and losses had been exaggerated. There was nothing wrong with the bank that a little fine-tuning could not cure, and Rob Campbell agreed. In recent months the BNZ board had wrestled with Campbell about the provisions for losses, with Campbell always wanting to present the best picture possible of the bank.

'One of our main quarrels with him was that we would agree to one thing in private and in public he would cut the ground from under our feet. We wanted to be preparing the public for bad news and let them down in a couple of stages to reality, and he would say publicly the bank was in good heart,' recalls Dr Lojkine.

Even when the bank announced in late January that its provision for bad debt was now $370 million for the year, Campbell boasted the outlook for the BNZ was still good. 'The medium-term earnings prospects for the bank are extremely strong . . . and we can say that with a great deal of confidence,' he was quoted as saying.

In the meantime the public was clamouring for news about the bank's exposure to Equiticorp, which had been placed in receivership a few days before. Editorials up and down the country were questioning the performance and health of the BNZ.

Pearson, Leeming and Lojkine saw the situation as critical. In January 1989 it was obvious to them the bank would post a loss that year, and they decided it was better to deal with the events in one hit, rather than let bad news seep out of the BNZ day by day.

They also had a plan of action which they conveyed to Campbell. They said he wrote down the various points and promised to speak to Brierley, who was in Sydney at the time. But Campbell returned with the news that Brierley didn't think there was any problem. He was busy and not returning to New Zealand until the next board meeting in February. The trio were dismayed and wondered whether Campbell had portrayed the situation with as much emphasis and urgency as they would have liked.

Pearson had reason to be especially frustrated. He had pinpointed the problems as far back as February 1988, and now, a year later, little had changed. He discussed his concerns with Dr Lojkine, and both worried that without a firm leader and decisive action the bank's fortunes would continue to drift dangerously downwards. The flow-on effects of this could be disastrous in the current climate, for the financial sector was still extremely fragile. There was talk, too, that the BIL team was trying to persuade Sir Ron to leave the bank, which would see Rob Campbell at the helm, and their trust in him had eroded to an all-time low.

In the end it was these concerns that prompted them to visit the Minister of Finance, David Caygill, on 2 February 1989. They told him he should be aware the BNZ would require a capital injection of up to $400 million. Lojkine thought it was more likely to be about $200 million and in hindsight she says Pearson was always ahead of everyone in foreseeing the future. Her comments are echoed by other board members such as Pat Morrison and Len Bayliss.

Lojkine and Pearson also told Caygill that if Sir Ron left or handed over responsibility to Campbell, then the hard decisions, vital for the long-term welfare of the bank, would not be taken.

Caygill was not surprised to see them. His sources had kept him up to date with the unfolding drama and he was grateful for their personal approach. He confirmed their intention was to urge the Government to take a closer interest in the bank's affairs and spur Brierley and Campbell into action.

He knew Brierley refused to acknowledge the problems facing the bank and he felt the bank was getting only a few days a month at best out of Brierley. The bank was in crisis and needed a chairman who could devote his energies to the problems.

On the afternoon of 13 February, the board met with Sir Ron as chairman for the last time. Dr Lojkine said she tried hard to convince Brierley the bank would make a loss that year. She suggested he listen to a report by an executive who had carried out a credit review, but he thought this was unnecessary. He said he thought the bank would break even and said it was a shocking thing for a bank to report a loss.

'Ron didn't like to face the unpalatable fact that the bank of which he was chairman was not doing well,' said Lojkine.

Brierley must have had an idea something was going on, for Leeming remembers that he accused board members at the meeting of going behind his back. Not knowing what had happened, Leeming rose to defend his colleagues.

After the meeting Brierley and Campbell had an appointment with David Caygill, who spoke to each man separately. He told Brierley he wanted to appoint someone else, and Brierley was given little less than a week to take the opportunity to resign gracefully. Brierley reiterated his view that the problems had been exaggerated and that he had been poorly advised. Caygill then asked Campbell to take over until the new chairman appointed his own deputy.

This was not at all what Pearson and Lojkine had expected. Their concern about Campbell's role had bounced back on Brierley, and they were as taken aback as he was. Pearson recalls: 'We went to the minister to get him to give Ron and Rob a prod and force them to face certain things. It was a very dramatic situation and what we did was a very unconventional act. We went behind the chairman's back to the minister and he reacted in a way we never would have guessed — he fired Ron.'

On 16 February Brierley officially resigned, leaving Campbell to take the reins. Campbell had already resigned from the Labour Party national executive three days before, and on 21 February he resigned as the acting chairman and deputy of the BNZ. His action forced the Government to rush forward the announcement of his replacement and, to Brierley and Campbell's chagrin, Frank Pearson and Dr Susan Lojkine were appointed chairman and deputy chair.

Campbell was still on the board, but he was an angry man and his outbursts made news for some weeks. He accused Caygill of being 'hell-bent on injecting instability' into the bank, and Caygill and the Prime Minister narrowly averted a press conference he had called to object to the new appointments.

Later that month Pearson revealed the bank's loss for the year could top $160 million. Campbell said the loss was overstated, but, when the figures came out in June, the loss was in excess of $600 million with a $1.2 billion provision for bad and doubtful debts.

In March, Campbell was sacked from the board and the Government put off all plans to sell the BNZ for two years.

But in June, Capital Markets, an offshoot of the merchant banking operation Fay Richwhite, promised to inject $300 million into the BNZ and in return took about 30 per cent of the Government's interest in the bank. The Government's holding was diluted from 84 per cent to 53 per cent and the public and bank staff controlled 18 per cent. A further $100 million was fed into the bank via new shares available to minority shareholders, and another $200 million was raised through the issue of capital securities. This $600 million capital injection effectively offset the more than $600 million loss.

That month Frank Pearson resigned as chairman, and, with the exception of Len Bayliss, all the other directors had departed from the bank by the end of 1989. Travers had already left and McCay had taken early retirement in May.

Brierley watched the developments with a consuming passion. He knew that, had the Government accepted the BIL bid in the first place, they would have been better off by several hundred million dollars. BIL had bid just over $1 billion for the bank, valuing the shares at about $1.20. Bruce Hancox later admitted they would have paid $1.45 per share for the bank, double the sum paid by the successful bidder — Capital Markets acquired their stake for 70 cents a share. Even though BIL had underestimated the losses by some $300 million, with assets of $17 billion that mattered little to them.

It appeared that the Government had sold off this stake too cheaply. Efforts to face the problems head-on had temporarily diminished the value of the bank, and on this basis Brierley might feel justifiably vindicated. But all the directors associated with the bank during the upheaval said it is impossible to know whether the losses and provisions were overstated, because of the subsequent action taken.

At BIL the mood was one of disbelief and disappointment with the news of Fay Richwhite's success. Collins said at that price they would have eagerly snapped up a chance at a part-share in the bank. Too much attention was being paid to the $1.2 billion bad debt provisions.

But Caygill said it would have been impossible to put the bank back on the market publicly. He could hardly trumpet the $600 million loss, plus the fact that the Government needed more money for the bank, and then ask, 'Is anybody interested?' Everybody would have withdrawn their money very quickly in that event.

The whole experience had been an extremely painful one for Brierley. Together with the knighthood, the chairmanship had been the ultimate validation of his achievements, and in some respects he had handled the role well. He had observed all the protocols and skilfully dealt with the diplomatic aspects of the role. His ability to respond with courtesy and discretion to shareholders' queries at meetings was, by now, finely honed. He had identified many of the poor loans and made changes to the way the board conducted business. His intention to shift their attention from routine to policy had been commended by all the directors.

However, it was questionable whether Brierley should have accepted the position as chairman at all. He had neither the time nor the expertise to warrant his accepting the appointment, and his contribution was always going to be minimal. But seduced by the status of the title, he took on the job of leading a board ready for change. The changes he introduced were not as sweeping as that board had hoped for, and his ethical standards were also put to the test when he refused to absent himself during the sales process. He took too long to stand down, and when trouble surfaced, he proved unwilling to act effectively and decisively. In the face of all the facts he stubbornly clung to the belief that the bank's situation was fine. His performance as chairman of the BNZ left much to be desired and his subsequent unceremonious dumping was hurtful and humiliating.

For months afterward Brierley read every newspaper clipping he could find on the bank and was aggrieved if some reports were not sent to him. The bank was never far from his mind and he could have been forgiven for nursing a deep resentment of the two directors who had dislodged him.

Frank Pearson certainly wondered what Brierley would say when they met by accident in a lift some months later. Brierley turned to Pearson and asked how things were going. 'Busy,' said Pearson. Brierley smiled and said, 'Well, Frank, I've got a lot of time to watch cricket now.'

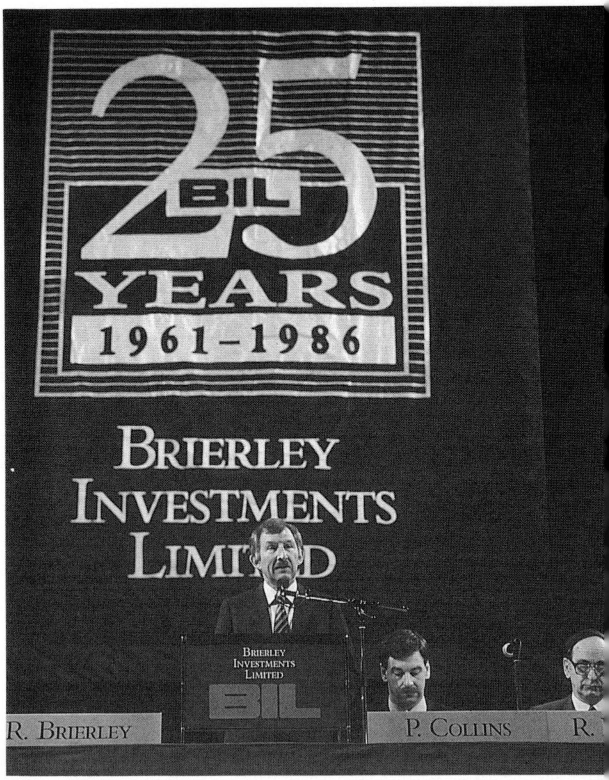

Presiding over the 25th annual general meeting of BIL

BIL shareholders crowding the refreshment tents at the Chase Stadium in Auckland, 1987
NZ Herald

Dancers express their gratitude for BIL's donation of $250,000 to the New Zealand Ballet Company in 1983

Craig Heatley, executive chairman of Rainbow, Ron Brierley and Paul Collins seal the BIL-Rainbow agreement with a glass of champagne
NZ Herald

May Brierley showing off her son in 1987

Brierley at the White House with Ronald and Nancy Reagan after a meeting of the International Council in 1987

Sir Ron Brierley handing over the chair to Bruce Hancox in 1989
NZ Herald

TWENTY-ONE

Coping with the Crash

THE FACT THAT Brierley had been predicting a crash for years counted for nothing when the crash finally struck in October 1987. His foresight could not diminish the contagious exhilaration of easy money and a bull market. Although the Brierley group was relatively restrained during much of the boom, in the year leading up to the crash their balance sheet ballooned with optimism.

In 1986 the entire Brierley group controlled assets worth $NZ5.6 billion funded by $3.3 billion of debt, but a year later they had salted away $12 billion of assets financed by over $8 billion debt. BIL had $1.81 billion in shareholders' funds, of which almost $800 million was invested in IEL and $331 million in IEP. BIL was therefore heavily dependent on its two overseas arms, and IEL was in an even more vulnerable position.

IEL owned 44 per cent of IEP, which it funded with a mixture of equity and loans at a low commercial rate in 1987, plus it had poured $A350 million into troubled retailer Woolworths. So its money was tied up in two permanent holdings and, since the size of the assets under the company's control was now too large for the shareholder base alone, it had to borrow to finance any other investments. When it came to borrowing, IEL was not frugal. In 1986 it had $2.4 billion of assets funded by $1.4 billion of debt, but just before the crash it had $5.9 billion worth of assets funded by $4.2 billion of debt.

IEL had always been the raider trader arm of the group, churning out one-off profits, but the new chief executive, Rodney Price, intended to alter this.

Price had spent fifteen years with the construction company Fricker Carrington and was its managing director when he became chief executive of the Southern Farmers subsidiary G. & R. Wills in January 1984. By October 1984 he was the chief executive of Southern Farmers. His rise within the IEL ranks continued, for in less than eighteen months he was appointed chief executive.

Price looked the model of the corporate executive with his thick, coiffured, steely grey hair, handsome face and freshly laundered appearance. He soon proved to be a tough operator with firm ideas about the direction the company needed to follow. He was convinced, just as Bruce Hancox had been when he entered BIL in the early 1980s, that the company needed a healthy operational base. Like Hancox, he too was faced with the difficulty of understanding a company as diverse and complex as IEL before he could implement his dream.

That was no easy task, for when Price took over the company it was already embroiled in two corporate battles, it had lost valuable staff to Goward, and Price also inherited a number of doubtful investments made in the Goward era. Price said it was also clear that there was nothing there to produce a profit in the future. Goward had 'depleted the cupboard'.

That year the North Broken Hill demerger and opposition to IEL's involvement in the Australian Gas Light Company took up more time than was warranted and had a detrimental influence on other activities. Investments in the oil industry in Australia in 1986 instigated by Russell Goward lost them some $50 million and the legacy of his property investments left a lot to be desired.

Nevertheless, the sale of IEL's insurance portfolio in 1986 contributed substantially to the record profit of $145 million, almost three times the 1985 figure of $51 million.

The form of IEL's new direction was already taking shape with the revival of 82 per cent owned subsidiary Acmex Holdings Ltd. Acmex was to become a mini-IEL, operating at the smaller end of the market and embodying the spirit and size of IEL in the 1960s and early '70s.

But the bigger picture was spelled out by Brierley in the 1987 IEL annual report when he said the group was looking overseas for acquisitions that complemented their Australian trading subsidiaries. Price was particularly keen to develop trans-Tasman bonds such as a Woolworths-Progressive link.

The company intended to build on its existing subsidiaries as a foundation for specialist, vertically integrated industrial units with high-growth potential. An example of this was the purchase of dairy company Consolidated Foods Ltd by Southern Farmers. Although it did not meet the company's traditional criteria for investment, its value was as a building block in the dairy industry.

As well, the company continued to provide the bottom-line profits with the sort of quick-turnaround deals that had earned him the reputation as a fast-buck artist. In 1986 IEL sold its 12 per cent in the *Herald* and *Weekly Times* to Rupert Murdoch's News Corporation

Ltd, just months after its entry into the company, for a $100 million profit. IEL's investment precipitated a renewed burst of interest in the company, and after it had departed, Robert Holmes à Court surfaced, bidding the shares up to $13.50 before giving in to Murdoch's $15 a share. Murdoch was clearly willing to pay a high premium to buy his father's old newspaper.

At the same time Brierley also managed to pick up 20 per cent of Advertiser Newspapers Ltd, which he sold in 1988 for a $50 million profit.

Although Brierley was credited for this wizardry, Price said the deal was not done by him. 'Brierley was not highly motivated even when I started there. He worked on whatever took his fancy, and that might be something that was not going to make a huge difference to the company.'

Price said Brierley often worked on the development of IEP but, as a director of IEP, Price said he did not see a lot of analytical work done by Brierley.

But with a $230 million profit in 1987 and the avowed intention to establish constant operating profits, it seemed IEL had little to worry about.

Although Brierley grumbled intermittently about the overheated market and the need to sell, he always baulked when others identified assets that could be jettisoned. Since he was unwilling to follow his own advice to sell, it was hard for others to take him seriously, and eventually his distress signals were dismissed as nothing more than a false alarm.

Besides, the investment team was on a high. They felt invincible and talked about how they were changing the world. Said one: 'We would come up with ideas and Rodney Price would go into bat to organise them. There would be money for anything we wanted to do. It was a tremendous opportunity.'

It took the crash to expose the danger of such unbounded confidence fuelled with unlimited money.

New Zealand was hit hard by the crash and it had the ignominious distinction of leading the world with its sharemarket plunge. By December the Barclays index had fallen almost 32 per cent since October's Black Monday, compared with London's drop of 23 per cent and Australia's 19 per cent. In New York the Dow Jones index was even recording an improvement of 1.6 per cent, and Tokyo was up by 3.5 per cent.

The Barclays index even went below 2,000, even though only three months earlier it had recorded an all-time high of 3968.89. It wasn't long before news of the closure of some stockbroking firms filtered through to the public, and the first of the listed company receiverships was announced by the end of 1987.

To Collins, Hancox and Price, it was abundantly clear they were dealing with a new and urgent situation. The rules had changed irrevocably and they could see immediate action had to be taken in order to avert a crisis within the group. By November they were drawing up a plan to reduce the level of assets and borrowing in the group.

For Bill Loewenthal, there was an element of *déjà vu* in the foreboding atmosphere at IEL. He had come through the recession in 1974/75 when IEL was even more stretched, but he remembered Brierley's decisive leadership then. He said to his colleagues, 'Ron was superb at handling that. Just wait. You'll really see Ron come into his own now.'

But Brierley and the company had changed since 1974. This time Brierley was numb with disappointment and overwhelmed by the enormity of the group. How could it happen? he asked himself over and over again. How could this happen to BIL? Simple, replied Bruce Hancox. The answer to that is because we buy shares. I can solve all of our problems. We just won't buy any more shares.

After twenty-seven years of ups and downs, after cautioning investors against speculation, talking about high-flying entrepreneurial stock, warning about an overheated market, he had still been caught out. He felt twenty-seven years of dedicated hard work had returned him to square one.

The BIL directors watched as he slowly absorbed the news and waited for the strength Loewenthal had told them about, but it never eventuated. Brierley was like a stunned animal. He was dazed and hurt, and retreated into his shell. With Brierley locked in his own thoughts, the directors found, as the BNZ board would, that he was in no mood to make decisions.

Instead, he took on the job of examining the accounts, but Price remembers how even that task was burdensome to Brierley. 'He didn't enjoy it at all,' Price says. As Brierley inspected the details and surveyed the damage, he was dismayed at what he found. He came to the conclusion that IEL had bought a lot of rubbish. Out of 136 stocks in their portfolio, 106 should never have been bought in the first place, he said.

What was the point of buying shares in CSR? Was there a long-term plan? he asked. No, there was not, although IEP spent $A152 million buying 35 million CSR shares that were worth $A108 million at 31 December. Then there was its investment in Consolidated Exploration. The company paid a fortune for it and at one stage it could have been sold. Instead it held on and this decision cost $A50 million.

IEL was so dangerously exposed that it had gone very close to the bank ratios set by its negative pledge funding. Some estimates on IEL's position since the crash suggested the investment fluctuation reserve had been wiped out and its position moved into the red to the tune of $100 million. IEL's share price was below its book value for the first time in twenty years, and by the time the AGM was held in November, the share price had slipped by 60 per cent, although the market had fallen by only 40 per cent.

Brierley's first response to the calamity was to write three special reports to shareholders. The first, on IEP as at 30 November, was released in January, and the BIL and IEL reports, as at 31 December, came out in March. Almost $HK400 million ($NZ278 million) was wiped off IEP's portfolio, but by the time the interim report was prepared its operating profit had increased by 364 per cent. BIL posted a $75 million profit for the half year, the first profit drop for twenty years, and its total sharemarket losses were $1600 million.

BIL's famous investment fluctuation fund, having shown a healthy $825 million in June 1987, was now recording a deficit of $753 million. Strictly speaking, this $1.58 billion drop in market values should have gone into the profit and loss account, but Collins argued this was unrealistic since a proper market did not exist at the time. And if the company had adhered to accounting standards, they would have to write down $92 million in investments, thus declaring a $17 million loss.

Brierley's harshest words were reserved for IEL, which suffered a profit fall of 55 per cent to $24 million. In his report he said the company had drifted from its founding principles and acquired stock that should never have been bought in the first place. His report was tougher than many at IEL would have liked, and, before it was published, Brierley was pressured to tone down the criticism. Bruce Hancox tried to explain to him why a public roasting was not in good taste. Just because you are at a party and you feel unwell halfway through, you don't have to be sick on the carpet. You can be sick in private without telling everyone about it, he said reasonably.

Brierley ignored Hancox's homely advice and chose the public route, with only minor modifications muting his judgment. With the benefit of hindsight, his executives have been able to applaud his reports, and they now see that this uncompromising, accurate assessment of the group helped allay the public's anxiety about his empire.

In the meantime the company had embarked on a sales programme that would earn it the epithet Brierley Divestments Ltd.

It started in early March when Winstones, Consolidated Metal Industries and BIL's stake in Petroleum Corporation Ltd were sold to FCL in a deal worth $661 million. Winstones had been one-third of BIL's New Zealand trading base.

BIL also increased its holding in New Zealand Newspapers, Kidd Garrett, Lanes Industries, Wellesley Resources and Acadia Corporation. But the sales continued with the disposal of former Rainbow company Argus Questar Corporation, its joint-venture company Printpac for more than $20 million, and Progressive Enterprises to Coles Myer for $477 million.

Few realised how good a deal BIL was getting when they sold their 37.8 per cent holding in NZI to Scottish-based General Accident for $2.45 a share, but a year later, when the shares fell to 65 cents and the company posted a $320 million loss, it was clear BIL had done well. Interestingly, BIL increased its shareholding from 32 per cent to 37.8 per cent at about the same time it had announced its intention to sell its stake in the insurance company.

BIL's new initiatives of 1986 also went under the hammer. Its 27.5 per cent share in the new domestic airline Ansett cost them more than $20 million and was finally sold, while its investment in the creation of the first new daily newspaper in the country for forty years, the *Auckland Sun*, lost BIL $34 million and a lot of goodwill in Auckland when the newspaper was closed after less than twelve months' production. The *Auckland Star* and *Sunday Star* were sold to INL. Finally, the launching of Pepsi-Cola by BIL subsidiary Dominion Breweries in 1986 also turned out to be a costly fizzer.

As a result of this rigorous sales programme the company had netted some $2 billion and wiped almost all its debt by July.

These were not the only changes in the group. Brierley's leadership role in the company had been minimal in recent years, but his abdication of responsibility after the crash paved the way for others to take control. Hancox, Collins and Price stepped into the breach and now, as a united force, they took decisions without him. It was either that or watch the company spiral into oblivion.

They knew Brierley would be opposed to their every move, and at times they deliberately withheld information on asset sales and simply waited until he read about events in the newspaper. Collins remembers vividly how angry Brierley was when he told him about the sale of New Zealand News newspapers, and the sale of NZI also upset him greatly.

'He remembered NZI as a completely different company,' said Collins. 'Remember, he had been away so much he saw it as the company it had once been. He didn't realise that things had changed.'

Brierley still went through all the accounts as he had done for years, sending queries and notes back to the accountants, but now he was too far behind to contribute effectively. He wanted to discuss the Winstones deal two and a half months after it had occurred. Collins was furious and told Hancox he wanted to convey his wrath in a letter to Brierley, but Hancox advised him not to bother. What good would it do, he asked with realistic resignation.

Said Hancox in August: 'He is still looking at the March accounts. He wouldn't have a clue about the accounts as they stand now.'

For the management of BIL and IEL, the current dilemma simply crystallised the dissatisfaction with Brierley that had been simmering for the past few years. Although his talents were much admired, these days his colleagues had come to question some of his judgments. They remembered incidents like Equity & Law, and how long it had taken Brierley to agree to the purchase of automotive company Tozer Kemsley & Millbourn (Holdings) Plc.

TKM had been identified by IEL's top analyst, Peter Pedley, and while Brierley and Pedley respected one another's abilities, the two had an uneasy relationship. It was Pedley who had sold all his IEP holdings before the crash and warned Brierley the downturn was imminent. Finally, IEP did move on TKM in 1985, and the company is now rated as the best takeover the company has ever done.

But the dispute that first caused a rift between IEL management and Brierley was a proposal to buy all of Woolworths in December 1986. Ten people sat in a boardroom and debated the merits of a full takeover. Nine voted for a part-scrip, part-cash offer. Only one was against the proposal but, as chairman, Brierley's vote was the only vote that counted. Perhaps he wanted to uphold his long-held principle of not issuing scrip in a takeover, or perhaps it was because he had not suggested the takeover himself that Brierley blocked the purchase of Woolworths. IEL had been prepared to offer one IEL share (worth about $7) plus 50 cents for every two Woolworths shares, worth $3.93 each. After the crash, when IEL's shares dropped to as low as $1.15 (in December) and Woolworths remained around the $2.10 mark, it appeared Brierley had made a grave mistake. At the time he blocked the bid, Brierley predicted the Woolworths share price would go down to $2 and he was right. But he kept procrastinating and IEL still didn't buy the shares.

Afterwards the IEL team were dismayed. Woolworths' performance had been dismal in recent years, but with the installation of new management its prospects began to brighten and in 1988 the retailer posted an unexpected profit.

After the crash, the missed opportunity was regarded as even more regrettable. They could have acquired the company on better terms in 1986 and without having to wrestle with Rainbow. Had IEL owned Woolworths, it would have had the quality cash-flow asset it so badly needed, and the acquisition might have forced the company to rationalise its smaller holdings earlier.

But despite the cooling of Brierley's relationship with management, he was still highly regarded by the IEL investment team. During the boom they had been the glamour boys of the group, and for a time they had developed an overblown sense of their own importance. They talked about being a brains centre and sometimes referred to themselves as the First XI of the world. Above all, they were convinced they were the key to IEL's sustained growth.

According to Price, since 1986 he had increased the contribution of operating subsidiaries to IEL's annual profit from 10 per cent to almost 70 per cent by 1989. But to the investment team this was a betrayal of the essence of Brierley's philosophy. IEL was an investment company. Its genius lay in its ability to select undervalued stocks, add value and eventually pass on that asset — at a profit to IEL — to the most effective owner. It had no special talent for managing companies. To them it seemed IEL had been hijacked by administrators and managers.

'Who would you rather meet,' asked one of Brierley's admirers in IEL, 'Billy Graham or the greatest book-keeper in the world? Ron is Billy Graham in a way. He is the spirit of analytical drive. Ninety-nine per cent of analysts are boring, but Ron has flashes of genius.'

So when these competent managers and administrators began to assert themselves after the crash, they watched Brierley's loss of power with alarm. Much to their chagrin, IEL's financial resources were now under the control of four men — Rodney Price, Herman Rockefeller, Brian Eggert, and Paul Collins at the helm. All decisions had to be referred to this group finance committee and, just as in New Zealand, the plan for IEL was a sell-down of assets and a reduction of debt.

Out went Brierley's cherished company Cascade Brewery Co. Ltd, as well as holdings in Advertiser Newspapers, ANZ Bank, AGC,

Bundaberg Sugar, Peko and Westpac. By July this had netted $500 million for the company, but there was still $1.9 billion of debt in the books.

The activities of the investment arm of IEL had virtually come to a standstill thanks to the firm hand of the finance committee. It was only when analyst Blake Nixon came up with a plan for an audacious market play involving Robert Holmes à Court that the committee relented. The bid for Bell Resources did more than just revive sagging spirits within the company, it boosted the image of Brierley as the master player once more. The two protagonists in the drama were Brierley and the raider he most resembled, the cool, cerebral Robert Holmes à Court. The media immediately dubbed the clash as the giants battling for recognition as king of Australia's takeover players.

Essentially it involved Brierley foiling Holmes à Court's plans to salvage his collapsing empire. Holmes à Court was one of the first entrepreneurs to come unstuck after the crash, and he was quick to sell assets to cover his yawning debt. His two major corporate entities were Bell Resources and Bell Group. At the top of the pyramid was his personal unlisted company, Heytesbury Holdings, which owned 40 per cent of Bell Group, which in turn owned 43 per cent of Bell Resources.

In what many analysts regarded as a cynical ploy to push his public corporation's cash flow and saleable assets closer to his personal holdings, Holmes à Court announced a $700 million takeover bid by the cash-rich Bell Resources for the debt-laden Bell Group. This would give his family company a much-needed cash injection, and it looked like a blatant case of robbing Peter to pay Paul.

But he hadn't counted on Kerry Packer and Ron Brierley acting as spoilers. Through a joint-venture company the pair made a cheap $825 million bid for Bell Resources in March and forced Holmes à Court to cancel a meeting to approve the proposed merger of Bell Resources and Bell Group. Later Brierley upstaged his rival when he held his own Bell Resources AGM a day before the meeting date set by Holmes à Court. Brierley argued that, because of delays, Holmes à Court's meeting the following day of 1,000 shareholders was invalid and only his meeting should be recognised.

As much as anything else, Brierley was scoring important psychological victories, and the media declared Holmes à Court had been outwitted in the endgame, though Holmes à Court had never been in any doubt about Brierley's ability. Only five years earlier he said of Brierley during the CUB takeover: 'Anyone who underestimates Ron Brierley does so at their own risk.'

The twists and turns in the Bell Resources saga continued, both in and out of court, until July, when the Brierley-Packer alliance sold their holding to Bond Corporation, delivering a tidy profit of $25 million.

However, apart from the Bell Resources play, new investment activity in IEL was practically dormant for the time being, and the IEL investment crew suddenly felt like observers in their own company. As if to underline their waning status, in June they were shifted to smaller, open-plan offices when IEL departed from the MLC centre in Martin Place to level 44 of a new building in Grosvenor Place. IEL occupied the top floor, which was decked out in marble and glass. While Price, Loewenthal and Brierley were each given an enormous office, and Brierley's even included a separate bathroom, the rest of the staff were slotted into smaller glass offices affording no privacy.

They were horrified. The offices at the MLC centre had been fairly egalitarian, but this new design immediately created a division between the haves and the have-nots. The general consensus was that the new premises consisted of three massive offices and thirty-three dog boxes.

It was not a change that would sit lightly on the shoulders of the investment team, and some, like Dr Gary Weiss, IEL's legal advisor and a director of IEL, took the changes as a personal snub. He campaigned ceaselessly against the new offices, and for him and others the spirit of IEL began to sour at this time.

Weiss was widely recognised as possessing one of the best legal minds in the business. Originally a Czech immigrant to New Zealand who had been an academic at Victoria University before he went to IEL, Weiss loved the challenge of an obstacle and worshipped Brierley. Unlike others, he shared Brierley's philosophy about the intangible benefits of a legal wrangle, and it was Weiss who identified the perceived flaw in Holmes à Court's meeting date in the Bell Resources bid. Weiss also believed that while IEL was a superb investor, it was at best an indifferent manager of assets.

So Weiss was particularly aggrieved when he witnessed the new dominance of the BIL and IEL management team. He, investment trader Graeme Cureton, chief investment analyst Peter Pedley and analyst Blake Nixon often talked to Brierley about their unhappiness.

After the Woolworths affair and after the crash, Brierley had become increasingly remote from BIL and IEL management. Instead of giving the group his support when it was needed, he was negative and carping, blaming everyone else for the company's problems. Weiss believed that deep down he was really blaming himself, but this forgiving attitude was not shared by many.

Once again Brierley had fallen out with his chief executive, and it was now said of him that he couldn't work with a chief executive, but neither could he work without one. Russell Goward had called this tendency to fall in and out of love with people the 'Brierley wheel of fortune'. This time the wheel had even turned against his old friend Bill Loewenthal. Only the investment team was in favour.

Brierley listened attentively to their complaints and, although he never baldly stated his position, they believed he was completely in sympathy with them. After all, they were on his side. Instead of seeing him as being unable to cope with the tough new conditions, they believed they were witnessing the emasculation of their hero and an about-turn in the company's philosophy. They wanted a return to the old Brierley investment philosophy, not this new management thrust led by Rodney Price.

The discontent fermented for a period of weeks and finally the four met with Loewenthal to thrash out the problem. Afterwards they were hopeful things might change, but, when nothing happened, the call for change began to gain momentum. During this period IEL was riven with ill-feeling and unspoken accusations, and the criticism focused largely on Rodney Price as the man responsible for sidelining Brierley.

Throughout the turmoil, Brierley was by no means an idle bystander. He, too, was actively fuelling the undercurrents threatening the company's internal stability. The dissent escalated and finally it was decided that the only solution to the fiasco was to get rid of Rodney Price.

The first Price officially knew about the planned coup was when Brierley raised the issue at a BIL board meeting. He said there was a lack of confidence in Price's management and a general unhappiness in the IEL office.

Goward had perceived Price correctly as a 'strong bugger'. He was not one to flinch from conflict and, while not enjoying Brierley's disclosure, he agreed with the board that it needed further discussion. He was glad it had been formally put on the table and he talked over the issues with Brierley in the company jet on the way back to Sydney. He said they hoped to continue the discussion with the investment team and to come up with resolutions to repair the damage.

But after their earlier discussions with Brierley, the investment team thought he had agreed to call Bruce Hancox over from New Zealand immediately to discuss their concerns.

The four waited anxiously for Hancox's arrival, but he did not appear for almost a week and when he did, he had Paul Collins in tow. Hancox and Collins were in no mood to discuss the group's difficulties with Rodney Price. Instead they announced BIL was going to take over IEL.

Merger talks at BIL or IEL were nothing new. From time to time it would be raised as a possibility, but there were always practical obstacles, just as there would be in this case. But, for the time being anyway, it appeared to be closer than ever to becoming a reality.

The four men who had planned to oust Price were aghast. 'Everyone said we are here to look after IEL, not sell it down the tubes,' said one.

Clearly their palace revolt had failed and suddenly their most important ally, Brierley himself, was nowhere to be seen. Bill Loewenthal had already told him that if Rodney Price went, he would go with him, and Brierley doubtless could see that Collins and Hancox were also right behind Price. Obviously any move to reinstate himself or his philosophy was doomed if he wanted to retain his management team.

Brierley must have realised he had little choice but to side with the New Zealanders. So in spite of his encouragement of the mutinous investment team, in the end he put his weight behind Collins and Hancox. In the circumstances, it may have been the wisest move, but it did nothing to enhance his standing within IEL.

Bill Loewenthal was saddened by what had happened. For years his avuncular tolerance had acted as a foil for Brierley, and his role as peace-maker had been invaluable. On this occasion he was honest enough to admit that the coup had highlighted real problems in the management's communication with staff. Price tended to have an autocratic style of leadership, and too often the need of staff to be kept informed had been overlooked. But this time there was little he could do immediately to smooth the waters, for even he had fallen out with his old friend Brierley.

'Gary [Weiss] and Ron got themselves a bit screwed,' Loewenthal says. 'They formed the view that the only people who can make money are the investment team, and that's wrong. They are all theory men. They've never had to make a quid out of the marketplace. They are good and bright, but they all sit in nice offices up here. When you have to deal with people and push a point of view at board meetings, it's not as easy as it sounds.

'Ron's role was unforgivable. He encouraged them and when it came to the crunch he sold them out. He left them like a shag on a rock.'

When it was over there was almost a feeling of relief, for the atmosphere until then had been unendurable at IEL. It was the worst kind of civil war and a negative form of leadership by Brierley, commented Ross Daniels. He was not alone in isolating Brierley as the perpetrator of the coup, and he wondered whether the events had snowballed out of his control or whether he had actually wanted to sustain the momentum.

The strong stance taken by Nixon, Weiss, Pedley and Cureton meant there was now only one honourable course of action. On 15 August, two days after the merger was publicly announced, the four resigned. Brierley had made it abundantly clear that he was not prepared to lead the company and, for some, this spelled the end of IEL.

'You take Ron out and you totally change the direction of the company,' said Peter Pedley. 'I interpreted that [his siding with the New Zealanders] as saying that he did not want to be the motivating influence anymore.'

As it turned out, only Pedley and Weiss actually left, and even that was not as it seemed. Price said that prior to the incident Pedley had already been working from home and was deciding whether to return to IEL, while Weiss left because 'in the final analysis we said he should'.

Meanwhile Nixon and Cureton had been canvassing other companies for new positions, but a promised option never came through. Since there were no alternatives that appealed to them, they decided to stay at IEL. Although initially their relationship with Rodney Price was tense, eventually the air cleared, and over time Price's handling of the crisis and the clean-up of the company would earn their respect.

The four men behind the coup sensed, too, that Brierley's reign of power was well and truly over. The coup had not only failed, it had back-fired. Instead of placing him back on the throne, it had succeeded only in casting him out further.

Rodney Price and Brierley resumed a polite working relationship. Price bore no malice about what had happened, even though he was certain Brierley had aided and abetted the coup. But as Price saw it, the coup was just a manifestation of Brierley trying to determine what he wanted and what his role was going to be. It was a function of his uncertainty, he said.

When Brierley indicated at the 1988 BIL annual general meeting that the company was wrestling with an identity crisis, his comments could have been construed by those who knew him as an oblique reference to his own place in the company. Brierley's question to the shareholders summed up the predicament neatly.

'Can the magic of the past be recaptured and extended over four or five centuries, or do we become an internationally represented but largely New Zealand-oriented financial institution of increasingly conventional character?' he asked.

Some within the company saw the problem in more personal terms.

'You wait,' said Peter Pedley in a gloomy outburst in early 1989, 'the next thing they'll do is change the name of the company to depersonalise it to BIL. After that, Ron won't turn up at a few more board meetings and they'll say why not make Ron president? They'll get in a new chairman who will last two years so Paul Collins can inherit the throne. In five years' time, no one will remember who Brierley is.'

TWENTY-TWO

The New Guard

BRIERLEY WAS OFTEN SILENT and withdrawn the year his top executives united to edge him out as chairman of BIL. He would snap shut, sealed by pride and distress from further confrontation. But this insularity, which had once protected and encased his ego like a mortar shell, was no match for the battering insistence of the new guard. He must have felt them advancing like an army with banners, and with his own revolt crushed, his only refuge was in a private resistance.

These days he was only one against many. Bruce Hancox, Paul Collins, Bill Loewenthal and Rodney Price were united on this issue. They all knew that, practically, Brierley had abdicated from the throne, though emotionally he was clinging to the last vestiges of control.

Of all the executives, Paul Collins was the most vocal critic of Brierley, and at times it seemed the battle centred entirely on the two men. Over the years his impatience with Brierley's quixotic behaviour had grown to the point where he was no longer able to contain his irritation, and he did not enjoy humouring Brierley as much as Bruce Hancox did. He had decided that Brierley was a reactive, not a proactive investor, and Hancox agreed. 'Ron reacts to things and that way he makes the minimum mistakes. He doesn't like making mistakes because he doesn't like losing, probably because of the fear of being seen to be wrong after all these years. That's why he doesn't take a lead role in anything,' says Hancox.

He was also an obstacle to their proactive philosophy, though this was nothing new. Woolworths represented just one more example of his intransigence. When the company grew and the decision involved taking over and managing a large asset, or perhaps simply because the idea was initiated by others, he proved almost impossible to persuade, and what some referred to as the 'dead hand of Brierley' would attempt to stifle these initiatives.

Selwyn Cushing well remembers Brierley's opposition to the takeover of the stationer Printing and Packaging Corporation Ltd (which traded as Whitcoulls) in the late 1970s. He said Brierley counted a string of uncertainties such as BIL's cash resources, the size of the company, and whether they had the ability to make it work and to handle any problem that would arise. Despite his anxieties, Cushing says the takeover of Printpac has proved to be one of BIL's most profitable investments.

What Paul Collins wanted was to clarify the lines of authority. With Ron as the titular head of the company, he was technically still able to block proposals and thwart initiatives without contributing to the day-to-day running of the company. Paul Collins simply wanted the reality of working with Brierley to be reflected in the structure of the company.

By 1988 Collins was daring to openly challenge him, and while Brierley had not been shielded from opposition, his authority had never been seriously threatened before. For the first time in his life he was being forced to yield his domain, and Paul Collins was a formidable opponent. His astonishingly retentive memory, quick delivery and aggressive nature have often created a barrier between him and other people. Paul Collins is so clinical and efficient he seems barely human and his high-speed, clipped speech simply affirms this impression. Anyone listening to him would be forgiven for suspecting that if a computer could talk it would surely sound like Paul Collins.

His appearance again underscores this impression. He is fighting fit (he jogs at least three times a week), his moustache is standard issue BIL, military-trim and authoritarian, and his dark eyes look almost malevolent in their concentration.

Hancox reckons that in terms of pure brain power, Collins has it all over him, and he likes to give the impression that he is the less dominant force of the pair. But the reality is that nothing happens in BIL without approval from Hancox.

Although he is spending more and more time at his new Nelson home, and he betrays a cynical detachment about the business world (which has led to the observation at BIL that he would be just as happy on the dole as running the company), Hancox is far less ingenuous than he appears. He knows Collins needs his personality, cunning and common sense as much as he needs Collins's financial ability.

The two complement one another nicely. Where Hancox rejects all invitations to business and social functions, Collins happily accepts these obligations. Collins moves easily in the circles of power and is comfortable presenting the public face of BIL.

Neither Brierley nor Hancox has ever sought this role and they have refused to fit the conventional mould of the businessman. Brierley, never married, has eschewed the formal entertainment circuit and prefers not to be obliged to attend functions. Hancox, who has two children with the woman he lives with, has taken a similar approach to Brierley. However, Collins, who is married to a very supportive wife and has three children, is in almost every way the most orthodox of the three men.

His life has always been secure and comfortable. Unlike Hancox and Brierley, he came from a well-off professional family. His father was a surgeon in Wellington, and Collins, born in 1953, was the youngest of four children. He left school after the sixth form and from 1971 to 1975 worked for the Wellington Gas Co., starting as a clerk and working his way up to be an accountant while also studying accountancy part-time at Victoria University.

His interest in BIL was stimulated by the company's holding in Wellington Gas in 1970. Collins was impressed with the way BIL approached the company from a board and management point of view, so when a position became available in 1976 he applied.

At BIL he worked closely with Bruce Judge in Christchurch, 'making terrible stuff-ups because I was just learning', and it was not until 1977 that he moved back to Wellington.

He arrived in the middle of the factional warfare between Judge and his critics. Collins's youth and close relationship with Judge meant that he automatically adopted Judge's point of view, and he thought those opposing him were trying to hamper his creative flair. So when Judge left to form his own company, Collins followed him enthusiastically.

He rejoined BIL in 1984 and two years later he was appointed chief executive. He was only thirty-three years old when he was elevated to this position, and he looked even younger, but his demeanour was that of a confident, serious, older man. Nevertheless, his responses are as honest and blunt as Hancox's, for BIL has never been a company to shy away from frank discussion.

Brierley openly admitted that it was hard to adjust to the changes being foisted upon him. In March 1989 he said, 'Some days I accept it more willingly than others. Some days we [Paul Collins and Brierley] are unhappy with each other.

'On the other hand, yes, I do accept it. What am I struggling to hold on to after twenty-eight years? Between Paul Collins, Bruce Hancox and myself I believe there is a very genuine and sincere effort to find the relationship which gets the best out of the three of us.'

The first change Brierley had to adjust to was handing over the role of IEL chairman to Bill Loewenthal in November 1988. Although Loewenthal was called acting chairman, Brierley had effectively relinquished the position.

Then in early 1989 Collins suggested selling the favourite arm of his triumvirate, IEL. The promised merger between BIL and IEL had never eventuated, owing to taxation and other practical obstacles, although in November 1988 BIL bought IEL's 51 per cent stake in IEP, lifting its holding in that company to 69 per cent. IEL received $A1.27 billion from this transaction, but notwithstanding this cash injection, IEL was still seen as a problem. While the rest of the organisation was operating under the direct control of Collins and Hancox, IEL had traditionally been an autonomous, publicly listed, high-profile company which did not take kindly to having its sphere of activity limited by the New Zealanders.

But its performance still left a lot to be desired. In 1988 IEL was the poorest performer in the group, posting a 75 per cent plunge in total consolidated group operating profit of $A58 million, while IEP had bounced back with a $NZ148 million profit, up 83 per cent on the year before, and further sales in the BIL empire had boosted its war chest to $4.46 billion. It must also be remembered that in November 1988 IEL had acquired 100 per cent of Woolworths for $NZ635 million at a time when Collins was trying to reduce the balance sheet of BIL. Despite the sale of IEP and IEL's own sales programme, it was still laden with debt and BIL was keen to rid itself of IEL's drag on the balance sheet.

Paul Collins had been the first person to suggest cutting IEL loose from the family business, but he advocated the sale of a 20 per cent stake. Loewenthal and Price told him he was being unrealistic. No one would want just 20 per cent. When it was analysed, they said, the only alternative was not a sell-down but a sell-out. Loewenthal was surprised and mildly disappointed by the suggestion, but was pragmatic enough to understand BIL's motivation.

It took time for a suitable buyer to surface, but in June, Pat Goodman and Bruce Hancox announced that Goodman Fielder Wattie would issue $A670 million worth of shares plus outlay $A1.12 billion in cash for 100 per cent of IEL. In turn, GFW would receive just over $1 billion in cash from BIL when BIL bought IEL's 57 per cent stake in Woolworths Ltd.

The first part of the deal had already taken place, with BIL selling 20 per cent of IEL for $2.40 cash per share. Its offer for the rest of IEL was one Goodman share and $A2.40 cash for every two shares in IEL.

For its total 52 per cent of IEL, BIL would receive $670 million in cash, 9.6 per cent of the enlarged Goodman capital, worth $A400 million, and it would also become the holding company for the new group.

This was a sweet deal for BIL, who had won control of Woolworths without having to outlay any money and had gained a 10 per cent stake in what would become Australia's thirteenth-largest company.

But GFW and IEL shareholders, including Loewenthal and Price, were wondering what was in it for them. While BIL's shares rose 7 cents to $1.77 the day after the announcement, GFW shares dropped 18c to $2.80. Over five million GFW shares were dumped that day.

The resistance of IEL management and GFW's shareholders finally defeated the audacious takeover bid, and IEL was once more back on the sales rack. This time a new deal was being hatched internally. Price and Loewenthal, with Melbourne textile magnate Abe Goldberg, were putting together plans for a management buyout of IEL at $A2.40 per share.

For the IEL executives it was the opportunity of a lifetime. Without risking their own capital they were promised a 25 per cent stake in the takeover company, Corama Pty Ltd, by Goldberg, who was bankrolling the whole venture himself. Ultimately the deal would be financed by selling IEL assets, leaving Southern Farmers, Acmex and Woolworths as the core investments.

Loewenthal and Price had no reason to doubt Goldberg, a sixty-year-old Polish immigrant. His experience and reputation were virtually minted in gold. He had begun his business career in the 1950s, managing and building up textile factories, and since then had become a key figure in the rationalisation of that industry in Australia. In 1989 *Business Review Weekly*'s 'Rich List' put his personal wealth at $A250 million, while *Australian Business* estimated it was closer to $A600 million. His solvency seemed assured.

So in July, BIL's 19.9 per cent stake in IEL was sold to Corama, who agreed to buy BIL's remaining 12 per cent and GFW's 19.9 per cent, subject to shareholders' approval.

But there was an unexpected fly in the ointment: John Spalvins's company Adelaide Steamship Co. Ltd had quietly built up a stake of about 12 per cent in IEL, which would have enabled him to defeat the proposal at a shareholders' meeting. This effectively forced Corama to make a full takeover bid for the company.

Spalvins had been regarded by IEL for years as a friendly rival. The tall, bombastic, fifty-three-year-old Latvian-born South Australian was the owner of more than a hundred companies including retailer David Jones (which, ironically, IEL had helped him acquire).

Spalvins's reputation, however, had suffered in recent years following a series of questionable judgments. His conviction that the bull market was drawing to a close in 1986, and subsequent decision to hedge his exposure in the futures market, had cost him millions. Complicated public battles with Holmes à Court and CUB helped muddy his reputation further, and for a time his move into the Australian banks was also viewed critically. But that strategy paid huge dividends, and now commentators were cautiously commenting on the neat symmetry of a possible merger with IEL, for its retailing and food assets dovetailed nicely with Adsteams's own holdings.

The funding for a full bid of Corama was proving to be more difficult than imagined. It was a highly leveraged deal because Goldberg was seeking to raise $A1.9 billion, $A1.5 billion of which was debt. IEL's own debt was over $A1 billion. If Corama was successful, it was looking at a $A400 million yearly interest bill.

But the worsening economic situation in Australia and growing nervousness about highly leveraged deals did not help Corama. Neither did Goldberg's own financial pickle. Loewenthal and Price were not alone in placing their faith in Goldberg. A number of Australian banks had done the same and, when his fortune crumbled, there were red faces all round.

Three months after BIL had sold its stake to Corama and two months after Corama had announced they would launch a $1.9 billion bid for IEL, the funding package was still not in place. The banks had forced Corama to come up with a further $100 million in equity to supplement the $400 million already raised.

IEL's record profit announcement in September was not even cause for congratulation. Over half of the net profit of $283 million was earned from the sale of IEP to BIL.

In the meantime Spalvins was becoming increasingly restive. He tired of waiting for Corama to move, and on 14 November he launched his own cash bid for IEL. His offer of $2.25 per share was less than the $2.40 Corama had bid. Brierley said it was less than he personally thought control of IEL was worth, a point of view supported later by an independent report from Coopers and Lybrand. By their calculations, IEL was worth between $2.63 and $2.87 per share.

Brierley's lukewarm response encouraged IEL to believe that BIL would not support Spalvins. This was confirmed the day after the bid, when Brierley and Collins publicly proclaimed they felt a moral commitment to support Corama because of their work and friendship with Rodney Price and Bill Loewenthal.

They were wrong. The next day BIL and Goodmans sold their shares to Spalvins. Their capitulation effectively ended the hopes of Price, Loewenthal and Goldberg. Adsteam now had 50.9 per cent of IEL.

The IEL crew were outraged by what they saw as a hypocritical betrayal. It seemed to them that the moral commitment of Brierley and Collins had a remarkably short shelf-life, but what was most galling was that no one from BIL had contacted them before settling the deal.

'They could have eased the pain a bit by letting us know,' says Loewenthal, while Price acknowledged that a phone call would not have altered the outcome but 'would have made it taste a bit better, that's all'.

But later Loewenthal, ever the reasonable man, admitted that he and Price had been hard to get hold of that day, and he said that in all fairness BIL had done everything they could to facilitate Corama's success. His only lingering regret was that they did not lobby Spalvins to buy Corama's shares, but for its part BIL could argue it had succeeded in pushing the price up 5 cents to $2.30 per share.

Spalvins's success created new problems for Corama. Corama had not paid for its stake in IEL acquired from BIL, but it was contractually bound to put up the $2.40 per share on 29 December. This meant Goldberg would be facing a loss of $15 million. There was also a question of a $25 million deposit paid on this transaction. But legal action that followed, with Corama suing BIL for $25 million and Goldberg suing Loewenthal and Price, came to nothing.

So after twenty-three years, BIL had finally sold its Australian alter ego, IEL. Bruce Hancox said it was like the teenager leaving home, but the IEL team were not thinking of the departure in such cosy familial terms. 'IEL supported BIL in plenty of bad years. Now, when the chips are down for IEL, they sell us out,' said one IEL staffer, echoing the sentiments of many in the company.

Those close to Brierley believed that selling IEL was an emotional wrench for him, although his feelings on the subject were difficult to divine. But they knew that IEL had been his favourite company and his personal flagship, so the loss must have been deeply felt.

Loewenthal remembers Brierley saying to him one day, 'God, I suddenly realised — what the hell happens now? Where is my office and what about the library?'

Brierley would eventually shift to the new BIL office in Sydney, but in the meantime he had been invited by Spalvins to remain on the IEL board and already had the use of an office in the company.

But sadly, his continued presence in IEL offended the sensibilities of many of his former colleagues. After Woolworths, Equity & Law, his abdication of authority and his role in the palace coup, his standing in the office was at an all-time low.

The latest development branded Brierley as a company traitor. Not only did he fly with Spalvins on the IEL jet to Adelaide to sign the deal, he did not even take the trouble to ring his two top executives at IEL to let them know what had transpired. It seemed all the more unforgivable when it was remembered that Bill Loewenthal had spent seventeen years working for Brierley and the company.

It was of little comfort to the people at IEL to know that Brierley had been a reluctant party to the sale, and Hancox virtually had to order him to finalise the deal. Brierley did not join Price and Loewenthal in recommending IEL shareholders reject Spalvins's bid and he did not align himself with Collins and Hancox, who were urging shareholders to sell. Brierley's response was typically ambivalent. He suggested they retain some shares in the company and sell others.

But throughout much of that year Brierley's own position had been under siege, and finally, as Peter Pedley had predicted, in August 1989 it was announced that Brierley would be removed as the chairman of BIL from 1990. It had taken a year for Brierley to agree to step down from the position he had held for twenty-eight years, but he finally succumbed and the news was broadcast that Sir Ron Brierley would from 1990 be known as 'founder president'. It was an unusual title in New Zealand and Australian business circles, and following the announcement, the New Zealand Stock Exchange decided that guidelines for bestowing this honour were required. Cynical observers commented it sounded like something out of a banana republic.

Some at IEL cast the event in a more sinister light. To them it was just one more example of Paul Collins extending his tentacles of control. They believed his guiding hand was behind moves altering the organisation of IEP. For years Brierley had worked on IEL's international portfolio, tackling the United States with Ron Langley and Great Britain with Peter Pedley. But New Zealander Rob Sutherland had since been shifted to the La Joya office in the United States, another New Zealander and BIL executive, Trevor Beyer, had gone to the London office, and Paul Forrester from BIL had gone to Hong Kong to head that office.

Brierley was clearly a reluctant party to his change in status, but the market barely reacted to the news. His mana in Australia had waned a little after the sale of IEL, and eyebrows had been raised when he started buying into Bruce Judge's old flagship, Ariadne Australia, in September 1989. Under Judge's leadership Ariadne had achieved the dubious distinction of chalking up Australia's biggest corporate loss — $A640 million in 1988. Thousands of shareholders had lost money with Bruce Judge, and a shareholder at the BIL annual meeting in 1989 echoed the view of many when he said it was sad to read of Sir Ron supporting the survival of Judge.

Everyone who knew Brierley and Bruce Judge was waiting to see whether Judge's self-nomination to the board of Ariadne would succeed. Bill Loewenthal remembers saying to Brierley as he left for the Ariadne meeting in Brisbane, 'For God's sake, don't vote Judge on to the board.' He was relieved when Brierley replied, 'Don't worry. That's all taken care of. I've talked him out of standing.'

But Bruce Judge did stand and he did get a seat on the board, and it appeared to observers that Brierley had not learned from his own, and others', experience of the arch-persuader.

In New Zealand the changes had little impact on Brierley's reputation, and in Australia the disenchantment was only temporary. Criticism turned to admiration when other Australian investment companies began to topple, and Brierley was suddenly credited with having avoided this ignominy.

But resurrecting his honour among his staff in Australia proved more difficult. The wheel of fortune had turned once too often for some who were beginning to wonder whether Brierley had any loyalties at all. As time passed, the IEL team would re-evaluate the actions of Paul Collins and Bruce Hancox, but their views on Brierley more often than not betrayed their disappointment with him on a personal level.

On the other hand, they were beginning to concede that the investment team might have been mistaken. There were no regrets that the coup had failed and Brierley had been displaced. In fact, people like Ross Daniels began to wish it had happened years ago. 'I wish Paul Collins, Bruce Hancox and Rodney Price had rebelled earlier. Had that happened in 1986, IEL would still be part of BIL. It would have avoided the problems of the crash. I'm sad it didn't happen earlier,' he said in March 1990.

To his shareholders, however, Brierley was still the company. No amount of jocular, disparaging comments about him by his executives or American-style relabelling could diminish his stature in the shining eyes of his adoring shareholders.

Brierley was still the god-head, the keeper of the faith, who had lifted the whole company out of the prosaic world of business into the luminous sphere of the extraordinary.

In November 1989, at the final BIL meeting over which Brierley would preside as chairman, people flocked to meet him and Dunedin greeted him like a long-lost hero. Streets were closed, a marquee was erected in one street for refreshments, huge streamers hung from the Town Hall and a band played as Dunedin honoured his presence. As soon as he walked onto the stage, the 2,700 shareholders present broke into a strong round of applause, and throughout the proceedings they laughed merrily at his jokes and gave him a standing ovation at the end. A founding shareholder stood up and thanked him on behalf of all those present, and the local newspaper, somewhat behind the times, dubbed the event a 'love-in'.

Afterwards he was engulfed by shareholders beseeching him for his autograph, just as if he were a retiring sports star or actor instead of a corporate investor. Brierley was only too happy to oblige, for he loved the attention. This was his yearly dose of undiluted adulation, his reward for working while others played. Besides, they weren't just shareholders. They were his family, of which he was the undisputed head.

It could be said that the shareholders' affection was dispensed in direct proportion to the share price — a greed quotient, if you like. Shareholders loved him because he had financed their world trip, holiday home, children's education or retirement, but when the good times ended, would they cease to love him? In fact, it is worth remembering that Brierley had a personal following even during the difficult years.

Although Brierley was an unlikely hero, devoid of power, good looks and the expansive optimism of the successful man, he has always had charisma. That charisma drew people to Brierley from the very beginning. He had always been able to inspire great trust and devotion from those around him, and few doubted he would succeed. Ken Douglas remembers reading about the Government's attempts to stop Brierley's deposit notes scheme in the early 1960s and thinking to himself, 'If there's a way, Brierley will find it.'

Like Ken Douglas, shareholders probably sensed that Brierley's will to win was indomitable and his commitment to his goal wholehearted. They could see that he had dedicated every fibre of his being, every thought and action, to his task, sacrificing all else, and they could not fail to be impressed. In the early days this commitment meant he rarely graced the social circuit, and such obscurity enhanced his appeal. It was the Brierley mystique in the making.

So, in part, his charisma was a product of the combination of commitment and obscurity, but there was one other factor: no matter how rich or influential Brierley became, and no matter who he was with, he treated everyone with the same deferential courtesy. He never vaingloriously flapped his cape, but people were drawn to him nevertheless. He was charming and never failed to impress people with his humility and gentleness.

Also to Brierley's credit is the fact that he has never equated success with his own personal wealth. Although wealth was undeniably a by-product of his activities, Brierley has never sought to increase his holding in the company at the expense of shareholders. During the boom he could have followed the example of many other directors by increasing his own personal debt to fund a bigger holding in the company, thereby putting the company at risk later when the crash occurred. But Brierley's holding has dwindled from a 15 per cent stake in 1961 to a 3.7 per cent stake today.

Fortunately, after all the changes, Brierley was still chairman of IEP and closely associated with the development of that company, even though his contribution to it was spasmodic. At one stage during discussions about his changing status, the suggestion arose that Brierley should be stripped of all his chairmanship roles, including IEP. But after further consideration it was agreed that Brierley's relationship with the shareholders should not be underestimated.

Not surprisingly, his loyal followers have accepted the changes reluctantly. 'BIL's not the same without Sir Ron,' they lament to brokers. Peter Pedley sees their dismay as further evidence of the betrayal of Brierley's philosophy by the new breed of managers. 'What shareholder ever gave money to BIL because of Paul Collins or Bruce Hancox?' he asks. He does not believe the company has a mandate from shareholders to follow this new direction, and he relates some of Brierley's lack of motivation to the changing nature of the company. Brierley, he says, is best suited to the smaller investment company of the 1960s and '70s, not the huge empire of assets created and run by the managers of the 1980s.

The argument that this spread of operating assets is required by a market that has become accustomed to annual profit increases does not impress Pedley. He believes that this is an expectation fuelled by BIL's management and says it could easily be altered to accommodate a more uneven growth pattern more appropriate for a speculative company.

Even Brierley's own executives would agree the company is not the same without him. Paul Collins says that Brierley definitely has something others don't have, and he rates his ability to analyse a company and research the salient points as outstanding. Selwyn Cushing respects Brierley's probability analysis and says that, although he appears to be a good gambler, he never really gambles. His thorough preparation is the key to his superb evaluation of financial risk. Don McDonald says Brierley is the only real genius he has ever worked with, and Bruce Hancox, in his inimitable vernacular, calls Brierley a 'smart little bugger' and acknowledges he is smarter than the rest of them.

However, it is Bill Loewenthal who best sums up Brierley's abilities: 'If you gave Ron, Bruce, Rodney or Paul all a sum of money and told them to do what they wanted with it, Ron would have more than them at the end of five years, that's for sure. Ron is a hoarder and does things his own way. You've got a basic difference.

'He's a brilliant analyst but he's more than that. Whatever you say about Ron, he created BIL, IEL and IEP. You can't take that away from him.'

Brierley's achievement in creating an entrepreneurial company in 1961 that is still in operation some thirty years later is considerable, though many attribute some crucial successes to luck. McDonald remembers worrying that the political debacle over the unsecured deposit notes could stimulate a run on the notes at a time when the company did not have sufficient funds to pay the noteholders. But Brierley's luck held then, as it did during the high-risk Equity & Law deal and the fortuitous sale of the troubled NZI Corporation, which, if it remained in the BIL portfolio, could have made life very uncomfortable for the company. Brierley could also be said to have been lucky in his selection of executives, since many people say that he is not a good judge of character.

Of course, there is another school of thought that argues there is no such thing as luck. People like Brierley are said to be so committed to their task that they see opportunities and outcomes ordinary mortals, encumbered by families and other concerns, would never see. As an ardent individualist, Brierley would no doubt subscribe to this theory, for he believes implicitly in the efficacy of his own actions. He pointed out to me that if the concept of luck is given credence then one had to accept that he would be equally as susceptible to bad luck as good luck.

Brierley is fond of surveying the past, particularly since BIL has played such a central role in the changing corporate economy in New Zealand. He sees BIL's history as 'almost a cameo of what has happened in the stockmarket. The two are almost totally intertwined.' He has said the role of his company has been as a monitoring organisation that continually evaluated the performance of various companies and acted as a catalyst to promote the most effective ownership of a company.

Few would argue that he has been an agent for change, holding up a mirror to management and boards alike, and urging them to improve their performance. But it would be a mistake to think that all the management teams Brierley threatened were incompetent. Sometimes it was just a realisation that a new management team could be more effective than the old team.

Brierley's achievement as a spur to management was not just limited to the firms he took over, but extended to all the firms threatened by his presence. There were many companies like Geo. H. Scales who set in motion a plan of action Brierley himself had intended to instigate.

On the whole the redistribution of assets and workers promoted by Brierley's activity worked well in the 1960s and '70s when there was near full employment and the redundant assets and workers generally found a new use. But in the late 1970s and '80s the benefits of this process have not been as obvious, because many of the assets and people released on to the market have not found a more productive use.

At the same time Brierley also assisted in creating a climate of acceptance for some of the less laudable aspects of the boom. His reluctance to respect any authority other than that of the marketplace, and his consequent success, was a signal of approval to others and set the tone for even greater abuse. It was a triumph of delinquency. During the 1980s Brierley contributed to the elevation of the entrepreneur as the hero of capitalism, at once rebel and conquistador. Suddenly it became smart to defy accounting conventions and regulatory bodies, to cloak your activities in mystery and try to avoid paying tax, as BIL had done for years.

But by 1990 it was clear to most observers that Brierley was no longer the force he had once been in the company, and it would have been reasonable to assume Brierley would be unhappy with his new role. After all, he had just survived the most testing year of his life. From his seemingly unassailable position as king of New Zealand business, friend of Government, captain of the nation's bank, he had tumbled into a humiliating, seemingly ever-descending spiral of rejection.

To reign over the biggest loss the BNZ had ever recorded, to be forcibly and publicly cast aside as its leader, to fail to come to terms with his own company's predicament, then reluctantly to hand over IEL's chairmanship to his deputy and finally relinquish the driving seat of the empire he had created all in the space of twelve months could have unhinged the most stable soul.

Brierley had been stripped of his power and institutionalised as founder president. He must have felt as if the Fates were conspiring against him, heaping their entire storehouse of ill fortune on him at once. It was a cruel coda to the knighthood of the year before.

Instead, to the surprise of his executives, Brierley appeared visibly relieved that a conclusion had been reached. Now that it was over the tension seemed to gradually ebb away from him, leaving in its wake a vast uninterrupted shore of freedom. Friends noticed that Brierley seemed to have a new spring in his step. He was chirrupy, smiling and joking and more relaxed than ever. He had been released from the daily grind, having sheeted home all the responsibility to Collins and Hancox, and with the continuing survival of his empire his reputation was intact. For the first time in almost thirty years Brierley was free to do more of what he liked, and although what he liked more often than not was work, his approach had changed. He no longer worked as hard as he had in the 1960s and '70s, but work was once again becoming his form of relaxation.

Brierley's blossoming appreciation of the material world, fostered during the boom years, also continued. He loved going to frivolous functions like the launching of a new French champagne and, after years of ignoring the IEL boat, he was even beginning to enjoy hosting parties on the water. He bought a new house in Point Piper and had extensive renovations done, and he followed cricket dutifully.

In what may become the first asset in his own portfolio, in 1989 Brierley also acquired a personal holding in the Australian subsidiary of the British stamp group Stanley Gibbons.

Weekends saw Brierley regularly travelling by boat with his friend Elizabeth Rich to their holiday home in the Pittwater area, north of Sydney. Elizabeth Rich had known Brierley long enough to expect little from him, but she appreciated his company. She was a capable, independent woman running her own small management business and she wisely allowed him as much freedom as he wanted. For her part, she found him a relaxing companion because he was so undemanding and non-judgmental.

When Brierley wasn't working, he was pursuing one of his many interests — stamps, reading newspapers, playing computer games, often computer chess or other mental agility games, and walking.

Brierley would wander off happily for hours on his own.

Although friends like Elizabeth Rich believe he is still capable of making a comeback, the reality is that Brierley is slowly dropping out of sight on the work front. Those who know him better are aware that Brierley has always had a tendency to seek out the solitary life and they worry that he is becoming more and more regressive as time goes by.

Certainly Hancox and Collins have been disappointed by his gradual withdrawal from the company. They hoped that the new arrangement would facilitate the release of his talents but they find Brierley is not to be pushed.

'He isn't doing anything at the moment. He just works when he feels like it. I reckon he must be spending an hour longer getting dressed in the morning. He gets out his papers, shifts them, reads a bit and looks out of the window,' says Hancox.

'The price he pays for this is that we will go without him. We're not doing it his way now, the way he would like.'

Although Brierley has recently showed flashes of his old self — for instance, at the British engineering group Vickers Plc's annual meeting in April 1990, where he attempted to get shareholder support for his plan to demerge the Rolls-Royce subsidiary — it seemed to Collins and Hancox that his interest was still at a low ebb.

But when he is motivated, he generally occupies himself with IEP's investment portfolio. During the 1980s it was Brierley who had the foresight to develop IEP, and today it is probably the most promising arm of the operation in terms of growth and profit potential. IEP most closely resembles the BIL and IEL of the 1970s in its aims, size and flexibility.

Today Brierley is no longer indispensable to the operation of the empire he created and he admits that he could disengage himself completely without any repercussions to the executive structure. The truth is that it has been years since his contribution was essential to the running of BIL. Nevertheless, Brierley still exerts a subtle influence on the company. His legacy to BIL is in his philosophy, which by now is deeply rooted in the ethic of the company.

Although his executives present an irreverently critical and comical view of Brierley, they do not deny he is still the psychological lynchpin of the operation. Selwyn Cushing described Brierley's pervasive presence as being 'like God. He is there even though he has left it all to you.' Hancox likens Brierley's influence to that of a parent you continue to want to please even though you have long reached adulthood.

To the man who has made the company his life and who regards the shareholders as his family, those observations are probably the kindest commendations of all.

READING LIST

The Ariadne Story, Bruce Ross. Greenhouse Publications, Sydney, 1988.

Eliott: A Biography of John D. Eliott, Peter Denton. Little Hills Press, Sydney, 1986.

Crash! Corporate Australia and New Zealand Fight For Their Lives, John McManamy. Pan Books, Sydney, 1988.

Behind the Mirror Glass, Bruce Jesson. Penguin Books, Auckland, 1987.

Clore: The Man and His Millions, David Clutterbuck and Marion Devine. Weidenfeld and Nicholson, London 1986.

Slater Walker, Charles Raw. Andre Deutsch, London, 1977.

The New Boys Network, Ruth Ostrow. Heinemann Australia, Melbourne, 1987.

INDEX